Winston Cup

1996

The 1996 NASCAR Winston Cup Yearbook
is dedicated to the fond memory of
Elmo Harrell Langley
1929 - 1996

Acknowledgments

Dear Racing Fan,

What a year in racing 1996 brought us! In February, who would have expected that Dale Jarrett, with a new team and a rookie crew chief, would triumph in some of the most important races of the season — the Daytona 500, the Brickyard 400 and the Coca-Cola 600 — and come so close to winning the Winston Select Million? Who could anticipate that, after starting the season with two straight DNFs, defending NASCAR Winston Cup Champion Jeff Gordon would recover to capture a series-leading 10 wins and would be in contention for a second straight crown until the closing laps at Atlanta? Who could ignore the drama of Dale Earnhardt's quest for a record-breaking eighth title, hampered by a mid-season setback at Talladega? And let's not forget the return of The King. Car owner Richard Petty was back in victory lane for the first time since 1984 with Bobby Hamilton's win at Phoenix. And, while everyone else was grabbing the headlines, Terry Labonte was carrying out his trademark quiet, steady performances each weekend that, at the end of the season, added up to the NASCAR Winston Cup championship.

The folks at NASCAR did an excellent job in providing us with another tremendous, action-packed season of racing. This book would not be possible without their help and guidance. We would especially like to thank Mr. Bill France, Mr. Jim France, Mr. Brian France, Mr. Paul Brooks, Mr. George Pyne, Mr. John Griffin, Mr. Kevin Triplett, Mr. Andy Hall and Mr. Paul Schaefer.

Also deserving our thanks and appreciation are all the members of the NASCAR Winston Cup team at the R.J. Reynolds Tobacco Company. Special thanks go to Mr. T. Wayne Robertson, Mr. Greg Littell, Mr. John Powell, Mr. Nat Walker, Mr. Larry Prillaman, Mr. Curtis Gray, Mr. Steve Tucker, Mr. Chris Powell, Mr. Dennis Dawson, Ms. Sara Ayers and Ms. Mary Reynolds.

Mr. Bob Kelly worked tirelessly to give us yet another fantastic recount of all the events of the season for your enjoyment. The beautiful photography in this book is the work of a very accomplished group of photographers — Mr. Don Grassman, Mr. Ernie Masche and Mr. David Chobat — and we thank them.

But our greatest appreciation and gratitude is reserved for YOU, the NASCAR Winston Cup racing fans. You are the reason for NASCAR racing's phenomenal growth and success. Without your support, NASCAR and this book would not be possible.

Please enjoy.

Staff

Publisher
Ivan Mothershead

Associate Publisher
Charlie Keiger

Controller
Lewis Patton

Managing Editor
Ward Woodbury

Senior Editor
Bob Kelly

Associate Editors
Betty Alfred Mackinson
Kathryn Hass

Art Director
Brett Shippy

Layout/Design
Mike McBride
Paul Bond

Administrative Staff
Mark Cantey, Mary Cartee,
Henry Boardman, Mary Costner,
Carla Greene and Mark Whitlock

Contributing Photographers
David Chobat, Don Grassman
and Ernie Masche

Foreword

Bill France

"One of the main reasons that sponsors join the sport — and remain in it — is directly attributable to you, the fan. Without your support of the series, its events and its drivers, none of this would be possible."

What a year this was!

It began with a brand-new team, with Dale Jarrett driving and Todd Parrott as the crew chief, sweeping both the Busch Clash and the Daytona 500, and ended with Terry Labonte and the Kellogg's Corn Flakes Chevrolet claiming the NASCAR Winston Cup championship in the final race of the season.

In between were some of the finest races in our sport's long history and the emergence of several teams and drivers who stamped themselves as contenders for future championships.

And who could possibly forget the splendid victory at Phoenix, when Bobby Hamilton brought the STP Pontiac to victory lane, giving Petty Enterprises its first trip to the winner's circle since 1983? What a very special way to celebrate the 25th anniversary of the association between STP and Petty Enterprises.

The championship chase took several turns during the course of the year as Jeff Gordon and Terry Labonte, the two drivers who would battle for the year-end title in the final race, both had problems in the first few races of the season. Dale Earnhardt looked as though he would figure into the championship picture for much of the season, and we'll always remember his superb performance at The Glen, when he won the pole and led the first half of the race. In the end, the stretch runs of Labonte and Gordon told the story of the championship, and Terry's gritty performances at Phoenix and Atlanta showed how much he wanted to win the title after 12 years of chasing a second NASCAR Winston Cup.

During the year, the sport continued to grow, television ratings continued to increase, and the popularity of NASCAR racing moved to an all-time high. New sponsors joined the sport, and the continued promotions of every company involved helped move us to a higher level. That movement will continue during the 1997 season as more companies join both established and new teams on the circuit. We feel we can only move ahead as these companies include us in their marketing programs.

One of the main reasons that sponsors join the sport — and remain in it — is directly attributable to you, the fan. Without your support of the series, its events and its drivers, none of this would be possible. The level of your loyalty to the companies who do participate is higher than that of any other professional sport, and every member of the NASCAR Winston Cup family — from drivers to corporate sponsors — thanks you for it.

The 1996 season was a great year, and all of us at NASCAR hope that this book brings the season back to life for you as you read it. We all look forward to seeing you along the circuit in 1997.

Bill France
President
National Association for Stock Car Auto Racing

Table of Contents

Acknowledgments 3

Foreword by Bill France 4

Preface 6

NASCAR Winston Cup Champion Story 12

Daytona 500 18

Goodwrench 400 24

Pontiac Excitement 400 30

Purolator 500 36

TranSouth Financial 400 42

Food City 500 48

First Union 400 54

Goody's Headache Powder 500 60

Winston Select 500 66

Save Mart Supermarkets 300 72

The Winston Select 78

Coca-Cola 600 84

Miller 500 90

UAW-GM Teamwork 500 96

Miller 400 102

Pepsi 400 108

Jiffy Lube 300 114

Miller 500 120

DieHard 500 126

Brickyard 400 132

The Bud at The Glen 138

GM Goodwrench Dealer 400 144

Goody's Headache Powder 500 150

Mountain Dew Southern 500 156

Miller 400 162

MBNA 500 168

Hanes 500 174

Tyson Holly Farms 400 180

UAW-GM Quality 500 186

ACDelco 400 192

Dura Lube 500 198

NAPA 500 204

Reflections 210

Autographs 215

1996 NASCAR Winston Cup Champion
Terry Labonte

Preface

Jeff Gordon prepares to open defense of his NASCAR Winston Cup championship.

From the moment the checkered flag fell at Atlanta in November to mark the end of the 1995 NASCAR Winston Cup season until the green flag unfurled at Daytona in February for the first official practice session of 1996, an unusual number of changes occurred among the teams preparing to contest the new year of competition.

When the cast of characters was unveiled in Daytona for the 1996 season, some teams had disappeared, new teams had been formed and more than 30 existing teams had changed significantly. Drivers and crew chiefs were working with new teams, sponsors had left one team for another and new sponsors had joined the sport. Pontiac had introduced a new Grand Prix for competition, and the Ford forces displayed a new nose based on the 1996 production model of the Thunderbird.

Heading the changes was longtime NASCAR Winston Cup competitor and car owner Junior Johnson, who divested himself of his two teams and retired from the sport. Brett Bodine worked a deal with Johnson and sponsor Lowe's home improvement stores to purchase the famed "11" team, and moved the equipment to its new home just north of Charlotte. In the process, Bodine lured crew chief (and brother-in-law) Donnie Richeson from the Stavola Brothers team. Richeson immediately began to put together the crew of new faces that would work with the Lowe's Fords for the 1996 season.

Johnson, leaving the sport that was his life for more than three decades, also completed the sale of his "27" team to Hooters president Bob Brooks, who immediately sold the team to Arkansas attorney David Blair and his wife, Suzanne. Blair, a longtime racing enthusiast and friend of car owner Bill Davis, entrusted the fortunes of his new team to crew chief Mike Hill and driver Elton Sawyer. Blair, Hill and Sawyer, losing the Hooters colors that graced the Fords in 1995, began beating the bushes in search of a new sponsor.

Hooters restaurants remained involved in racing at the NASCAR Winston Cup level by replacing Skoal as the sponsor of the Richard Jackson-owned team and driver Rick Mast. Jackson switched from Fords to Pontiacs during the winter, giving Mast an entirely new stable of mounts to drive this year.

Bill and Mickey Stavola hired Hut Stricklin as their driver and enrolled the services of Circuit City, the appliance superstore chain, as the team's new sponsor. When Richeson left the Stavola Brothers to join Brett Bodine with his new effort, he was quickly replaced by Philippe Lopez, who toiled during the previous season for Alan Dillard's team.

Dillard began the 1995 season with Ward Burton behind the wheel of his Hardee's Chevrolets, but, by the end of the year, he lost the restaurant sponsorship, his driver and his crew chief. By the time the teams assembled at Daytona, Dillard had sold the team and it disappeared from week-to-week competition.

Dillard's team wasn't the only one to close shop. In late November, Kenny Bernstein auctioned off his King Racing effort piece by piece, with two of his Fords moving to Ricky Rudd's stable of Tide Thunderbirds. Richard Broome, Bernstein's team manager for the Quaker State-backed Thunderbirds driven by Stricklin, signed as Rudd's new crew chief and team manager, replacing Bill Ingle.

Ingles' new package with the Diamond Ridge team included his role as Steve Grissom's crew chief and an occasional ride in the NASCAR Busch Series and NASCAR Craftsman Truck Series when the schedule permitted. A promising NASCAR Busch Series driver until an accident turned him into a full-time crew chief, Ingle welcomed the opportunity to return to the wheel. Gary and Carolyn Bechtel, owners of the Diamond Ridge team, and the Cartoon Network joined forces to make Grissom's Chevrolets the most colorful on the circuit, with several of the Hanna-Barbera cartoon characters incorporated into the new paint and sponsorship schemes. Diamond Ridge also signed World Championship Wrestling to sponsor a limited season of races for Grissom in the NASCAR Busch Series.

While Fred Flintstone and Dino the Dinosaur on the Diamond Ridge Chevrolets brought smiles to everyone's faces, there was little laughter in the camps of three teams planning to contend for the 1996 NASCAR Winston Cup championship. For Rusty Wallace, Dale Earnhardt and Kyle Petty, the new year offered varying reasons to attack the work at hand cheerlessly.

After losing the 1995 championship to Jeff Gordon, the Goodwrench Service-sponsored team owned by Richard Childress vowed to return to the top rung of the point ladder. When crew chief Andy Petree left the team to rejoin Leo Jackson's Skoal team with driver Robert Pressley and realize his long-sought-after dream of becoming a NASCAR Winston Cup car owner, Childress, after considering all the options, promoted from within his own operation. He named David Smith as the crew chief and Bobby Hutchens as the team manager for Earnhardt's venerable black Chevrolets. With the contracts of both Goodwrench and Earnhardt extended through the year 2000, everyone expected the Childress team to be at the front of the point battle for a record eighth championship for some time to come.

Although Rusty Wallace had a new splash of color on the sides of his Miller-sponsored Thunderbirds, the big changes for the Penske South team came within the crew. Late in 1995, Miller team engine builder David Evans and

(Right) Dale Earnhardt had the winter months to reflect upon his 1995 season, in which he finished second to Jeff Gordon in the point race. By the time the 1996 season rolled around, Dale was the odds-on favorite to capture an unprecedented eighth NASCAR Winston Cup championship, even with a new crew chief and team manager. (Below) Among the new looks for 1996 were Bud Moore's revamped "15" Ford with Wally Dallenbach behind the wheel and Hayes Modems on the hood, and the Stavola Brothers' Circuit City Ford with Hut Stricklin behind the wheel.

mechanic Billy Woodruff moved across the street to the revamped Felix Sabates team. Rusty was quick to name Mike Ege as his new head engine builder. The team also lost several other crew members to different teams, but Robin Pemberton remained as Wallace's crew chief.

Petty, despite his Dover victory in 1995, continued to plummet in the point standings. Kyle finished fifth in the 1993 points, fell to 15th in 1994 and, at the end of last season, found himself 30th. Clearly needing to guide the team in a different direction in 1996, owner Sabates put together a new cast of crew members headed by Woodruff and Evans. With a new crew chief, a new engine builder and an updated paint scheme from sponsor Coors Light on the new Pontiac Grand Prix, SABCO expected to see its fortune change immediately.

Petty and Sabates were not the only driver and car owner

son. He changed manufacturers, motor oils and colors and hoped the transformation would also bring a change in his racing luck.

Waltrip's move was just the beginning of upheavals within Ford teams. Exide Batteries left Geoff Bodine's team and joined forces with Jack Roush to form a third Roush Racing team. Jack hired veteran crew chief Buddy Parrott as head wrench and team manager of the new effort fielding the No. 99 Fords for 1994 Rookie of the Year Jeff Burton.

Within his two original teams, Roush worked with Valvoline to change the appearance of Mark Martin's Thunderbirds and cut a deal with The Family Channel and satellite television service

(Above) For his first full season of racing since sustaining injuries at Michigan in 1994, Ernie Irvan, here with wife Kim, returned to Robert Yates Racing and his trademark Texaco Havoline Ford.
(Right) Irvan's teammate, Dale Jarrett, acquired the sponsorship of Quality Care and Ford Credit and joined with new crew chief Todd Parrott for the 1996 season.

betting on the new Pontiac Grand Prix to move them to a higher competitive plane during the coming season. Petty Enterprises and driver Bobby Hamilton, showing flashes of brilliance during the 1995 season, hoped the new car would vault them into a position as a race-to-race contender for victory. STP would celebrate its silver anniversary as the team's sponsor this year, and the Pontiacs would carry five different paint schemes during the season to commemorate the long-standing association. And, during the 1996 season, car owner Richard Petty would campaign to be North Carolina's next Secretary of State.

Ward Burton, who joined the Bill Davis team late in 1995, rocketed to his first career NASCAR Winston Cup victory in October at Rockingham. With MBNA bank returning as the team's sponsor and a slightly different paint scheme, Burton hoped to move into contention for the championship with the new Grand Prix.

The fifth Pontiac team — Bahari Racing — inked Pennzoil for another season and replaced departed driver Michael Waltrip with former NASCAR Busch Series champion Johnny Benson Jr. Benson, a winner at every step in his climb to the Cup level, was labeled a "can't miss" prospect. In 1996, he would campaign for the NASCAR Winston Cup Rookie-of-the-Year title in the bright yellow cars owned by Charlotte businessmen Chuck Ryder and Lowrance Harry.

After spending a decade with the Pennzoil-backed team without winning his first NASCAR Winston Cup race, Michael Waltrip felt that it was time for him to change the direction of his career. Leaving Bahari Racing was difficult for Michael, but he grabbed the chance to work with one of the most famous teams in the history of the sport when the Wood Brothers' Citgo Ford ride opened up late in the sea-

PRIMESTAR to co-sponsor Ted Musgrave's red-white-blue-and-yellow Fords.

Roush was not the only Ford team owner to create an additional effort for the track. As Robert Yates and crew chief Larry McReynolds prepared to celebrate the return of Ernie Irvan to the driver's seat in their famed No. 28 Texaco Havoline Fords, they put the finishing touches on a deal combining the sponsorships of Ford's Quality Care and Ford Credit for their 1995 driver Dale Jarrett. Todd Parrott left Penske South to become the new crew chief for the red-white-and-blue Fords carrying "88," the same number the old DiGard Racing team wore during its glory years in the early '80s when Yates was the head engine builder for the team.

Geoff Bodine and longtime car owner Bud Moore faced the 1996 season with some trepidation. With Exide gone to the new Roush team, Geoff began searching for a new sponsor for the season. He secured a sponsorship from television's shopping giant, QVC, and quipped that the company's initials really stood for Qualifying, Victory and Championship." Bodine named Gary Preziosi as the head of his engine program, replacing Danny Glad, who joined the Wood Brothers as an engine development specialist.

Moore and driver Wally Dallenbach headed for Daytona with a refrigerator-white Ford, still in search of a sponsor to replace departed Quality Care. By the conclusion of Speedweeks, Moore had inked a full-season package with computer modem-maker Hayes, and plans were underway for a sparkling new paint scheme. Dallenbach also had extended his contract to a full year. When longtime crew member Donnie Wingo left Moore's Spartanburg, S.C., shop to work for Travis Carter, Moore promoted former racer and '95 hired hand Jimmy Means to the crew chief position for the famous "15" cars.

Butch Mock named Morgan Shepherd as the replacement for recently released Todd Bodine to drive his Thunderbirds for '96. The association marked the third time Shepherd, himself recently released from the Wood Brothers team, and Mock would work together. When Factory Outlet Stores dropped to an associate sponsorship

(Right) Rusty Wallace would sport a more colorful Miller design on his "2" car in '96 and named Mike Ege as his head engine builder when former motor man David Evans and mechanic Billy Woodruff headed to Felix Sabates' SABCO team.

(Below) Bristol International Raceway was purchased by Speedway Motorsports Inc., who promised many improvements to make the half-mile oval a world-class facility.

level with the team, Mock signed Remington Arms as full sponsor, changing the colors from blue and orange to the green and gold of Remington.

With Wingo now reporting to the Smokin' Joe's shop near Lake Norman to prepare the yellow-and-purple Fords for car owner Carter and driver Jimmy Spencer, another new combination was at work within Harry Melling's team. Driver Lake Speed hired Jim Long (formerly with Sabates' team) as his new crew chief when Peter Sospenzo and five others headed out the door and up the road to the TriStar team. Mark Smith became the sole owner of TriStar after purchasing the portions owned by Dave Fuge and George Bradshaw. Healthsource boosted its sponsorship of the team to include a full program for driver Loy Allen for the coming season, and Jeff Hammond was hired as the head wrench for the effort.

At Bobby Allison Motorsports, driver Derrike Cope celebrated his re-signing with the team by walking down the

aisle with former Miss Winston, Renee White, on December 3.

In a Hickory, N.C., airport hangar, Mike Beam's new shop was preparing to receive delivery of parts and pieces from Bill Elliott's shop in Dawsonville, Ga. Bill and team co-owner Charles Hardy decided to field the McDonald's Fords from Beam's shop, but would continue research and development and fielding entries in selected NASCAR Busch Series and ARCA races for Ron Barfield Jr. in Dawsonville. Elliott also finalized the details to run a team in the NASCAR Craftsman Truck Series shortly after wife Cindy presented him with their first son, William Clyde, immediately nicknamed

of the Hendrick teams, including Terry Labonte's Kellogg's-sponsored Chevrolets.

Darrell Waltrip had a new look for his Western Auto Monte Carlos, changing the paint to reflect the opening of a new line of stores owned by the company under the Parts America name. The familiar tones of gray-fading-to-black were replaced by varying shades of blue. Waltrip also successfully underwent surgery to remove a plate and 18 screws from his leg inserted after his 1990 accident in the Pepsi 400 at Daytona.

Dave Marcis greeted new full-time sponsor Prodigy Services by hiring veteran ARCA crew chief

(Above) Dave Marcis got the full-time sponsorship of Prodigy Services and hired veteran ARCA crew chief Terry Shirley to replace the departed Dale Fischlein. (Right) Hoping to turn a lackluster season (in which the team finished 30th in the point standings) around, car owner Felix Sabates hired a new crew chief, a new engine builder and changed the paint scheme on driver Kyle Petty's Coors Light Pontiac Grand Prix. Bahari Racing hired reigning NASCAR Busch Series Champion Johnny Benson to drive the Pennzoil Pontiacs that Michael Waltrip had driven for years.

"Chase." Sadly, just five weeks later, Bill's nephew and brother Ernie's son, Casey, died after a valiant battle with an extended illness, casting a pall over the family's efforts for the coming season.

Bob Johnson returned as the crew chief for Junie Donlavey's Heilig-Meyers Fords based in Richmond, Va., with Mike Wallace back behind the wheel of the black-and-teal Thunderbirds. A consortium that included Jasper Engines' Doug Bawel and driver Bobby Hillin purchased the "77" team from D.K. Ulrich's U.S. Racing. USAir no longer sponsored the team, but Bawel and Hillin prepared to run the full season with Jasper's sponsorship and a new paint scheme that incorporated red, white, blue and yellow.

Kenny Wallace became the third Wallace brother to compete at the NASCAR Winston Cup level for the entire season when FILMAR Racing announced plans to step up from the NASCAR Busch Series ranks. Wallace and car owner Fil Martocci signed Square D electrical components as its sponsor and proudly pulled the cover off its new blue-and-yellow Thunderbirds.

Changes were also occurring within the Chevrolet camps.

Hendrick Motorsports re-dedicated its efforts to get Ken Schrader and the Budweiser Monte Carlos back on the winning track by naming NASCAR Winston Cup champion crew chief Ray Evernham as team manager for both Schrader's effort and that of defending champion Gordon. When Ken Howes, Schrader's crew chief in '95, moved to a research and development program within Hendrick Motorsports, Evernham named Phil Hammer as the new head wrench for Schrader's red-and-white cars. Quaker State replaced Valvoline as an associate sponsor on all three

Terry Shirley to replace Dale Fischlein, who left to pursue a driving career of his own after working with Marcis for several years and driving in an occasional race when time and preparation permitted.

Ricky Craven, winner of the 1995 NASCAR Winston Cup Rookie-of-the-Year title, saw some changes occur in his Kodiak-sponsored team owned by Larry Hedrick. Waddell Wilson left the group to join forces with longtime friend Harry Ranier, who was returning to racing with the formation of a NASCAR Busch Series team scheduled for a limited season and featuring driver Tony Stewart. Hedrick named Scott Maxim, who worked with Craven in the past, as the team's new manager and Gregg Wilson as the new head engine builder. Charley Pressley signed on as the new crew chief for Craven and the Kodiak team after Andy Petree's return to Leo Jackson's team.

At the Interstate Batteries shop, John Wilson (formerly at SABCO) was busy at work establishing a new engine-building department for Bobby Labonte's Monte Carlos. Everyone in the shop took a break from work to celebrate car owner Joe Gibbs' induction into the National Football Hall of Fame in Canton, Ohio.

Joe Nemechek's Burger King-sponsored Chevrolet team would have a new crew chief to go with the flames recently added to the rear quarter panels of the Monte Carlos. Jeff Buice was named as the leader of the Double-Whopperwith-Cheese effort, replacing Mike Boerschinger, who wore the head wrench cap during 1995 for Nemechek's family-owned team.

During the off-season, other circumstances changed that would alter the face of the sport in 1996. Dick Brooks disbanded his team that he bought from Sabates during the 1995 season. Dean Myers and his Active Motorsports team had little success finding a new sponsor for the season and all but closed shop.

NASCAR announced its intention to hold an exhibition race in November of 1996 at the Suzuka circuit in Japan and also unveiled plans for NASCAR-themed stores and cafe restaurants to be opened during the coming season.

Series' sponsor R.J. Reynolds pulled the wraps off a new bonus program, announcing that $10,000 would be paid per race to the winning driver if he was also the point leader. If not, the money would roll over until the point leader won a race. A total of $310,000 would be paid in the leader bonus program during the 1996 season.

Silver Anniversary NASCAR Winston Cup Champion Gordon was busy, flying from site to site to accept the National Motorsports Press Association, the Eastern Motorsports Press Association and the national Driver-of-the-Year awards to go with his special silver NASCAR Winston Cup trophy. His winnings of more than $4.3 million during his spectacular championship season dwarfed the previous record held by Earnhardt by nearly $1 million.

Dave Marcis won the Busch Clash "wild card" drawing, and Charles Hardy accepted the NMPA's Most Popular Driver award for Bill Elliott. Bill was unable to claim his 10th MPD trophy in person as he was home with wife Cindy attending the birth of their son.

Construction continued at the new Texas Motor Speedway and the California Speedway, while New Hampshire's Bob Bahre bought half-interest in North Wilkesboro Speedway, immediately setting off speculation regarding the future of the historic five-eighths-mile track in North Carolina's Brushy Mountains. Bruton Smith purchased half-interest in the track late in the 1995 season, and many thought that the Smith/Bahre ownership of North Wilkesboro spelled the end of NASCAR Winston Cup racing at one of the most famous short tracks in the history of the sport. Immediately, media members began saying that Smith would take one NASCAR Winston Cup date for Texas, while Bahre would claim the other for a second race at New Hampshire International Speedway. Someone forgot to tell the media members that the track does not own the dates — NASCAR does.

Within weeks, Smith stunned the sport by announcing the purchase of Bristol International Raceway from owner Larry Carrier. Smith underscored his intentions for the spectacular half-mile in Thunder Valley by saying that there would be no changes in Bristol's schedule in the future.

On an unhappy note, the NASCAR Winston Cup family was saddened by the news that pioneer Darlington founder and retired area businessman Harold Brasington fell victim to a fatal heart attack during the winter.

From November to February, hardly a day passed without NASCAR Winston Cup racing showing up in newspaper headlines around the country as change after change occurred within the sport and teams worked their way through extensive testing sessions in preparation for the start of the new season.

Finally, it was time to race!

After all the upheavals – with drivers and crew members shifting from team to team and tracks changing hands – everyone on the NASCAR Winston Cup circuit breathed a sigh of relief when the green flag finally fell at Daytona to signal the beginning of the 1996 season.

NASCAR
Winston Cup Champion 1996
Terry Labonte

"... to stand there and look down at all the faces of the guys who had worked so hard for the entire year, and to see them so happy after winning the championship, really brought home to me what this was all about."

Terry Labonte

As a driver, you're never sure if you are going to win a race or not when you roll off the line on Sunday. You hope it will be your day — that everything will go right for you both on the track and on pit road. Performance in those two areas has to be near perfect in NASCAR Winston Cup racing, as competitive as it is today. It's the same way with winning the NASCAR Winston Cup championship. You can hope, but seldom does it really happen.

I know because I won the title in 1984 — and I've been chasing the second Winston Cup ever since. I've been through the peaks and the valleys of racing — from running well and winning to running well and losing to running poorly.

The point is that if you ever get into the position to have a chance to win the title, you really need to take advantage of everything you can because your opportunities are pretty limited. I've been very fortunate in some ways. In my entire NASCAR Winston Cup racing career, which began almost 20 years ago in 1978, I've been in the position at the end of the season to win the championship only twice.

And now, after this year, I have capitalized on both of those opportunities.

That's why I'm even more proud than I thought I might be to be writing this as the 1996 NASCAR Winston Cup champion.

I'm proud of the accomplishments of the season, proud

Championship team owner Rick Hendrick helps Terry hoist the championship trophy in the winner's circle at Atlanta. Hendrick, who also owns the championship runner-up DuPont Chevrolet team, is the first owner to end the season with his teams in the No. 1 and No. 2 spots in the point standings.

off, and that's the way I've always been.

But I must admit that this championship really brought out the emotion in me Sunday night at Atlanta after this was all over. Maybe part of the whole situation was the circumstances of the race — with Bobby winning the event, finally breaking through for a win in 1996 after the team had struggled at the beginning of the season and then really started to get everything together later in the year.

The fact that he dominated the race, leading the most laps and then holding off Dale Jarrett in the closing laps, was special for him, and for my mom and dad, too. So, to have him become the first Labonte to win at Atlanta was great.

The fact that I was able to clinch the championship in the same race, after running extremely well all day, was an even bigger bonus. Pulling alongside each other for our "double victory lap" made the day even more special for both of us. Bobby said it was the coolest thing we've ever done together as brothers, and I think I might agree with him. It was something that was so special and so spontaneous, that I'll never forget those few minutes we drove around together. I know he won't, and I know I won't.

When I was standing on the back of the trailer that was taking our entire crew around the track for our championship victory lap, I guess it began to sink in that we actually had won the championship. We tried not to think about what it would be like to be champions before the race because we didn't want to jinx ourselves. But to stand there and look down at all the faces of the guys who had worked so hard for the entire year, and to see them so happy after winning the championship, really brought home to me what this was all about.

My first championship came in my fifth year of driving in NASCAR Winston Cup, and, like a lot of drivers who win the title early in their career, I probably didn't appreciate and understand just how important it is. It's not just the money. It's what the championship really means and how much of a reward it truly is for a team.

It's so hard to win the championship. It's hard to win races. There are so many good teams, good drivers, good sponsors and good crew members out there. Just winning races is difficult, and it gets harder, really, every year. To win the championship takes such dedication, such hard

of my family who will share the honor with me when we go to New York in December, and proud for our sponsor, Kellogg's Corn Flakes. Most of all, however, I'm proud of the team that put together the program and then did all the work putting the Kellogg's cars under me and giving me chances to run well and to win at every track on the schedule all year long.

Everyone always says that the crew and the team are the most important part of a championship, and I wish there was some way that each of you reading this could spend a season with my crew chief, Gary DeHart, and all the rest of the Hendrick Motorsports team. Spending time with them is probably the only way that you could ever understand the dedication, the harmony, the hard work and the perseverance that every one of those crew members has when it comes to putting the best cars possible on the track for the driver every week.

You just can't put into words the amount of hard work it takes to make an effort like this happen. Unless you live with it and work with it every day, all year, there's no real way to tell you how deserving this team is of the championship and how rewarded they are because we won. Every crew member on every team works hard all year, and some teams have more success than others, for one reason or another. I've seen hard work not result in either wins or championships.

That's why this championship season means so much to my Kellogg's team.

Last year, the team worked hard all year but watched its Hendrick Motorsports teammates enjoy being named the champions at the end of the season when Jeff Gordon won the title. This year, they get to enjoy it themselves as the champions. That's one of the nicest parts of this whole situation, as far as I'm concerned.

I'm usually not a very emotional guy — as everyone knows. I don't show much to people, either on the track or work, and such good luck during the course of the entire season that it's difficult to describe.

That's what makes this title so sweet. After winning the first one in 1984, I figured I might get another in '85 or '86. I thought, "Well, we've got the first one, and we've got the same team pretty much intact, and there's no reason it won't be the first of several Winston Cups."

But that's not the way it is. And as each year goes past, and you don't win again, you begin to appreciate just how fortunate the team is that does win a championship.

Year after year went by. I'd win some races and run pretty well at times, but the championship stayed out of my reach. Then, I went four years without a single victory. It wasn't that the teams weren't trying and working hard. It's just that we didn't have everything right to win.

It got pretty frustrating for me, really. I didn't doubt myself or my ability, but nothing seemed to be working the right way. Not winning at all was very difficult, and so I can empathize with drivers who are trying to break that winless streak. It's not that you're not trying and can't win. It's just that things aren't working and you're not getting the breaks you need. That's the way it was for me, too.

When Ricky Rudd decided to leave Hendrick Motorsports and form his own team with Tide, a great opportunity opened for me. Rick Hendrick called and asked me if I would consider joining his team and taking over the "5" car, and I realized that this might be the chance of a lifetime for me.

There wasn't any question that the cars, the crew and the opportunity to win races and championships were there. I felt honored in some ways that Rick would think of

Terry Labonte's victory at the fall race in Charlotte, his first points win in 37 tries, set the stage for his ultimately successful run at the NASCAR Winston Cup championship. He managed to cut Gordon's lead to one point with three races remaining in the season. (Right) For the UAW-GM Quality 500, Terry's car sported another special paint scheme courtesy of his sponsor, Kellogg's Corn Flakes.

me and offer me the chance to drive for his team. Here I was in a four-year nonwinning streak, and he thought enough of me to ask if I would drive his cars.

Kellogg's came with me to the Hendrick team, and I'll never be able to thank them enough. The folks there are so great to work with, and we have developed such a good relationship through the years, that it has been very special for me to have been able to carry them on the cars all the way to a championship.

We gave them their first top-10 finish, and then their first victory, and it's very, very special for me to be able to give them their first championship. Kellogg's has been so supportive of our sport and has done so much with a variety of drivers to help promote NASCAR Winston Cup racing that I think it's only fitting that they get to enjoy winning a championship with us. I know they are excited about the championship, and I also know that they will continue to help support racing in the years to come. Having Kellogg's at the head table with us in New York will be a great way to thank them for all they have done for the sport in the past.

After we finished sixth in the point standings last year, we knew that we had a very good chance to figure into the championship this year. But after we finished 24th at Daytona and then 34th at Rockingham with a cracked cylinder head, we weren't quite sure what to think. We had led almost all of the first half of the race at Rockingham before

the engine problem, so we knew that we had what it took to win there, but we really wondered if we were in for a season of bad luck.

Our luck turned around a little at Richmond, where we finished eighth, and at Atlanta, where we were second behind Dale Earnhardt. Those two finishes early in the season moved us to seventh in the point standings, after we had been as low as 30th.

Then we began hitting our stride. We won at North Wilkesboro in the "Iron Man" car after sitting on the pole there — our third of the young season. That win moved us to third in the standings, and although we had brake problems at the next race in Martinsville and finished 24th, we still felt pretty good about the way we were running week after week.

Then we really got things going. For the next eight races, from Talladega to New Hampshire, we finished out of the top five just twice — seventh at the first Pocono and sixth at New Hampshire. In that string were second places at Dover, Michigan and Daytona in the Pepsi 400. When New Hampshire was over, we had moved into the point lead for the first time in the season.

We struggled with the handling of the car at Pocono — I guess we just brought the wrong car there — and finished 16th. The following race at Talladega, we were 24th after being involved in a multicar accident that we had no control over, and we fell to second place in the standings.

Then came a third at The Brickyard and we were back in the lead. We finished second at The Glen, third at Michigan and fifth at Bristol. Then came Darlington and the Mountain Dew Southern 500, where we thought we would run really well. We did run in the top five for the majority of the race, but in the final 100 laps, we had an oil leak develop that ended up with the crew making repairs.

Under the direction of veteran crew chief Gary DeHart (below), Kellogg's team members provided Terry with competitive, reliable equipment from their shops at Hendrick Motorsports. At the track, DeHart and the crew were among the very best in the garage and on pit road, helping Terry to two wins, 21 top-five finishes and a NASCAR Winston Cup championship.

We finished 26th, but still held onto the point lead.

After a fifth place at Richmond, we went to Dover. Although we had a really good car there, we had two different cut tires that needed to be replaced under the green flag, and we lost laps with each. We finished 21st in the race and fell out of the point lead when Jeff won there again.

If we wanted to win the championship, there was little doubt about what we had to do the rest of the year. We needed to really run well and finish well if we had any hopes of the title.

At Martinsville, we felt we had a really good chance — but then we lost a lap early in the race and had to fight our way back into contention. It turned out to be one of the most important races of the season for us. We could have been way down the list in the final rundown, but instead, we were able to get the lost lap back. Then we fought hard all day and ended up finishing second. It was the kind of performance that really showed how determined our race team

was, and it kept us in contention for the championship.

The following weekend at North Wilkesboro was another good example of how much this team wanted the championship. We struggled with the car all weekend. It really didn't handle as well as we had hoped it would, but we managed to finish fifth with it. We headed to Charlotte still in hopes of finding a way to catch up with Jeff, who was having a great stretch run.

I had never won at Charlotte before in my entire career, but this time everything went right for us and we came out of there with the victory. Jeff cracked a cylinder head and finished low, and we were right back in the middle of the battle for the championship, just a single point down as we headed for Rockingham.

We felt we had a good car, and, after the way we ran there in the spring, we went with high hopes. But at the same time, we had problems there with the engine in the spring, and we knew that we had to have a good day. We did just that, finishing third. Jeff struggled a little, and we went to Phoenix in the point lead again.

Other than Atlanta, Phoenix turned out to be probably the most important race of the year. On my second lap of practice, the throttle hung in our primary car and I crashed very hard, breaking a bone in my left hand in the process. The team scrambled around, pulled the spare car off the transporter and I started working with a group of doctors and sports medicine specialists to get my hand in some kind of shape so I could drive in the race on Sunday. Here we were with a spare car and an injured driver — and the championship hanging in the balance.

That was hardly the way anyone wanted to go into the two most important races of the year. With a lot of work and a lot of painkillers, I was able to run the entire race and actually had a chance to win it at one point. At the end, I lost second place to Mark Martin with just over a lap to go. But to finish third there and also gain a few points on Jeff under such difficult circumstances testifies to the outstanding performance by the crew.

Then we began to prepare for Atlanta. Gary and the crew did everything they could to make sure that we would have the best car we could for the track. They brought all kinds of spare parts, including a rear clip with a fuel cell already installed. They made arrangements for a frame-straightening device to be on hand if we should be involved in a wreck early in the race and needed to fix the car. Everything we could think of that we might possibly need was all there in Atlanta.

As it turned out, we didn't need any of them. The car was very strong, and we had a really solid run. The car might have been capable of winning, but I'm not sure about the driver because my hand was hurting a lot, particularly in the second half of the race. I didn't need to really push things too much, because I knew all along that all I needed to do was to run in the top eight and the championship was ours.

In the closing laps of the race, I might have been able to improve my finish by one position, but it really didn't matter. Instead, I chose to back the car off just a touch, running just a little bit conservatively to make sure that we finished the race where we needed to. Once Jeff got his laps back and clearly was going to finish in the top three in the race, we knew where we needed to finish. If we had a problem, he could still win the championship, and we needed to run all the way to the end to clinch the title.

And with 17 cars still on the lead lap, we didn't need to take any unnecessary chances. We just played it close to the vest in those final laps, and in the end, that was the right decision to make.

As I said earlier, I didn't think that the second championship would take so long to win. But I learned a lot in the 12 years between NASCAR Winston Cups. I learned that you don't take anything for granted in racing and that what you do one year really doesn't have a whole lot to do with what you do the following year. You can have all the pieces in place, and have the best cars, motors and team members, and still not win the title.

This second title is very, very special to myself and to my family.

When I won the first one, it wasn't as big a deal. The sport wasn't as big as it is now, and the competitive level now is much higher than it was then. My children were very young when I won the championship before, and to them, the Winston Cup was just another trophy in our house. They really didn't understand what it meant and how hard it was to win.

Now they are older, and they have lived through this season. They know more about the sport and how hard it was to win the championship. They have been through the ups and downs with me during the last several years. The Winston Cup has a lot of meaning to them, and one of the most special parts of this championship will be taking them to New York with Kim and me and having them enjoy this with us and the team.

I would like to close this by thanking the fans who have supported me and our efforts through the years. I was really surprised at how many of you wrote cards and sent things to me and the team during the stretch run to the championship, particularly during the weeks since Phoenix.

Not all of you were Terry Labonte fans, but at the same time, you wished us well in our quest for the Winston Cup. The fact that you were either Earnhardt fans, Rusty fans, Mark Martin fans, or Bill Elliott fans and wished us luck as long as your favorite driver was not in contention for the championship this year, was very touching to Kim and me.

Our sport is a very special one, and the fans who support it are special, too. I am proud to have won the championship, and I hope that in the year to come, you will feel that I have been a good champion for our sport.

Terry Labonte
1996 NASCAR Winston Cup Champion

Daytona 500

Dale Jarrett (88) and Terry Labonte (5) team up on the inside of Daytona's tri-oval in pursuit of Jeremy Mayfield (98) as Robert Pressley (33), Sterling Marlin (4) and Bobby Hamilton (43) draft together on the outside. **(Right)** *Dale Jarrett and his first-year team had a stellar Speedweeks performance with victories in the Busch Clash and the Gatorade Twin 125 that culminated in Dale's second career trip to a Daytona 500 victory lane.*

For nearly three months, teams had worked day and night in their shops, tested at Daytona and Talladega, spent hour after hour in the wind tunnel, fine-tuned aerodynamics, and tested chassis settings over and over in preparation for the NASCAR Winston Cup season-opener.

No other sport opens its year with the biggest event of the season. The Super Bowl brings the NFL season to a close. The World Series crowns Major League Baseball's champion. Hockey fans revel in the drama of the Stanley Cup where NHL players battle for supremacy.

NASCAR Winston Cup racing's most prestigious race, the Daytona 500, marks the beginning of the new season, and no stone is left unturned as teams try to notch a victory in the sport's biggest event.

Some car owners and drivers will tell you that the Daytona lid-lifter is merely the first event of the schedule, and that it pays the same amount of points as Rockingham, Richmond or Atlanta, the next races of the season. In the next breath, however, the same car owner or driver, as well as the team's sponsor, will tell you that winning the Daytona 500 is everything.

To win this one makes a season.

For nearly every team in the garage area, this year's Daytona 500 was the first test in the fire of battle after the changes that occurred (see Preface) during the off-season. New crew chiefs, drivers, crew members and — in some cases — car owners, would receive an immediate reading on what the season held in store for them and what remaining pieces of the puzzle were needed in order to bring their program to the razor-sharp winning edge.

Jeff Gordon arrived at Daytona ready defend his NASCAR Winston Cup championship, but the majority of the eyes in the huge grandstand crowds were focused on a black-white-and-silver Chevrolet Monte Carlo bearing the No. 3.

After the spirited 1995 championship battle left Dale Earnhardt sitting at a floor table at the Waldorf-Astoria Hotel instead of in the champion's seat on the raised dais, the seven-time champion and his mates at Richard Childress Racing had grimly re-dedicated themselves to winning the title in 1996. The fire had not been missing in Earnhardt's eyes during the 1995 season, and the loss of the title to Gordon had fanned those flames to a white-hot incandescence over the winter.

The front row for this year's Daytona 500 is a mirror image of last year's, when Dale Jarrett secured the pole in the "28" and was joined on his right by Dale Earnhardt. This year, Earnhardt and Irvan led the field under the green flag to kick off the 1996 NASCAR Winston Cup season. Earnhardt underscored his determination to conquer the Daytona 500 and return to championship form by seizing the first Busch Pole Award of the new season (left). Irvan, in a triumphant return to the Texaco Thunderbird, also showed his determination to return to competitive form with a front-row qualifying effort and a win in his Twin 125.

Coupled with Dale's fierce determination to win the crown again was the fact that he had never won the Daytona 500. Time after time during the weeks leading to the season-opener, Dale had been asked if this was the year that he would finally claim the elusive victory. Most thought it would be and ranked Earnhardt as the favorite for the win at The Beach.

Although young Jeremy Mayfield had topped the speed charts during the preseason testing sessions driving Cale Yarborough's RCA Ford, no one disregarded the potent duo from the Robert Yates shops: Ernie Irvan and Dale Jarrett. They would have the best power plants that master engine builder Yates could produce, and many thought Ford's best shot for the Daytona 500 pole would come in

the form of the Texaco or Quality Care Thunderbirds.

Meanwhile, no one forgot that Sterling Marlin, with Runt Pittman building another hand grenade engine, would head for Florida with a history-making "three-peat" in mind. The Morgan-McClure Kodak Chevrolet was also remembered as the class of the field at restrictor-plate tracks in 1995, and a well-tweaked yellow Monte Carlo was ready for the current season.

Still, the money was on Earnhardt to grab the Daytona 500 pole, and he didn't disappoint his legions of black-clad

Ken Schrader (left) and Jeff Gordon compare notes in Daytona's garage area. Prior to the season, Rick Hendrick named Ray Evernham (Gordon's crew chief) as team manager for the Budweiser Chevrolets in an attempt to make them more competitive. The strategy seemed to pay off immediately: Schrader started fourth and finished third in the biggest race of the year.

fans. When the first qualifying session of the year was completed, Dale claimed the first Daytona 500 pole of his storied career, although he needed every split second on the track to do it. His margin over Irvan, who claimed the outside front-row starting position, was just over 14/100ths of a second; an infinitesimal difference that only an electronic watch could measure.

Jarrett and Marlin gave a good accounting for themselves, posting the third- and fifth-fastest laps, and Mayfield proved his preseason testing times were on the money as he hustled the red-and-white Ford to the fourth-fastest lap. Gordon was in the hunt as well, rocketing his DuPont Chevrolet to sixth position on the time sheet. Other strong runs were recorded by Robert Pressley, Rick Mast (with the fastest Pontiac in qualifying), Terry Labonte and Ken Schrader.

After establishing the Goodwrench Monte Carlo as the fastest car in the garage area, Earnhardt turned his attention to the team's other car which he entered in the Busch Clash, the annual dash for cash featuring the previous season's Busch Pole winners. Included in the Clash field this year were Dave Marcis (with a Childress engine in his Prodigy Monte Carlo) and David Green. Marcis was the lucky "wildcard" winner, gaining a spot in the race when his name was drawn from the pool of drivers who were fastest in second-round qualifying in 1995. Green claimed the most Busch Poles during 1995 in the NASCAR Busch Series division to earn an entry in the Clash for the second-straight year. Buz McCall, owner of Green's NASCAR Busch Series effort, purchased a special Monte Carlo for the race and hired former Childress championship-winning

(Right) Ernie Irvan waits while his crew makes repairs to the Texaco Ford after a mishap on lap 28 that also involved Earnhardt and Wally Dallenbach. Irvan returned to action and was credited with 35th place after completing 145 of the scheduled 200 laps. (Below) Dale Jarrett's team, led by first-year crew chief Todd Parrott, provided excellent service on pit road and kept Dale in the lead pack throughout the afternoon.

crew chief Kirk Shelmerdine to ramrod the Busch-sponsored effort.

This year, the Busch Clash again would be run in two segments, with the second 10-lapper featuring an inverted start based on the finishing positions of the first 10 laps. Rick Mast drew the pole for the opening lap of the race but, when the first 10 laps were over, Marlin had stormed to the front to claim the $25,000 prize. Jarrett had rolled through the field from 12th to second, just ahead of Terry Labonte. Earnhardt, surprisingly, was toward the rear of the field after the first 10 laps, and started from the inside of the second row for the second 10-lapper. Tens of thousands of fans figured victory was a cinch for the black No. 3, and their cheers grew louder as John Andretti and Bobby Labonte fell

to the back of the pack for the start. Andretti had developed an oil leak in the first-segment laps, and Labonte was struggling with engine problems. Dale had clear sailing.

Earnhardt, however, found his engine bogging down slightly. Not realizing that Dale had hurt the qualifying engine during his run to the Daytona 500 pole, his team had inserted the damaged power plant in the Clash car for the race. With the bulk of the field lined up behind him fighting for position, "The Other Dale" whipped his red-white-and-blue Ford into the inside lane and shot through the pack to claim second place by the end of the segment's first lap! With a push from Ken Schrader, Jarrett then cleared Earnhardt on lap 14 and began looking in his rearview mirror.

The Chevrolet phalanx was lined up to challenge him, but the three Hendrick Motorsports drivers, along with Marlin and Earnhardt, began fighting for position, allowing Jarrett to build and maintain a two-car-length lead for the remainder of the race.

Giving car owner Yates the Clash victory, Jarrett also provided Todd Parrott with his first Cup victory of any kind in his new role of crew chief. Marlin held off Earnhardt for second place, with Labonte and Schrader filling the top five. Ford-driving Ricky Rudd, Mark Martin and Bill Elliott beat Gordon to the line.

When the competing cars in the Gatorade Twin 125s rolled out Thursday to determine the remainder of the starting field, Earnhardt was again the favorite for victory. And this time, there was no denying the black No. 3. as Earnhardt trounced the field in the Gatorade Twin for the seventh-consecutive year. His winning margin, however, was just 0.16 seconds over second-place Marlin after a multicar tangle prompted a late-race caution that set the stage for a three-lap, green-flag dash to the checkers. Behind Earnhardt and Marlin, Terry Labonte claimed third place.

Reporters didn't know what to lead their stories with

(Right) Sterling Marlin (4), shooting for an unprecedented third straight Daytona 500 victory, looked strong in the early going and took the point briefly before his engine failed uncharacteristically and sent Sterling to the garage in 40th place. Michael Waltrip showed off his new ride in the Citgo Ford by running with the lead group, which included Dale Earnhardt and Ken Schrader.
(Below) In a virtual repeat of 1994, Dale Jarrett powered past Dale Earnhardt late in the race and hung on to take the checkered flag. Ken Schrader followed with a close third.

after the finish of the second Gatorade Twin. Earnhardt's seventh-straight Twin 125 victory earlier in the afternoon was enough to rate a bold headline, but Ernie Irvan had completed his storybook comeback by scoring a fabulous rock-'em, sock-'em victory over Schrader in the second event. Irvan's finish in the Texaco Havoline Ford, a half car-length ahead of the red Budweiser Chevrolet, was one of the most popular wins of his career. It underscored the fact that Ernie was back to his competitive form.

Earnhardt continued to be the favorite when he went to the line for his 18th start in the Daytona 500. Bolstered by a dramatic victory in the first round of the IROC series, Dale hoped to add the long-sought-after Daytona 500 trophy to his haul when he boarded his Lear jet later that afternoon.

He almost got it. Dale went to victory lane at the conclusion of the 500, but his last name was not Earnhardt — instead, the name on the winning car was Jarrett!

After Gordon slapped the wall on the 11th lap to finish 42nd, and Marlin headed to the garage before quarter-dis-

Dale Jarrett stands with team owner Robert Yates (center) and crew chief Todd Parrott as they display their trophies after the Daytona 500 win. Robert Yates collected his second trophy as the Daytona 500's winning car owner. (Davey Allison drove the No. 28 Ford to victory in 1992.) Todd Parrott collected his first trophy, following in the footsteps of his dad, Buddy, who wrenched Derrike Cope to victory in 1990.

tance with engine failure, Jarrett and Earnhardt locked up in a titanic duel late in the race. Schrader was in the mix, and Martin drafted his slow Ford into contention as well. Behind Mark, seven more Fords were lined up, and the Valvoline Thunderbird driver could only hope a freight train would push him to victory. Unfortunately, it didn't happen that way this day for a fourth-place Martin.

With 23 laps left in the race, Jarrett took the lead from Earnhardt and, as in the Clash a week earlier, looked in his rearview mirror to see Earnhardt and Schrader lined up in their Chevrolets. Knowing that the Bowtie Brigade would make a run at him, trying to steamroll their way past his Thunderbird, Jarrett could only hope the ace in his sleeve would be enough to win the high-stakes game. Throughout the day, Parrott and the Quality Care team had worked on the handling on Jarrett's Ford and, on the last stop, dialed the car in perfectly. Jarrett also knew that he had the best motor from the Yates shop under his right foot. The combination of power and handling, along with Jarrett's skill and nerve, would now be put to the toughest test.

Jarrett maintained the point and, on the final lap, drove as much with his mirror as he did with his windshield. Everywhere Earnhardt attacked, Jarrett countered. When the last 2.5 miles were complete, the patriotically-painted Thunderbird headed for victory lane as Jarrett's second-career Daytona 500 victory was in the books. Earnhardt, suffering yet another Daytona 500 disappointment, finished second, just over a car-length behind Jarrett, yet ahead of Schrader and Martin. Jeff Burton, making his debut with the new Jack Roush team, finished fifth, while Wally Dallenbach battled to sixth, ahead of Ted Musgrave, Elliott and Rudd. Michael Waltrip, in his first outing for the Wood Brothers, claimed the final position in the top 10, just ahead of Jimmy Spencer.

In victory lane, Jarrett was jubilant. His first Daytona 500 victory had come in 1993 when he once again beat Earnhardt to the checkers. Now, with another victory at The Beach, Jarrett became only the sixth driver in history to win the event more than once. As he high-fived his crew chief, the victory became even more meaningful as Dale had given Parrott a victory in his first NASCAR Winston Cup race as a crew chief.

Todd also got his own page in the history book as it was the first time that a second-generation crew chief won the Daytona 500. In 1990, Parrott's dad, Buddy, had been the head wrench for winner Derrike Cope.

The victory was the second Daytona 500 win for Yates Racing, the first coming in 1992 with Davey Allison behind the wheel.

Daytona 500

Fin. Pos.	Str. Pos.	Car #	Driver	Team
1	7	88	Dale Jarrett	Quality Care / Ford Credit Ford
2	1	3	Dale Earnhardt	GM Goodwrench Service Chevrolet
3	4	25	Ken Schrader	Budweiser Chevrolet
4	15	6	Mark Martin	Valvoline Ford
5	16	99	Jeff Burton	Exide Batteries Ford
6	9	15	Wally Dallenbach	Hayes Modems Ford
7	20	16	Ted Musgrave	Family Channel / PRIMESTAR Ford
8	21	94	Bill Elliott	McDonald's Ford
9	10	10	Ricky Rudd	Tide Ford
10	11	21	Michael Waltrip	Citgo Ford
11	19	23	Jimmy Spencer	Camel Cigarettes Ford
12	34	44	Jeff Purvis	MCA Records Chevrolet
13	36	41	Ricky Craven	Kodiak Chevrolet
14	32	9	Lake Speed	Spam Ford
15	23	71	Dave Marcis	Prodigy Chevrolet
16	43	2	Rusty Wallace	Miller Ford
17	35	18	Bobby Labonte	Interstate Batteries Chevrolet
18	29	42	Kyle Petty	Coors Light Pontiac
19	14	98	Jeremy Mayfield	RCA Ford
20	39	43	Bobby Hamilton	STP Pontiac
21	33	81	Kenny Wallace	Square D / T.I.C. Ford
22	42	8	Hut Stricklin	Circuit City Ford
23	27	30	Johnny Benson	Pennzoil Pontiac
24	5	5	Terry Labonte	Kellogg's Corn Flakes Chevrolet
25	18	27	Elton Sawyer	David Blair Motorsports Ford
26	13	22	Ward Burton	MBNA America Pontiac
27	26	29	Steve Grissom	Cartoon Network Chevrolet
28	31	1	Rick Mast	Hooters Pontiac
29	40	17	Darrell Waltrip	Parts America Chevrolet
30	25	33	Robert Pressley	Skoal Bandit Chevrolet
31	12	75	Morgan Shepherd	Remington Arms Ford
32	41	11	Brett Bodine	Lowe's Ford
33	30	97	Chad Little	Sterling Cowboy Pontiac
34	38	7	Geoff Bodine	QVC Ford
35	2	28	Ernie Irvan	Texaco Havoline Ford
36	24	19	Loy Allen	Healthsource Ford
37	17	90	Mike Wallace	Heilig-Meyers Ford
38	6	37	John Andretti	Kmart / Little Caesars Ford
39	37	87	Joe Nemechek	Burger King Chevrolet
40	3	4	Sterling Marlin	Kodak Film Chevrolet
41	22	12	Derrike Cope	Mane 'N Tail Ford
42	8	24	Jeff Gordon	DuPont Refinishes Chevrolet
43	28	63	Dick Trickle	Purina Hi Pro Ford

Goodwrench 400

Jimmy Spencer and hot-running Jeremy Mayfield (98) race door to door through Rockingham's high banks while Ricky Rudd (10) and Rick Mast (1) look for an opening. Spencer was very fast in the race's first half, working his way from a 28th starting spot to the lead in the first 100 laps, but a faulty engine sent Jimmy to the garage early. **(Right)** *Dale Earnhardt dives into the first turn leading a pack that includes Mike Skinner, driving a white Monte Carlo owned by Richard Childress, and second-place finisher Dale Jarrett.*

As one of the sport's biggest stars, graced with McDonald's Golden Arches across the hood and flanks of the Ford Thunderbird that he owns with Georgia businessman Charles Hardy, the red-headed Bill Elliott leaned against his transporter in the spanking-new North Carolina Motor Speedway garage area, just days after his solid eighth-place finish in the season-opener at Daytona. Thinking about his NASCAR Winston Cup debut that took place right here at Rockingham two decades before, Elliott grimaced and then allowed a small, embarrassed smile to crease his face.

"Oh, man, I don't know if I want to remember that first race," the lanky Georgian said in his trademark drawl. "It's still a little embarrassing to all of us."

With some prompting, Elliott drifted back 20 years and talked about his family-run team's first foray into NASCAR Winston Cup competition.

"We were so green back then that the word 'rookie' really didn't apply," Bill said softly. "The car we were using was a '73 Ford Torino that my dad, George, bought from Bobby Allison for less than $5,000. We had updated it to '76 specs as best we could, and we worked on that car day and night,

trying to get it ready for the race. I looked like I was a member of a rock group. I had hair sticking out all over the place because I had been working on the car and hadn't had time to get a haircut. We'd send someone out to get food for us because we didn't take a break for working on the car.

"That wasn't bad enough. The car had 'Dahlonega Ford Sales' hand-painted on the sides of it for my dad's Ford dealership that sold four, maybe five, cars a month. We weren't exactly high rollers, that's for sure. We had an old truck that we sold parts off at short tracks in North Georgia, and we put that old Torino on an open trailer and towed it to Rockingham behind that old truck. When we got here, there were no rookie meetings or anything. You were left to try to figure out what to do by yourselves.

"The car was so bad, so grungy, that I tried to clean it up so it didn't look like such an eyesore sitting there in the garage, but there's only so much that could be done. We made the field during the third round of qualifying, and we were so happy to get into the race that we forgot to unblock the oil cooler after qualifying. On race day, we lasted just 32 laps before the oil pump broke, and we won the grand total of $640! Looking back, it really was unbelievable that we

scheduled to practice and qualify the QVC Ford, as well as take over the driving chores from Geoff on the earliest possible lap during the race. Making matters worse, Geoff sat in 35th place in the point standings.

With only one race complete on the 1996 NASCAR Winston Cup schedule, many other teams also faced an uphill struggle in the point battle. Defending series champion Jeff Gordon finished 42nd last week at Daytona and was at the bottom of the point table. Ernie Irvan, John Andretti, Sterling Marlin, Morgan Shepherd and Darrell Waltrip also finished well down on the Daytona results sheet and each needed to have a strong Rockingham outing to keep from digging an early-season hole that would be difficult to emerge from as the year rolled on.

(Above) Jeff Gordon looks over his DuPont Monte Carlo prior to the start of the Goodwrench 400. Jeff bounced back from a disappointing run at Daytona to claim a spot on the front row alongside pole winner Terry Labonte. (Right) The Fords of Kenny Wallace (81), Jimmy Spencer and Dale Jarrett give chase, but none had the muscle to keep Earnhardt's Chevrolet from making its final stop in victory lane.

even made the race, considering what we were working with — both mechanically and mentally!"

Since then, Elliott and his team have grown into their role as one of the best competitors in the sport, with Bill claiming the 1988 NASCAR Winston Cup championship and securing a part of the sport's history when he became the only driver to win the Winston Million by grabbing 1985 victories at Daytona, Talladega and Darlington.

While Elliott was taking media members on a trip down memory lane, Geoff Bodine stood in another area of the new garage, wincing from the injuries he suffered in a multicar accident the previous weekend at Daytona. Geoff knew he would be unable to complete the weekend's grueling 400-mile test at Rockingham and enrolled the services of younger brother Todd Bodine for the weekend. Todd was

At the top of the point standings were a pair of Dales, with Jarrett five points ahead of Earnhardt based on their Daytona finishes. Jarrett and car owner Robert Yates made the trip back to the Charlotte, N.C., shop without the Daytona 500-winning Ford Thunderbird. They had turned the car over to the Daytona USA exhibit for the upcoming year, and the Ford would be one of the focal points of the new attraction scheduled to open in July.

As teams prepared for the first round of qualifying in the

(Above) Terry Labonte led from the pole and looked nearly unbeatable before pulling into his pit trailing a cloud of tell-tale smoke. Terry was credited with a 34th-place finish at the end of the day.
(Right) During one of the race's ten caution periods, pit crews provide service under the watchful eyes of video cameras that dangle on poles over each pit stall.

Sandhills region of North Carolina, teams were heartened by NASCAR's announcement that the structure for the use of provisional starts had been changed, allowing teams to gain and use provisionals earlier than last year. Each team would begin the season with four provisionals and would receive an additional slot after every eight qualifying attempts. In the past, teams only received an additional provisional after each third of the season. With qualifying continuing to grow in importance every week, the new provisional system would benefit all the teams.

One driver who wouldn't need provisionals of any type at

Rockingham was Terry Labonte, who upstaged Hendrick Motorsports teammate Jeff Gordon by snatching the pole with a blistering run of nearly 157 mph. The Kellogg's Corn Flakes Chevrolet driver had gone more than three years without a pole before he snapped the string in 1995. Notching his first pole of the young season, Labonte ensured his team of a slot in the 1997 running of the Busch Clash.

One look through the remainder of the top-10 qualifiers caused veteran garage watchers to wonder just exactly what was going on this February afternoon at Rockingham. Rookie contender Johnny Benson was the fastest Pontiac qualifier, locking down the inside of the second row, with Hut Stricklin and the Stavola Brothers' Ford alongside. Bobby Labonte and young Steve Grissom made up the third row, with the Yabba Dabba Doo Chevrolet on the outside of the green-and-black Interstate Batteries-sponsored Monte Carlo. John Andretti and Kenny Wallace placed their Fords in the fourth row, followed by the Pontiacs of Kyle Petty and Bobby Hamilton. Ward Burton made it four Pontiacs in the top 11 slots, and Jeremy Mayfield backed up his Daytona effort by barely missing the

MacDonald and Gary Bradberry, home to watch the race on television.

From the drop of the green flag at Rockingham, it was clear that Labonte's speed during qualifying was no fluke as he led the field away from starter Doyle Ford and held the point for all but 37 of the first 235 laps. Labonte looked like he was ready to make a shambles of the race until the motor in his yellow-and-red Chevrolet began overheating and spitting water out of the header pipes. Terry peeled off the track and headed for pit road with a cracked cylinder head, ending his day after 236 laps.

When Labonte arrived in the garage area, he found teammate Gordon already there with engine failure that further escalated his woes in the point standings. The Hendrick fortunes took another lump on the jaw when Ken Schrader's Budweiser Chevrolet struggled with brake problems and eventually finished 29th.

With Labonte out of the lead, the battle for the victory turned into a tussle that included Earnhardt, Jarrett, a strong-running Jimmy Spencer, and an impressive Hamilton driving the STP Pontiac that carried the 1972 paint scheme that Richard Petty drove to the NASCAR Winston Cup championship.

Hamilton fought his way to the lead for the first time on lap 296 and then locked horns with Earnhardt in a brilliant battle that had the capacity crowd on its feet, roaring in

top 10 at Rockingham and qualifying 12th.

Elton Sawyer turned the David Blair Motorsports Ford over to Dick Trickle for the second round of qualifying in hopes of getting the Thunderbird into the field, but Trickle was unable to muster the needed speed. Bobby Hillin, Dave Marcis and Loy Allen used provisionals to make the field, sending the Blair team, along with the entries for Randy

By the race's three-quarter mark, Bobby Hamilton (above), carrying a paint scheme reminiscent of Richard Petty's 1972 championship-winning car, had worked his way to the front of the field where he locked horns with Dale Earnhardt. In a furious battle at the point, the two cars tangled, leaving Hamilton to wonder what might have been.

Unocal's Bill Brodrick juggles hats with Dale Earnhardt in Rockingham's victory lane. Dale's win, combined with his second place in the Daytona 500, put him in a tie for the point lead with Dale Jarrett, who finished second at Rockingham.

approval. It was the first time a Petty Enterprises car had led a lap at Rockingham since 1986!

The two drivers swapped the lead back and forth five times in as many laps, thrilling the thousands on hand watching the event. Then, on lap 345, with Hamilton on the outside in turn 4, the black Chevrolet and the red-and-blue Pontiac tangled. Hamilton slid into the wall and scrubbed along the concrete barrier, falling to fifth. Earnhardt, meanwhile, pulled away while debris from the Pontiac brought out the seventh caution of the race. On lap 366, Hamilton spun in the second turn, hitting the wall and ending his hopes for his first career victory.

Jarrett, looking for a second-straight win for his new team at the beginning of the season, was at the point following the next-to-last caution period. When the green flag fell, the Daytona 500 winner hoped that he was good enough to hold off the expected challenge from the black Chevrolet that he beat to the finish line last weekend. On the restart, however, Derrike Cope, doing his best to get a lap back, dove into the third corner in the low groove. Following Cope underneath Jarrett's Ford, Earnhardt emerged at the point with the intentions of staying there. With just two laps remaining in the race, the final yellow flag of the day flew when Bobby Hillin's Ford collected the second-turn wall and handed Earnhardt his 69th career victory.

Ricky Craven, who struggled during the middle of the race with a brake master cylinder problem until his crew made repairs, posted the best finish of his brief career by coming home third, beating Ricky Rudd and Grissom. Marlin and Kenny Wallace, the final cars on the lead lap, took sixth and seventh place. Cope soldiered to eighth place, ahead of Joe Nemechek and Rick Mast.

Although Todd took over the wheel from brother Geoff during the first caution of the race, the Bodine's hopes for a strong finish ended after just 141 laps when the engine failed. Shepherd continued to struggle in the Remington Arms Ford and finished 37th. Andretti was another driver in the garage early with engine failure, lasting just 159 laps. Mark Martin, after a staunch fourth-place run at Daytona, and after winning the NASCAR Busch Series race the previous day at Rockingham, saw his hopes for a Sandhills sweep end with a broken camshaft halfway through the Goodwrench Service 400.

One of the most pleasant surprises of the day was the performance of NASCAR Craftsman Truck Series Champion Mike Skinner in a white "research and development" Chevrolet fielded by Richard Childress Racing. Skinner made the field easily, qualifying 35th and then drove a smooth and consistent race to finish a solid 12th, two laps behind at the conclusion of the 400-mile race. It was the first of a handful of races that Skinner would campaign this year in Childress' "second" team.

Goodwrench 400

Fin. Pos.	Str. Pos.	Car #	Driver	Team
1	18	3	Dale Earnhardt	GM Goodwrench Service Chevrolet
2	13	88	Dale Jarrett	Quality Care / Ford Credit Ford
3	30	41	Ricky Craven	Kodiak Chevrolet
4	25	10	Ricky Rudd	Tide Ford
5	6	29	Steve Grissom	Cartoon Network Chevrolet
6	31	4	Sterling Marlin	Kodak Film Chevrolet
7	8	81	Kenny Wallace	Square D / T.I.C. Ford
8	29	12	Derrike Cope	Mane 'N Tail Ford
9	16	87	Joe Nemechek	Burger King Chevrolet
10	24	1	Rick Mast	Hooters Pontiac
11	9	42	Kyle Petty	Coors Light Pontiac
12	35	31	Mike Skinner	RCR Chevrolet
13	23	99	Jeff Burton	Exide Batteries Ford
14	34	28	Ernie Irvan	Texaco Havoline Ford
15	15	94	Bill Elliott	McDonald's Ford
16	14	17	Darrell Waltrip	Parts America Chevrolet
17	32	90	Mike Wallace	Heilig-Meyers Ford
18	39	77	Bobby Hillin	Jasper Engines Ford
19	12	98	Jeremy Mayfield	RCA Ford
20	3	30	Johnny Benson	Pennzoil Pontiac
21	40	71	Dave Marcis	Prodigy Chevrolet
22	21	2	Rusty Wallace	Miller Ford
23	37	15	Wally Dallenbach	Hayes Modems Ford
24	10	43	Bobby Hamilton	STP Pontiac
25	38	9	Lake Speed	Spam Ford
26	19	33	Robert Pressley	Skoal Bandit Chevrolet
27	28	23	Jimmy Spencer	Camel Cigarettes Ford
28	17	11	Brett Bodine	Lowe's Ford
29	20	25	Ken Schrader	Budweiser Chevrolet
30	4	8	Hut Stricklin	Circuit City Ford
31	27	16	Ted Musgrave	Family Channel / PRIMESTAR Ford
32	22	6	Mark Martin	Valvoline Ford
33	5	18	Bobby Labonte	Interstate Batteries Chevrolet
34	1	5	Terry Labonte	Kellogg's Corn Flakes Chevrolet
35	26	21	Michael Waltrip	Citgo Ford
36	41	19	Loy Allen	Healthsource Ford
37	36	75	Morgan Shepherd	Remington Arms Ford
38	7	37	John Andretti	Kmart / Little Caesars Ford
39	33	7	Geoff Bodine	QVC Ford
40	2	24	Jeff Gordon	DuPont Refinishes Chevrolet
41	11	22	Ward Burton	MBNA America Pontiac

Pontiac Excitement 400

*Larry McReynolds performs some impromptu body work on the hood of the Texaco Havoline Ford after an on-track altercation. Eventually, the car left the race with over-heating problems, one of only two cars that failed to finish the event. **(Right)** After a disappointing start to the season that had ranked them 43rd in the point standings, crew chief Ray Evernham (left) and driver Jeff Gordon discuss their strategy to return to the front at Richmond.*

The furor following the Dale Earnhardt/Bobby Hamilton altercation last weekend at Rockingham had barely subsided when the teams unloaded at Paul Sawyer's splendid three-quarter-mile Richmond mini-super-speedway.

Hamilton's brilliant day ended in an accident that included the second-turn concrete wall which paved the way for Earnhardt's victory later in the race under the final caution flag. The days between Rockingham and Richmond had provided plenty of time for the fans of both teams to discuss the varying implications of the incident.

One team with considerably more to worry about than the dispute between "3" and "43" was the Hendrick Motorsports effort of defending champion Jeff Gordon and his Rainbow Warriors. Although it was early in the season and there was no reason to push the panic button yet, Gordon's premature departures from the first two races had combined to mire him in 43rd place in the point standings. But their position on the point ladder wasn't the team's concern, rather, it was the number of points they had fallen behind. Gordon sat 275 markers in arrears to the hot-running cars of "The Dales" as Earnhardt and Jarrett were tied

for the point lead. Another poor performance by Gordon would make the journey out of the early-season hole much more difficult. He and his DuPont team were determined to finish well at Richmond and begin a move toward the top of the point table.

Terry Labonte, who suffered engine problems at Daytona and Rockingham after leading the most laps in both races, was also well down the point list in 30th place, 183 points behind. Labonte's finishes did not reflect the strength of his Kellogg's Chevrolet but instead demonstrated poor luck which Terry hoped to turn around at Richmond, where he was the defending event champion.

The biggest question of the weekend, however, was not how well the teams in the bottom half of the point standings would fare in the Pontiac Excitement 400, but rather would the event even take the green flag at all on Sunday. The weather was raw, with temperatures barely breaking the mid-30s, and snow was forecast for the weekend.

Crew members resembled Eskimos with their bulky jackets zipped tight and caps pulled low around their ears as they worked their way through Friday's practice sessions and prepared for the first qualifying session.

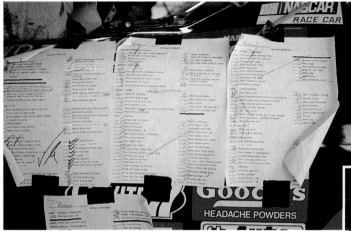

(Top) This checklist, taped to the side of the Texaco Ford, illustrates the preparation and attention to detail required of any team that wishes to be competitive at racing's highest level. (Right) The minimum height requirement is checked as teams push their mounts through inspection prior to qualifying.

With 10 minutes left in the final practice session, Ernie Irvan hammered the wall in the third turn when he locked up the left-front brake in his Ford. The Havoline team frantically unloaded the backup car from the transporter, and Ernie belted into the Thunderbird, hoping to get in a practice lap or two before the end of the session. Just as Irvan was rumbling out of the garage area, however, the red

flag flew, ending practice and leaving Ernie to attempt to qualify a car that had yet to make a lap around the track. Although he failed to make the field during the first round, Irvan turned the fastest lap of the second session on Saturday to grab the Busch Clash "wild card."

With just 30 minutes between the end of Friday's practice and the beginning of first-round qualifying, cars were hastily prepared and pushed through technical inspection. The short time frame coupled with weather problems scrambled the qualifying order, and cars went onto the

track as they lined up after inspection rather than in the order drawn earlier in the day.

The near-frigid temperatures made the first lap of qualifying tricky business indeed. Driver after driver skated around the 0.75-mile oval during that first lap, trying to generate enough heat in the Goodyears so that they would grip the cold surface during the banzai lap the second time around.

When the session was completed, Terry Labonte had duplicated his Rockingham pole and nipped teammate Gordon on the results sheet. The difference between the two drivers was 0.041 seconds — a blink of a gnat's eyelash — but was enough to give Labonte the Busch bonus. The pole came with a car that Terry had not driven for more than a year. It was the same Chevrolet that he drove to victory in the 1994 Phoenix race when the car was bodied as a Lumina rather than its current Monte Carlo configuration.

Hamilton was on form with the STP Pontiac, holding the top spot until late in the qualifying session before he was dropped to the inside of the second row by the two Hendrick Chevrolets. On Bobby's right was Ricky Craven with another outstanding performance in the Kodiak Chevrolet. Mark Martin and Bill Elliott posted the fastest Ford laps to grab the third row. Steve Grissom, with Fred Flintstone riding on the hood of his Cartoon Network Monte Carlo, rolled to the seventh-place starting position, with Joe Nemechek and his Burger King Chevrolet on the

Dale Jarrett prepares for 400 laps at Richmond, perhaps by reflecting on the outstanding start to the season his team has made. When the day was over, Dale claimed his second straight second-place finish and sat alone atop the point standings.

Hendrick stablemates Terry Labonte and Jeff Gordon lead the field under the green flag for the second straight week. Terry Labonte, attempting to bounce back from early-season woes, jumped out to lead the first three laps before yielding the point for good.

outside. Earnhardt and Kenny Wallace claimed the final top-10 positions, just ahead of Jarrett and a strong-running Darrell Waltrip.

On Friday night, crew members and drivers ate supper and settled into their motel rooms early as the expected snow began falling. As much as four inches was anticipated but, fortunately, never arrived. The skies gradually cleared by Saturday morning, bringing blue skies and sunshine that melted the white stuff that did fall. Temperatures, however, remained in the 30s.

Jeff Purvis posted his first career NASCAR Busch Series victory and headed to the winner's circle to celebrate. While Jeff was spraying champagne at everyone, three teams were loading their NASCAR Winston Cup efforts onto the transporters for the journey back home.

One of those teams was the TriStar Motorsports effort. Trickle was enlisted as the interim driver of the Healthsource Ford after Loy Allen's injuries in an

After tangling last week at Rockingham, Bobby Hamilton and Dale Earnhardt found themselves side by side once again. This week, Hamilton continued – without incident – to lead the most laps and finish a solid sixth, while Earnhardt fell to a 31st-place finish.

accident the previous Sunday at Rockingham kept him from racing. Exacerbated by the weather problems and shortened practice sessions, the TriStar team had been trapped on the sidelines.

Bobby Labonte, John Andretti, Lake Speed and Bobby Hillin were all forced to use provisionals to get into the race, while Randy McDonald and Robby Faggart failed to make the field and would have to join millions of fans who watched the race unfold on television as the Pontiac 400 was broadcast by ESPN for the first time since 1983.

During the weekend, Pontiac and Richmond's track management announced that the event would continue for another three years with sponsorship from the General Motors brand, delighting everyone in the garage area. As

race time neared, however, the object was to get this Pontiac 400 in the record book. A cold wind, blowing between 15 and 25 mph and gusting in the 40-mph range, had every crew member shivering on pit road and looking forward to the completion of the race and a chance to thaw out.

The Pennzoil team was the first to fall in action, with Johnny Benson needing a push around the track. During pre-race preparations, the drive shaft had not been hooked up, and crew members dove under the car to attach the missing bolts.

Few doubted that Rusty Wallace and Dale Earnhardt would figure high in the final results sheet when the field growled its way under the green flag. Wallace has one of the best records ever compiled at Richmond, posting five victories, a pair of seconds and 12 top-five finishes in his 16 starts since the track was reconfigured to its present length and shape. Earnhardt was working on a string of 12 consecutive top-10 finishes that stretched back into 1995, and his

practice times put him among the fastest cars in the field during Saturday afternoon's final "Happy Hour" session.

While Gordon and Hamilton were battling at the point for the first third of the race, Wallace rocketed to the top five in his Miller Ford. Without question, he had one of the strongest cars in the field, and Wallace delighted his fans with his run to the front. Those watching the black Monte Carlo, expecting the same charge from Earnhardt, were disappointed when Dale was never able to put the Goodwrench car in the lead. Struggling with brake problems midway through the race, he ultimately spun and hit the second-turn wall with less than 30 laps to go. With only two cars falling from the race, Dale was forced to settle for 31st place, seven laps off the pace at the end, dropping him to fourth place in the point standings.

Trailing the STP Pontiac, Gordon was repeatedly reminded by team manager Ray Evernham to "take care of the tires." Although Gordon was chomping at the bit to pass the Petty Enterprises car, he responded by not overusing the Goodyears. All weekend, Gordon and Evernham had plotted their strategy, setting up the chassis under the DuPont Chevrolet to run consistently during long, green-flag sessions on the track. As the laps clicked off during a 266-lap stint under green, the strategy paid off, and Gordon remained in the battle for victory, while Hamilton slid backwards.

(Left) Ernie Irvan's "28" car shows the results of smacking the wall just minutes before pre-qualifying practice ended. Ernie was forced to qualify the backup car, which he drove to the fastest second-round qualifying speed. (Below) On the fourth caution of the day, the Rainbow Warriors set to work and sent Gordon back to the track in the lead with just 50 laps remaining.

Gordon flashes past the capacity crowd along Richmond's back-stretch on the way to his first victory of the young season.

As the second half of the race began, the Fords of Elliott, Jeff Burton, Wallace and Jarrett surfaced at the front of the field, with Gordon falling to fourth place on the track. Gordon was dismayed at the burst of speed shown by the Blue Oval contingent, and the radio crackled as he and Evernham exchanged thoughts about what to do with the Chevrolet in the closing laps to make it the class of the field.

The green-flag stint finally ended when Ward Burton and Darrell Waltrip collided on the frontstretch with just 50 laps left in the event, and the lead-lap cars headed for pit road for tires and fuel. As the defending Series titlist, Gordon has the choice of the pits and, like many before him, his selection was the first pit which is closest to the first-turn exit of pit road.

Evernham had altered the air pressure in the new set of Goodyear Eagles, changing the handling of the Monte Carlo from a "long green" machine into a car ready to handle short sprints.

The Rainbow Warriors were ready. The pit crew put the new tires on quickly, and Gordon accelerated over the timing line, just beating the charging horde behind him and moving into first place. With four caution periods in the final 50 laps, the DuPont team's strategy worked perfectly as the changes in the tires worked to Gordon's advantage, allowing him to power away from the field on the restarts. Maintaining the point for the final 50 laps, Gordon withstood everything his competitors could muster in the short spurts of green-flag racing.

Jarrett was Gordon's strongest challenger, but his Ford needed some 15-18 laps on new tires to come into its own. In the final 30 laps, however, the longest green-flag period was just six laps, and Jarrett could not mount a challenge. The red-white-and-blue Ford finished more than a half-second behind Gordon. Roush Racing teammates Ted Musgrave, Jeff Burton and Mark Martin clawed their way past Hamilton and Wallace to grab the third, fourth and fifth place spots in the closing laps. Terry Labonte finished eighth, ahead of Ricky Rudd and Elliott.

Jarrett, although denied victory, was happy with his new team's continued performance at the front of the pack. During the first three races of the season, Dale had now finished first, second and second to be well in command of the point lead, 86 points ahead of second-place Jeff Burton who was closely trailed by third-place Rudd, only three points behind Burton in the standings.

In victory lane, Gordon was mobbed by his teammates. After dismal showings in the first two events of the season, the team had triumphed at a track where it least expected to. It was Gordon's 10th career win, and his first at Richmond. More importantly, it was his first victory since Dover last September, and the 180 points he claimed as the race winner sent him leap-frogging from 43rd to 27th in the point table.

Pontiac Excitement 400

Fin. Pos.	Str. Pos.	Car #	Driver	Team
1	2	24	Jeff Gordon	DuPont Refinishes Chevrolet
2	11	88	Dale Jarrett	Quality Care / Ford Credit Ford
3	15	16	Ted Musgrave	Family Channel / PRIMESTAR Ford
4	21	99	Jeff Burton	Exide Batteries Ford
5	5	6	Mark Martin	Valvoline Ford
6	3	43	Bobby Hamilton	STP Pontiac
7	14	2	Rusty Wallace	Miller Ford
8	1	5	Terry Labonte	Kellogg's Corn Flakes Chevrolet
9	34	10	Ricky Rudd	Tide Ford
10	6	94	Bill Elliott	McDonald's Ford
11	16	4	Sterling Marlin	Kodak Film Chevrolet
12	38	37	John Andretti	Kmart / Little Caesars Ford
13	28	22	Ward Burton	MBNA America Pontiac
14	13	25	Ken Schrader	Budweiser Chevrolet
15	10	81	Kenny Wallace	Square D / T.I.C. Ford
16	23	33	Robert Pressley	Skoal Bandit Chevrolet
17	4	41	Ricky Craven	Kodiak Chevrolet
18	39	9	Lake Speed	Spam Ford
19	18	1	Rick Mast	Hooters Pontiac
20	36	42	Kyle Petty	Coors Light Pontiac
21	7	29	Steve Grissom	Cartoon Network Chevrolet
22	27	12	Derrike Cope	Mane 'N Tail Ford
23	37	18	Bobby Labonte	Interstate Batteries Chevrolet
24	25	90	Mike Wallace	Heilig-Meyers Ford
25	24	11	Brett Bodine	Lowe's Ford
26	40	77	Bobby Hillin	Jasper Engines Ford
27	12	17	Darrell Waltrip	Parts America Chevrolet
28	29	98	Jeremy Mayfield	RCA Ford
29	30	23	Jimmy Spencer	Camel Cigarettes Ford
30	20	27	Elton Sawyer	David Blair Motorsports Ford
31	9	3	Dale Earnhardt	GM Goodwrench Service Chevrolet
32	22	75	Morgan Shepherd	Remington Arms Ford
33	19	7	Geoff Bodine	QVC Ford
34	8	87	Joe Nemechek	Burger King Chevrolet
35	32	71	Dave Marcis	Prodigy Chevrolet
36	35	21	Michael Waltrip	Citgo Ford
37	33	30	Johnny Benson	Pennzoil Pontiac
38	26	28	Ernie Irvan	Texaco Havoline Ford
39	31	8	Hut Stricklin	Circuit City Ford
40	17	15	Wally Dallenbach	Hayes Modems Ford

Purolator 500

The cold Atlanta weekend started in grand fashion for Johnny Benson: The rookie contender captured the Busch Pole Award just hours after attending the birth of his first child. **(Right)** *As the weekend drew to a close, Dale Earnhardt assumed the lead and drove to Atlanta's victory lane to claim his second win in only four starts. The win put Dale atop the list as Atlanta's winningest driver.*

During the last two years, qualifying has become increasingly important to every team in the NASCAR Winston Cup garage area. With the number of teams on hand larger than the number of available starting positions at nearly every race, the importance of a crew having its qualifying act together has turned the Friday and Saturday sessions into dramatic events where hundredths of seconds — immeasurable to the human eye — have meant the difference between staying around for the weekend or loading the car on the transporter and making an early exit from the track.

Qualifying sessions for the Purolator 500 at Atlanta Motor Speedway became even more important for the several teams that had no available provisionals to use if they didn't make it into the field on speed alone. Teams finishing in the top 40 in car owner points the previous season were given four provisionals at the beginning of the year, with the usage of those provisionals for the first four races of the season based on the final 1995 owner point standings. After the fourth race of the season, taking place at Atlanta, the current 1996 point standings would go into effect in determining the use of provisionals.

For Dick Trickle (TriStar Motorsports) and Kenny Wallace (FILMAR Racing), there were no provisionals to use. Both teams campaigned a limited number of events in 1995, and neither team was in the top 40 at the conclusion of last year. Jeff Burton (Roush Racing), Dale Jarrett (Robert Yates Racing) and Chuck Bown (Sadler Racing) had no provisionals to use because their teams were new at the beginning of the season. And, although both Elton Sawyer (Blair Motorsports) and Brett Bodine (BDR Racing) finished the 1995 season in the top 40 in points, both teams were sold by Junior Johnson at the conclusion of the 1995 season, and their new ownership made them ineligible to use last year's owner point standings for provisionals.

All of these teams were faced with either making the field on speed or heading up the interstate at the end of Saturday's activities. They brought the best equipment they had in the shop, knowing that a fraction of a second lost during a qualifying lap could mean they would miss the race.

It's a vicious cycle. If a team doesn't make the race, it falls further behind in the point standings. Later in the season, if the team needs to use a provisional, the race it missed and

the points it lost may have put it below other teams that also didn't qualify but have the first option for using a provisional. The team is forced to go home again, losing even more points. It's easy to see why qualifying has gained such importance!

Crew members preparing for Friday's first timed sessions probably thought they were still in Richmond. The weather at Atlanta was just as cold and blustery, with temperatures once again in the mid-30s. Johnny Benson, the only rookie contender to make a race in 1996, was still fighting a bout of pneumonia he had contracted before the Richmond event, but even the effects of the virus couldn't wipe the grin off his face as he headed for his Pennzoil Pontiac for

the first qualifying session. Benson stayed up until 1:30 a.m. with his wife, Debbie, while she gave birth to their first child, Katelyn Rae. After four hours of sleep, he jumped on an airplane and headed from Charlotte to Atlanta in time for the track activities.

Benson's grin was even wider following the first qualifying session. Whipping his Pontiac around the 1.5-mile oval, Benson won the Busch Pole! Only the 10th rookie driver since 1971 to post the fastest qualifying time, Johnny was also the first Pontiac driver to win a pole since 1993.

Mark Martin, 0.040 seconds behind Benson, claimed the outside of the first row. Terry Labonte continued his torrid qualifying performances, posting the third-fastest lap of the session, just a tick faster than Jeremy Mayfield. Geoff Bodine plunked his black QVC Ford on the inside of the third row with his best qualifying effort since the February Rockingham race more than a year ago when he started fourth.

The sixth and seventh-fastest cars were Bobby Hamilton's STP Pontiac and the Kmart/Little

(Left) Bobby Hamilton, Steve Grissom (29), Michael Waltrip (21) and Ken Schrader (25) appear to be driving in formation as they head for Atlanta's turn one. Schrader and Waltrip both finished in the top 10, while Hamilton was 16th and Grissom retired early with engine failure. (Below) After Benson's practice accident forced him to start at the rear of the field in a backup car, Terry Labonte moved up from his third qualifying position to lead the field at the start for the third straight week.

Caesars Ford driven by John Andretti, bringing a chuckle from several garage observers when the official results were posted. At Richmond the previous weekend, the two cars had tangled in the closing laps, and Andretti, venting his frustration when the event was over, had hammered the rear bumper of the blue-and-red Pontiac on the "cool down" lap

pulled the backup car off the tractor-trailer, and Joe would have to go to the back of the field for Sunday's race.

Darrell Waltrip was 13th fastest after a roller-coaster emotional week. Darrell's father-in-law, Frank Rader, who had been helpful to Darrell's early NASCAR Winston Cup career, died on Sunday. Funeral services were held on Wednesday, the same day that Darrell's parents, Leroy and

(Left) Jeff Gordon looks for position on the outside of Jeremy Mayfield, who was driving Cale Yarborough's No. 98 Thunderbird. Gordon took the spot on his way to a third-place finish, while Mayfield finished with a career-best fifth. (Below) Bobby Labonte (18) leads fellow top-10 starters Wally Dallenbach (15) and Hut Stricklin (8) in the early going as Dale Earnhardt charges through the field after starting from the 18th position. Darrell Waltrip (17), Ward Burton (22) and Jeff Gordon also give chase.

— a move that cost him a $2,000 fine from NASCAR.

Bobby Labonte, Hut Stricklin and Wally Dallenbach completed the top 10 in qualifying, just ahead of Lake Speed and Joe Nemechek, whose official time came from the first of his two qualifying laps. During Nemechek's second lap, he stuffed the Burger King Chevrolet into the wall, destroying the car. His team headed for the transporter and

Margaret, celebrated their 50th wedding anniversary.

The qualifying worries for Trickle and Brett Bodine ended after the first session. Both were safely in the top 25, with Trickle 17th and Brett 19th. Chuck Bown, Elton Sawyer, Dale Jarrett and Kenny Wallace all made it into the field during the second round. Jimmy Spencer, Mike Wallace and Dave Marcis exercised provisionals to make the field.

Dale moved from his 18th starting position to the point.

By the time the first yellow of the race appeared on lap 165, Earnhardt, along with Gordon and Labonte, had shown that the Monte Carlos and the downforce built into the bodies of the Chevrolets would be difficult to beat in the long, sweeping Atlanta turns.

Ernie Irvan, after starting from 37th position, mounted his own charge through the field. By the end of the first 80 laps, he was in the top 10. Moving into the top five some 80 laps later, he eventually fought with Earnhardt and Labonte for the lead and headed the field three times for six laps before the event was completed.

(Above) The Flying Aces put it all together on Earnhardt's final stop of the day, giving Dale the track position he would need to secure the victory over Terry Labonte. (Right) Rusty Wallace and Dale Earnhardt have one of their familiar, spirited exchanges at the point. Rusty was strong, swapping the lead with Earnhardt on several occasions, before engine failure sent the Miller Ford to the garage shortly after mid-distance.

The ax fell on the Jeff Burton team headed by veteran crew chief Buddy Parrott. After a sparkling fourth-place finish the previous weekend that helped place him second in the point standings, Burton's fastest Atlanta lap was 40th on the list, and he had no provisionals to use. Burton, along with Steve Seligman and Randy MacDonald, would be forced to watch the race on television.

Halfway through "Happy Hour," Benson's giant bubble suddenly burst when his yellow Pennzoil Pontiac crashed into the third-turn wall, shortening the Grand Prix by some three feet on the right-front corner. Like Nemechek's team, the Pennzoil crew pulled the backup car off the transporter, and Benson's pole position was negated. The team began preparations on the backup car, which would start from the rear of the field for Sunday's 500-mile test.

Benson's poor luck moved up Terry Labonte to lead the field under the green flag. He wasted no time in displaying the power in his Kellogg's Chevrolet, pulling the field around the track for the first 49 laps. Behind him, Earnhardt was picking his way toward the front. After only 50 laps,

However, the Texaco Havoline Ford had nothing left in the final 50 laps, and the battle for the victory came down to a final series of green-flag stops. With Labonte leading by nearly 1.5 seconds, Earnhardt gave up his runner-up position, becoming the first of the leaders on pit road for a final stop for tires and fuel.

Only 38 laps remained in the race, and the "Flying Aces" hit the ground running when the black Chevrolet slid to a stop in its pit stall. After a brilliant, 19.72-second stop for four tires and a load of Unocal, Earnhardt was rolling back down pit road, headed for the first turn. The stop was so fast that the soft drink that Earnhardt was drinking sloshed all over the front of his driver's suit when the jack dropped on the right side. 'Wow,' Earnhardt thought to himself as he tossed the paper cup out the window. 'I'd better get ready quick. This one's a fast one!'

After coming back up to racing speed, Earnhardt headed down the front straight on lap 292, and a quick glance to

A crew member puts a round of bite in the right-rear of Irvan's car while the rest of the team adds tires and fuel. Ernie charged through the field from his 37th starting spot to fourth place and was the highest finishing Ford.

his left showed that Labonte was just beginning to roll out of his pit stall after his four-tire stop. Terry's crew had done their work, but jammed lug nuts slowed them and they had taken two seconds longer than Earnhardt's team. The problem in Labonte's pit gave Dale just the amount of breathing room he needed, and the Goodwrench Chevrolet was not passed for the remainder of the race.

At the end, the margin of victory was just over four seconds, and Earnhardt frolicked in victory lane with the crew that gave him the stop that proved to be the difference between first and second place. It was Earnhardt's 70th career victory (his 10th at Atlanta), and it broke his tie with Cale Yarborough for all-time leader at the track. It had been a powerful performance with the same car he drove to a dominating victory at Atlanta last November in a futile effort to beat Gordon for the point championship.

Labonte's hopes for victory took an early-race hit when the front spoiler of his car was damaged by a piece of debris from Stricklin's Ford. Terry drove around the problem and stayed competitive, but the extra two seconds lost on pit road during his final stop ended his charge and he was forced to settle for second place.

Gordon closed on Irvan in the final laps, passing the Texaco-sponsored car to make it a 1-2-3 Chevrolet finish. Behind Irvan, Mayfield took Yarborough's RCA Ford to fifth place, ahead of Ken Schrader, who gave the Hendrick team three cars in the top six with his performance. Jimmy Spencer was seventh, beating Ricky Rudd, Michael Waltrip and Bill Elliott in their own battle of lap-down cars. Jarrett, struggling with handling problems throughout the race, finished 11th and maintained the NASCAR Winston Cup point lead.

Earnhardt's second victory in the first four races of the season vaulted him back into second place in the standings, 50 points behind Jarrett. Rudd's fourth straight top-10 finish held him in third place, 72 points behind, and Elliott climbed to fourth place, 45 points behind Rudd. Ricky Craven stayed in fifth, 10 points behind Elliott and 11 markers in front of Schrader. Labonte moved to seventh in the standings while Ted Musgrave, Hamilton and Martin completed the top 10. Gordon's third-place finish pushed him up to 16th in the points.

How expensive was Jeff Burton's failure to qualify? He fell from second place in the standings to 14th.

At the conclusion of the race, NASCAR inspectors quickly moved to Labonte's Chevrolet, Hamilton's Pontiac and Rusty Wallace's Ford (blown engine and all) and claimed the cars for NASCAR's wind-tunnel tests the following day. Hoping to find a way to make all three cars more aerodynamically competitive with each other, time had been scheduled in Lockheed's nearby wind tunnel Monday and Tuesday following the Atlanta race.

Purolator 500

Fin. Pos.	Str. Pos.	Car #	Driver	Team
1	18	3	Dale Earnhardt	GM Goodwrench Service Chevrolet
2	3	5	Terry Labonte	Kellogg's Corn Flakes Chevrolet
3	21	24	Jeff Gordon	DuPont Refinishes Chevrolet
4	37	28	Ernie Irvan	Texaco Havoline Ford
5	4	98	Jeremy Mayfield	RCA Ford
6	30	25	Ken Schrader	Budweiser Chevrolet
7	39	23	Jimmy Spencer	Camel Cigarettes Ford
8	20	10	Ricky Rudd	Tide Ford
9	27	21	Michael Waltrip	Citgo Ford
10	23	94	Bill Elliott	McDonald's Ford
11	36	88	Dale Jarrett	Quality Care / Ford Credit Ford
12	15	41	Ricky Craven	Kodiak Chevrolet
13	28	4	Sterling Marlin	Kodak Film Chevrolet
14	17	19	Dick Trickle	Healthsource Ford
15	16	22	Ward Burton	MBNA America Pontiac
16	6	43	Bobby Hamilton	STP Pontiac
17	12	87	Joe Nemechek	Burger King Chevrolet
18	25	16	Ted Musgrave	Family Channel / PRIMESTAR Ford
19	35	27	Elton Sawyer	David Blair Motorsports Ford
20	10	15	Wally Dallenbach	Hayes Modems Ford
21	7	37	John Andretti	Kmart / Little Caesars Ford
22	33	42	Kyle Petty	Coors Light Pontiac
23	5	7	Geoff Bodine	QVC Ford
24	19	11	Brett Bodine	Lowe's Ford
25	9	8	Hut Stricklin	Circuit City Ford
26	2	6	Mark Martin	Valvoline Ford
27	14	33	Robert Pressley	Skoal Bandit Chevrolet
28	29	77	Bobby Hillin	Jasper Engines Ford
29	41	71	Dave Marcis	Prodigy Chevrolet
30	32	75	Morgan Shepherd	Remington Arms Ford
31	8	18	Bobby Labonte	Interstate Batteries Chevrolet
32	13	17	Darrell Waltrip	Parts America Chevrolet
33	40	90	Mike Wallace	Heilig-Meyers Ford
34	31	1	Rick Mast	Hooters Pontiac
35	26	12	Derrike Cope	Mane 'N Tail Ford
36	22	2	Rusty Wallace	Miller Ford
37	38	81	Kenny Wallace	Square D / T.I.C. Ford
38	1	30	Johnny Benson	Pennzoil Pontiac
39	24	29	Steve Grissom	Cartoon Network Chevrolet
40	34	95	Chuck Bown	Shoney's Inn Ford
41	11	9	Lake Speed	Spam Ford

TranSouth Financial 400

Pit crews had a busy day at Darlington as 11 caution flags flew during the running of the TranSouth Financial 400. Here, the crews of Jeff Gordon, Ward Burton, Dale Jarrett, Bill Elliott and Rusty Wallace compete to give their drivers an advantage on the track. **(Right)** Not a single fan sits as Dale Earnhardt (3) and Jeff Burton (99) chase Mark Martin at venerable Darlington Raceway.

With four races on the books and the crews headed for tradition-rich Darlington for the TranSouth Financial 400, several teams found themselves on the wrong end of the point standings — a long way from where they expected to be.

Morgan Shepherd and the Butch Mock-owned team took a look at the point standings following the Atlanta race and shuddered. Sponsored by Remington Arms, Shepherd's name was toward the bottom of the list in 40th place. Yet to post a finish higher than 30th, Morgan was 398 points behind point leader Dale Jarrett.

Geoff Bodine's own QVC Ford team, for which he had high hopes at the beginning of the season, was struggling in 38th place. Johnny Benson and the Pennzoil team were 36th. Brett Bodine, running his own team, was 33rd in the point standings. Despite several promising runs, poor finishes dumped John Andretti in 32nd. Darrell Waltrip in 30th place and Derrike Cope in 31st realized that they needed to turn their seasons around in a hurry.

The top 10 in the standings, on the other hand, offered a few surprises. Dale Jarrett's first-year Ford team, under the tutelage of rookie crew chief Todd Parrott, strung together three top-two finishes and an 11th place at Atlanta to maintain the point lead. Ricky Rudd and Bill Elliott held down third and fourth places and hoped that Darlington would be the track where they would make their first trip to victory lane this season. Ricky Craven had a solid lock on fifth place. Bobby Hamilton was the highest Pontiac driver in the standings, holding ninth place by a mere seven points over Mark Martin.

Another Ford looking for its initial foray into the winner's circle was Bud Moore's Thunderbird. When the car was rolled out of Moore's transporter, the veteran car owner and his driver, Wally Dallenbach, stood to the side, hearing the 'oohs' and 'aahs' from every person who walked by the gleaming car. A new paint scheme, incorporating varying shades of blue and a futuristic globe symbolizing Hayes Modems technology, was instantly judged as one of the finest in the garage area.

During pre-event testing, Pontiac drivers Hamilton and Ward Burton were the fastest on the charts, and both drivers hoped to be able to duplicate those practice speeds during the first qualifying session. With Goodyear bringing a new, softer compound tire to Darlington for the event,

Ward Burton (left) joined Fireball Roberts and Tim Richmond as the only Pontiac drivers ever to take the pole at Darlington. **(Below)** During the race, Ward guides his MBNA Pontiac around Dave Marcis' Prodigy Chevrolet. Ward led from the pole and ran well before leaving the race due to damage sustained in an accident.

there was little question that the track record would fall. But many wondered just how many drivers would crack the mark and how fast the pole speed would be.

The answer to the first question was 20 drivers, and the answer to the second was nearly 3 mph faster than the old mark held by Jeff Gordon. When the first session was complete, Burton had backed up his pre-event test speeds by becoming only the third Pontiac driver in history to claim the pole for the spring event at venerable Darlington. He was the only driver to crack the 28.3-second mark and wrote his name into the record book alongside Pontiac drivers Fireball Roberts (1960) and Tim Richmond (1983).

Gordon did his best to win his first pole of the season, but his effort came up just 0.030 seconds short. Jarrett claimed the inside of the second row and was joined on his right by Shepherd, who was determined to turn his season around. Elliott and Ken Schrader occupied the third row, while Kenny Wallace surprised many by grabbing the inside of the fourth row with his Square D Ford, just a tick of the watch faster than older brother Rusty and his Miller Ford. Jeremy Mayfield gave hometown hero Cale Yarborough

Brothers Kenny (left) and Rusty Wallace confer in Darlington's garage as they prepare to begin the race side by side from the fourth row. They also were ranked next to each other in the standings (17th and 18th) going into the race, with Rusty holding a mere seven point margin over his younger brother.

something to cheer about by turning the ninth-fastest lap, and Elton Sawyer had a strong run to claim the final top-10 position, just faster than Rick Mast and Jimmy Spencer.

Making the field in the first day of qualifying means more than not having to worry about it for the rest of the weekend at Darlington. The fastest 25 drivers have the privilege

of pitting on the front side of the track. The remainder of the field is forced to pit on the back side, which is viewed by most teams as a detriment to winning. Among those who failed to make the field on the first day and would set up shop along the backstretch for Sunday's race were Michael Waltrip, Darrell Waltrip, Ernie Irvan, Sterling Marlin, and none other than the seven-time champion and nine-time Darlington race winner Dale Earnhardt.

The world's leading money-winner in motorsports would start 27th in the field but, despite the handicap of pitting on the backstretch, no one believed that Earnhardt would not quickly be in the thick of battle once the green flag dropped on the TranSouth Financial 400.

Bobby Hillin was the fastest of the drivers who ran in the second session, posting a speed good enough for the 26th starting position. But, more importantly to the Jasper Motorsports team, the speed secured a "wild card" entry for the Busch Clash lottery. If Hillin failed to win a pole during the remainder of the season, he would at least be one of the drivers eligible to draw for the one Busch Clash slot available to the 1996 fastest second-round qualifiers.

Kyle Petty, Joe Nemechek and Mike Wallace used provi-

(Right) Bill Elliott, who came to Darlington fourth in points with his McDonald's Fords, directs his thoughts toward a strong Darlington run. He would start fifth, but finish 13th, one lap off the pace.
(Below) Provisional starters Kyle Petty (42) and Joe Nemechek (87) race side by side after starting together from the 20th row, while John Andretti gives chase. Kyle fought all the way to a 12th-place finish.

sionals to make the field, while Chuck Bown, Randy MacDonald and Robby Faggart were forced to watch their cars being loaded onto the transporters.

For the second straight race, "Happy Hour" turned into disaster for the Busch Pole winner. With minutes to go in the final practice session, Burton's MBNA Pontiac tangled with Lake Speed's Spam Ford, sending the Ford spinning and backing into the wall. Speed took one look at the blue-and-yellow Ford and told crew chief Jim Long to start unloading the spare car. "This one's about three feet too short in the back to pass inspection," Speed said humorlessly. Burton's team, refusing to give up the hard-won pole position, fell to work on the black-and-green Pontiac, and by Sunday morning, the car was ready to take its place on the inside of the front row.

Sunday morning, Mast and Craven eased over to Elliott's garage area and beckoned to the McDonald's driver. Bill, with a quizzical look on his face, could only wonder what the two drivers wanted from him.

"C'mere, we need some advice," Mast said.

"About what?" Elliott asked, walking over to the Pontiac and Chevrolet drivers.

"You have any luck chasing a diaper sponsor?" Mast grinned, referring to the recent birth of Elliott's first son, Chase. "We thought if you had, well, you might give us the guy's name, and we could contact him."

"What in the world would you need a diaper sponsor for?" Elliott asked.

"Well, Ricky here and his wife are going to have a baby in the fall," Mast said. "And I'm gonna need that diaper sponsor more than Ricky."

Elliott simply stared at Mast. "Nah. Now you're kidding me," the redhead said.

Robert Pressley (33) took the lead on lap 149 during the seventh caution of the race and held the position until lap 161, when he brought out the eighth yellow flag of the day after tagging the wall. Craven (41) and Elliott (94) split the race track to avoid Pressley's damaged Monte Carlo.

"Nope. Sharon and I are going to have a baby, too. In fact, the reason I need that sponsor more than Ricky does is that Sharon and I are going to have three babies — triplets."

The look of surprise on Elliott's face was priceless. And suddenly, all three drivers began roaring with laughter.

"Well, if I find one of those sponsors for Pampers or Huggies, I'll send him your way," Elliott said through his grin, turning to walk away.

Of the three drivers, Craven would have the best reason to smile at the conclusion of the 293-lap test at tricky Darlington. He equaled his best career finish by fighting to a third place in his green-and-white Chevrolet, while Elliott finished 13th and Mast 19th.

Burton led the field under the green flag and lasted seven laps at the point before drifting back through the field with

his damaged Pontiac. Gordon pulled past Burton on the eighth lap to take over the lead, establishing his Monte Carlo as the best car in the field this sunny Sunday afternoon. Dominating the competitor, Gordon led the first third of the event handily. Returning to the point on lap 197, the rainbow-hued Chevrolet threatened to make a shambles of the race.

Earnhardt fought handling problems throughout the day, leading a single lap to claim the five bonus points during

(Left) *Ricky Craven ran well throughout the race and was rewarded with a career-best third-place finish in his Kodiak Chevrolet, moving him up to fourth in the point standings.*
(Below) *Jeff Gordon, who started from the outside of the front row, takes the lead from pole winner Ward Burton on lap seven, as third-place starter Dale Jarrett tries to keep pace.*

the fourth caution flag of the afternoon. Dale eventually finished 14th, a lap behind, unable to mount his expected challenge.

The Other Dale, however, found his Ford riding better and better as the afternoon wore on, thanks to hard work by Parrott and the Quality Care crew. The strong-running red-white-and-blue Thunderbird was a contender all day and, when Gordon struggled for three laps to put Earnhardt a lap behind, Jarrett closed on the reigning champion's car. On lap 278, with just 16 laps left, Jarrett thrust the Ford in front of Gordon's Chevrolet and began to ease away.

The radio instantly crackled in Gordon's ear as crew chief and team manager Ray Evernham began telling Jeff not to lose his concentration and not to worry about Jarrett. "He's gonna have to stop for gas. He can't make it all the way," Evernham reassured his driver. "Just keep on doing what you're doing, and things will be okay. We've got plenty of fuel to make it to the end, but he's got to stop."

Gordon watched and waited and, on lap 286, fuel stopped being an issue at all when Jarrett, passing Dave Marcis on the high side of the fourth turn, was pinched into the wall and pancaked the right side of his Ford. Two laps later, Gordon fought his way past the struggling Thunderbird and pulled away from Jarrett.

Evernham was right about Jarrett being unable to make the entire distance without a stop. On the final lap, the Ford coughed and choked. Jarrett dove for the backstretch pit road, coming to a stop in teammate Irvan's pit. The crew sluiced some Unocal into the car, and then, along with a couple of members of the Wood Brothers team, gave Jarrett a push to help start his stalled Ford. The push turned out to be costly as Jarrett, already in second place when he headed onto pit road, was penalized for receiving assistance on the final lap of the race and was dropped to 15th place in the final rundown.

With cars heading for the pits for fuel in the final five laps, the running order underwent considerable change, but it didn't matter to Gordon, who rolled to a 1.4-second victory over Bobby Labonte. Behind Craven, Rusty Wallace came home fourth ahead of Terry Labonte and Mark Martin. Ted Musgrave finished seventh, the final car on the lead lap, while Shepherd ran steadily to an eighth-place finish, his best of the year. Rudd and Jeff Burton claimed the final positions in the top 10, just ahead of Marlin and Kyle Petty.

The victory was Gordon's second in the last three races, and helped him climb to ninth place in the point standings. It was his second straight triumph at Darlington where he had won the prestigious Mountain Dew Southern 500 on his way to the championship last September.

TranSouth Financial 400

Fin. Pos.	Str. Pos.	Car #	Driver	Team
1	2	24	Jeff Gordon	DuPont Refinishes Chevrolet
2	13	18	Bobby Labonte	Interstate Batteries Chevrolet
3	14	41	Ricky Craven	Kodiak Chevrolet
4	8	2	Rusty Wallace	Miller Ford
5	17	5	Terry Labonte	Kellogg's Corn Flakes Chevrolet
6	16	6	Mark Martin	Valvoline Ford
7	18	16	Ted Musgrave	Family Channel / PRIMESTAR Ford
8	4	75	Morgan Shepherd	Remington Arms Ford
9	24	10	Ricky Rudd	Tide Ford
10	21	99	Jeff Burton	Exide Batteries Ford
11	33	4	Sterling Marlin	Kodak Film Chevrolet
12	39	42	Kyle Petty	Coors Light Pontiac
13	5	94	Bill Elliott	McDonald's Ford
14	27	3	Dale Earnhardt	GM Goodwrench Service Chevrolet
15	3	88	Dale Jarrett	Quality Care / Ford Credit Ford
16	23	43	Bobby Hamilton	STP Pontiac
17	7	81	Kenny Wallace	Square D / T.I.C. Ford
18	9	98	Jeremy Mayfield	RCA Ford
19	11	1	Rick Mast	Hooters Pontiac
20	34	8	Hut Stricklin	Circuit City Ford
21	41	90	Mike Wallace	Heilig-Meyers Ford
22	19	7	Geoff Bodine	QVC Ford
23	37	71	Dave Marcis	Prodigy Chevrolet
24	38	30	Johnny Benson	Pennzoil Pontiac
25	25	9	Lake Speed	Spam Ford
26	28	29	Steve Grissom	Cartoon Network Chevrolet
27	15	11	Brett Bodine	Lowe's Ford
28	6	25	Ken Schrader	Budweiser Chevrolet
29	29	21	Michael Waltrip	Citgo Ford
30	10	27	Elton Sawyer	David Blair Motorsports Ford
31	40	87	Joe Nemechek	Burger King Chevrolet
32	12	23	Jimmy Spencer	Camel Cigarettes Ford
33	32	28	Ernie Irvan	Texaco Havoline Ford
34	30	17	Darrell Waltrip	Parts America Chevrolet
35	22	19	Dick Trickle	Healthsource Ford
36	31	33	Robert Pressley	Skoal Bandit Chevrolet
37	36	15	Wally Dallenbach	Hayes Modems Ford
38	1	22	Ward Burton	MBNA America Pontiac
39	20	12	Derrike Cope	Mane 'N Tail Ford
40	35	37	John Andretti	Kmart / Little Caesars Ford
41	26	77	Bobby Hillin	Jasper Engines Ford

Food City 500

Bill Elliott, after starting last with a former champion's provisional, took the lead on lap 70 using some brilliant pit strategy during the first three cautions. Jeff Gordon slips underneath Bill Elliott in turn four to take the lead for the first time on lap 108. Jeff went on to lead 148 of the remaining 235 laps in the rain-shortened event to take his third win in the last four races. (Right) Three straight poles at Bristol? Hey, no big deal for Mark Martin, who also grabbed the first pole of the season for Ford. Mark led the first 59 laps and finished a strong third behind Gordon and Terry Labonte.

It's no different than changing managers on a baseball team or coaches in a basketball program. Sometimes, the existing system isn't working properly, and a breath of fresh air and new blood is what's needed to trigger an upward swing in fortunes.

When your team is 34th in the point standings after the first five races, and the car owner and driver feel that the team is considerably more competitive than that statistic shows, it's time for a change.

That's what happened at Darrell Waltrip Racing two days after the TranSouth Financial 400 at Darlington. Tuesday morning, Jeff Hammond reported for work as the new team manager for the Parts America-sponsored Chevrolet team, hoping to move Darrell's effort to a higher plane. In the past, the driver and crew chief worked together at Junior Johnson's shop during Darrell's successful run at three championships. He later joined Waltrip at Hendrick Motorsports in 1987. When Darrell formed his own effort in 1991, Jeff worked with the new team for two years. Overall, Waltrip won nearly 50 times while working with Hammond in the past. The first test of the new pairing came at Bristol where Waltrip was the leading career win-

ner with a dozen triumphs on the high-banked half-mile.

Darrell explained his reasoning behind reuniting with his former crew chief by saying, "There's a chemistry between some drivers, and in this case, team managers, that allows them to get the best out of a car by getting the most out of a driver. Jeff and I have that bond."

Hammond's move to the Waltrip shop opened the crew chief's slot at TriStar Motorsports where Jeff had been working with Loy Allen and, most recently, interim driver Dick Trickle. TriStar owner Mark Smith quickly named Peter Sospenzo to fill the crew chief's role with the Healthsource Fords. Sospenzo, who worked as Lake Speed's crew chief the previous year, left the Harry Melling-owned team when Speed named former SABCO crew chief Jim Long to the post at the end of the 1995 season.

While Hammond was getting acquainted with his new teammates on Waltrip's team, The Dales were studying the point table. Their Darlington finishes — 14th for Earnhardt and 15th for a penalized Jarrett — had been costly. The gap between the two point leaders was a mere 47 markers but, more importantly, others had crept to within striking distance. Ricky Rudd's fifth consecutive top-10

The Bristol event was the first under the new ownership of Speedway Motorsports. Bruton Smith had purchased the track from founder and longtime owner Larry Carrier and named Jeff Byrd to head the management team. As always, the sold-out facility attracted a premier field of competitors.

Mike Skinner hoped to make his second race of the season with Richard Childress' research and development team. Childress announced that the white car, carrying the number 31, would be campaigned a total of six times during 1996, including the upcoming Winston Select Open, carrying sponsorship from Realtree Camouflage. Childress said he expected the team to become a full-fledged second team from his Welcome, N.C., shop either in 1997 or 1998, depending on how things fell into place in the coming months.

With 43 cars on hand to compete for a maximum of 37 starting positions, qualifying once again took on enormous importance to every team. Clearly, some of the regular runners would not make the field. With only 20 pits on the frontstretch, a fast lap was needed to avoid being forced to pit on the backstretch for Sunday's race.

After two straight Pontiac poles at Atlanta and Darlington, the Ford and Chevrolet forces were determined to see one of their own cars turn the fastest lap during the first session of qualifying on Friday. When the timed period was complete, Valvoline Ford driver Mark Martin had grabbed his third consecutive Busch Pole on the concrete oval, his fifth at Thunder Valley. Martin's pole was not only

finish of the season put him just 10 points behind the second-place Earnhardt. Ricky Craven, bolstered by two strong finishes in his last pair of races, was just 28 points behind Rudd. Bill Elliott, in fifth place and only 116 points back, looked in his rearview mirror to find Terry Labonte, Ted Musgrave and Mark Martin clustered close behind him in the standings.

Then there was Gordon. After a pitiful start in the first two races of the season, Gordon's surge in the last three events, including a pair of victories, had allowed the reigning champion to rocket through the point standings, moving all the way from 43rd to ninth in just three events! He was a mere two points behind Martin in their battle for eighth place, and Jeff had chopped and hacked his way to 168 points behind point leader Jarrett. Another stumble for The Dales like Darlington, coupled with another solid Gordon finish, would bring the DuPont Chevrolet driver right back into the point battle.

Bobby Labonte, celebrating his 100th career NASCAR Winston Cup start, gets some words of encouragement from crew chief Jimmy Makar before qualifying. Makar's advice must have been good: Bobby charged to the fifth-fastest qualifying speed. After staying among the leaders for most of the race, Bobby finished seventh, the first car not on the lead lap.

his first of the season, it was also the first for a member of the Blue Oval contingent.

Martin's speedy lap was well off his track record, but he beat second-place Terry Labonte's lap by nearly a tenth of a second. The magic between Hammond and Waltrip appeared to be working as Darrell posted his best qualifying position since his pole in the season-ending race at Atlanta last November. Sterling Marlin gave his locally-based Morgan-McClure team plenty to brag about with his fourth-fastest lap, while Bobby Labonte claimed the fifth-fastest lap, just ahead of a surprising time turned in by Skinner in the second Childress car.

Jarrett and Gordon were seventh and eighth fastest, but Jarrett was forced to yield the inside of the fourth row when the field prepared to take the green flag. Completing his second qualifying lap, Dale lost control and smacked the wall. By the time he returned to the garage area, his team was already pulling the backup Quality Care Ford off the transporter.

Ricky Rudd and Kenny Wallace completed the top 10. Rusty Wallace qualified 11th and Ward Burton posted the fastest Pontiac qualifying lap, good enough for the outside of the sixth row. Earnhardt qualified 19th, barely keeping the black Chevrolet on the frontstretch, and Joe Nemechek's qualifying crash came after he posted the 20th-

Ernie Irvan, Ricky Rudd and Dale Jarrett take Bristol's high-banked turns nose to tail. Jarrett, who qualified seventh, was forced to start from the rear of the field in his backup car, and he charged all the way to a sixth-place finish, protecting his lead in the point standings.

fastest lap. The Burger King crew fell to work repairing the car so that they would not join Jarrett in the back of the starting pack.

Trickle grabbed the Busch Clash "wild card" with his second-round lap. Bill Elliott chose to exercise his former champion's provisional spot, allowing Steve Grissom to use the final provisional and join Jeremy Mayfield, Kyle Petty and Jeff Burton as the four provisional starters for Sunday's event.

John Andretti, Dave Marcis, Johnny Benson, Mike Wallace, Bobby Hillin and Chuck Bown would not take the green flag when the race began. Just 0.31 seconds separated the field, with Andretti and Rick Mast tied for the final spot. Mast's car owner, Richard Jackson, celebrating his 59th birthday during the weekend, was higher in the standings than Andretti's Michael Kranefuss/Carl Haas-owned team, so Mast would take the green flag.

As teams began pushing their cars through the Sunday inspection line at Bristol, the biggest question in everyone's mind was whether the event could dodge the rain that the NASCAR radar showed to be hovering around the race track. With Rusty Wallace, Earnhardt, and a contingent of team and NASCAR personnel scheduled to leave for a test in Japan the following day, every effort would be made to get the full 500-lap distance in the books. But with rain everywhere, including on the track, it was clear, as race time approached, that the start of the event would be delayed at the very least.

(Right) Darrell Waltrip walks away from his Parts America Chevrolet after backing it into the wall. The incident occurred shortly after a restart, with threatening skies hinting of an early end to the race.
(Below) Ward Burton takes a wild ride down the frontstretch in his MBNA Pontiac on lap 58. Ward eventually continued, but finished a distant 33rd in the race.

The Food City 500 began more than 30 minutes later than its scheduled start and, after winning the NASCAR Busch Series event the previous day, it looked like Martin was on his way to a sweep of the weekend races when he pulled away from the field to lead the first 59 laps. Making his 300th career NASCAR Winston Cup start, he yielded the point to Skinner during the third caution of the race and, despite remaining in contention for the victory for the rest of the event, Mark could never get back to the front.

Gordon moved into the lead for the first time on lap 108 and held the point for the next 100 laps before making a green-flag pit stop. The green stretch went on and on for 258 laps — unusual for the close-quarter racing at Bristol where caution flags seem to wave as often as green ones. Bobby Labonte, Ricky Rudd and Rusty Wallace held the leader's role during the clean and green racing until the awaited rain storms began pelting the track, bringing out the yellow flag on lap 321.

When the yellow waved, Terry Labonte dove for pit road to get tires and fuel from his Kellogg's Corn Flakes team.

One can only imagine what Dale Jarrett (left) and Ernie Irvan are discussing here, but the two drivers for Robert Yates Racing seem to be getting comfortable with the team concept in 1996.

Just as he was rolling back out of his pit stall, starter Doyle Ford waved the red flag to stop the race because of the rain. The cars stopped on the backstretch, and Labonte fell in line at the back of the pack. Terry figured that he would have the advantage if the race resumed because he had already made his visit to pit road. The remaining cars on the lead lap would make their stops as soon as the race rolled again.

Some 33 minutes later, the track was dry enough for the race to restart under the caution flag. NASCAR officials, knowing another storm was approaching, opened pit road to give the drivers the opportunity to make their stops for service, and the lead-lap cars at the front of the field immediately headed to their pit stalls. By the time Labonte made it to the frontstretch trailing the long line of cars that remained on the track, the leaders had completed their stops and were rolling back onto the track.

Gordon, pitting in the first stall chosen with his champion's option, was the first out, and took over the point. Behind him, Wallace also brought his Miller Ford out ahead of Labonte, while Earnhardt and Martin fell in behind the Kellogg's car.

With the green flag waving, and the radar showing another storm headed for the track, Gordon spurted away from the field. Three laps later, Waltrip hammered the frontstretch wall, ending his day and bringing out the yellow flag which eventually turned red for 18 minutes while fluids from the car were washed off the track. The race resumed under caution and just as the green was ready to wave, rain began pelting the track again. This time, there was real doubt whether the event would be restarted. After 67 minutes, at 5:45 p.m., NASCAR officials closed the book on the race after 342 of the scheduled 500 laps were complete.

Gordon led 148 of those laps, including the most important one: the last lap of the race. At the front when the final red flag flew, Gordon took his 12th career victory and his third in the last four races. Labonte had managed to fight his way to second place, ahead of Martin and Earnhardt, while Wallace fell to fifth. Jarrett was sixth and maintained his point lead, finishing on the lead lap after making up a lost lap during the final caution of the afternoon. Bobby Labonte, in his 100th career NASCAR Winston Cup start, won the battle of lap-down cars despite strong runs from Trickle and Craven. Michael Waltrip's 10th place was his third top-10 finish of the season with the Wood Brothers' Ford, and Hut Stricklin celebrated his 200th career NASCAR Winston Cup start with an 11th-place finish in the Stavola Brothers' Circuit City Ford.

As the water-logged teams loaded their cars for the trip back to their shops, Earnhardt, Wallace and the remainder of the contingent of drivers headed for Japan began making their way through the huge crowd toward the airport.

Food City 500

Fin. Pos.	Str. Pos.	Car #	Driver	Team
1	8	24	Jeff Gordon	DuPont Refinishes Chevrolet
2	2	5	Terry Labonte	Kellogg's Corn Flakes Chevrolet
3	1	6	Mark Martin	Valvoline Ford
4	19	3	Dale Earnhardt	GM Goodwrench Service Chevrolet
5	11	2	Rusty Wallace	Miller Ford
6	7	88	Dale Jarrett	Quality Care / Ford Credit Ford
7	5	18	Bobby Labonte	Interstate Batteries Chevrolet
8	29	19	Dick Trickle	Healthsource Ford
9	13	41	Ricky Craven	Kodiak Chevrolet
10	25	21	Michael Waltrip	Citgo Ford
11	14	8	Hut Stricklin	Circuit City Ford
12	32	1	Rick Mast	Hooters Pontiac
13	15	23	Jimmy Spencer	Camel Cigarettes Ford
14	9	10	Ricky Rudd	Tide Ford
15	34	42	Kyle Petty	Coors Light Pontiac
16	16	28	Ernie Irvan	Texaco Havoline Ford
17	23	33	Robert Pressley	Skoal Bandit Chevrolet
18	4	4	Sterling Marlin	Kodak Film Chevrolet
19	21	7	Geoff Bodine	QVC Ford
20	22	11	Brett Bodine	Lowe's Ford
21	35	98	Jeremy Mayfield	RCA Ford
22	17	12	Derrike Cope	Mane 'N Tail Ford
23	33	99	Jeff Burton	Exide Batteries Ford
24	31	15	Wally Dallenbach	Hayes Modems Ford
25	30	16	Ted Musgrave	Family Channel / PRIMESTAR Ford
26	3	17	Darrell Waltrip	Parts America Chevrolet
27	36	29	Steve Grissom	Cartoon Network Chevrolet
28	37	94	Bill Elliott	McDonald's Ford
29	28	25	Ken Schrader	Budweiser Chevrolet
30	18	75	Morgan Shepherd	Remington Arms Ford
31	20	87	Joe Nemechek	Burger King Chevrolet
32	24	43	Bobby Hamilton	STP Pontiac
33	12	22	Ward Burton	MBNA America Pontiac
34	10	81	Kenny Wallace	Square D / T.I.C. Ford
35	26	9	Lake Speed	Spam Ford
36	6	31	Mike Skinner	RealTree Camouflage Chevrolet
37	27	27	Elton Sawyer	David Blair Motorsports Ford

First Union 400

Rusty Wallace gets quick service from his Miller teammates, who helped him charge to the head of the field. After taking the lead on lap 241, Rusty dominated the second half of the event and looked unbeatable until lady luck betrayed him and abruptly ended his day.
(Right) *Terry Labonte shed his "Iceman" nickname in favor of "Ironman" when he unveiled this special-edition paint job to commemorate his 513th consecutive NASCAR Winston Cup start.*

The rain and cold that plagued Richmond, Rockingham, Atlanta and Bristol were quickly forgotten on a brilliant spring weekend in the North Carolina Brushy Mountains as the teams assembled after the Easter holiday break at North Wilkesboro Speedway.

As crew members worked their way through practice, the pervading question of the weekend kept coming up: Was this the last time the NASCAR Winston Cup tour would make a spring stop at North Wilkes, whose five-eighths-mile track had hosted NASCAR Winston Cup events since Rex White claimed the first trophy with his Chevrolet back in 1961?

There really was no answer to the question. Ever since Bob Bahre bought the remaining half interest in the track in December to share the operation with Bruton Smith, who had purchased the other 50 percent earlier in 1995, speculation ran rampant that Smith wanted one of the North Wilkes dates for his Texas Motor Speedway which was under construction near Fort Worth. Bahre also made it clear that he would like to have two dates at his New Hampshire International Speedway.

Even though the dates belong to NASCAR, not to the track owners, NASCAR also creates the schedule on a year-to-year basis, leaving talk that the First Union 400 would not only be the last spring NASCAR Winston Cup race at North Wilkesboro, but it would also be the last NASCAR Winston Cup event at the track, period, with the fall date moved to Texas for a November running at TMS.

However, North Wilkesboro's management put an end to that part of the speculation by announcing that the tickets for the fall race had already been printed and would go on sale Monday morning following the running of the First Union 400.

Still, there was a feeling of impending change among the fans in the grandstands. It was far too early in the season to speculate, but they turned out in droves every day of the weekend, just in case it was the final time they would see the cars on the unique uphill-downhill track on an April afternoon.

SABCO Racing used the North Wilkesboro weekend to introduce a second team, with Jay Sauter driving and First Union Bank as the sponsor. They planned to campaign five races toward the conclusion of the current season, then expand the schedule for the team in 1997.

After six races in 1996, Ricky Craven arrived in North Wilkesboro riding a wave of consistently strong performances that had him fourth in championship points. In the race, Ricky continued the run by starting – and finishing – in seventh place.

A visit to the Robert Yates Racing transporter revealed a smiling Ernie Irvan who had quickly recovered from the minor eyelid surgery he underwent immediately after the Bristol race. It was a simple thing, Ernie explained, saying that the procedure improved his vision by lifting his eyelid, which tended to droop a bit when he was tired. "Everything's great," Ernie pronounced. "We just need a

good finish here to lift us up from our 22nd place in the point standings."

The test in Japan was a huge success, according to Rusty Wallace and Dale Earnhardt, who made the trip to the other side of the globe. "The fans there are simply unbelievable," Earnhardt said, "and we had a great time working with them and with the Goodyear engineers figuring out the tire combination for the November event. The setup for the event is going to be much the same as at Sears Point, and there's no doubt in either Rusty's or my mind that it's going to be a great show for everyone the whole time we're there."

The trip to Japan was one reason for Earnhardt's grin. The other was that he had moved to within 37 points of Dale Jarrett in the point standings following the Bristol race and was now where he wanted to be — in a position to apply pressure to the first-year team that led the standings. Right behind the two Dales was Ricky Rudd who had seen his top-10 streak, dating back to last season's fall race at Rockingham, end at Bristol. Ricky's 14th place in the rain-soaked event at Thunder Valley dropped him to 81 points behind Jarrett.

Ricky Craven held on to a comfortable fourth in the standings, 97 points behind Jarrett and 17 points ahead of Terry Labonte. Both were feeling the hot breath of the defending NASCAR Winston Cup champion on their necks

Terry Labonte takes the green flag to start the First Union 400. No one was surprised at Terry's third pole of the year – especially with it coming at North Wilkesboro. But Elton Sawyer shocked many by taking the other front row spot in David Blair's unsponsored Thunderbird.

as Jeff Gordon's second straight victory, his third win in the last four events, moved the reigning titlist to sixth place in the points. He was now just 133 behind — almost, he confided to his team, within striking distance.

A total of 42 cars were in the garage area for the first round of qualifying, and one of them looked much different than it had during the course of the season. The First Union 400 would mark Terry Labonte's 513th-consecutive NASCAR Winston Cup start, tying the record set by Richard Petty. It was a mark no one had expected to ever see matched, much the same as The King's 200 career victo-

of the session to claim his third Busch Pole of the year.

Labonte's quick lap ended a fairy tale moment for Elton Sawyer and the Mike Hill-led David Blair Motorsports team. With a spanking-new car, Sawyer ran early in the session and put the quickest time on the scoreboard. Still in search of a sponsor for the season, Sawyer and Hill hoped the lap would stand to put the black-white-and-gold Ford on the pole. Although bumped to the second starting spot, Sawyer would still start the race from the outside of the front row — a great accomplishment for the meagerly-funded team.

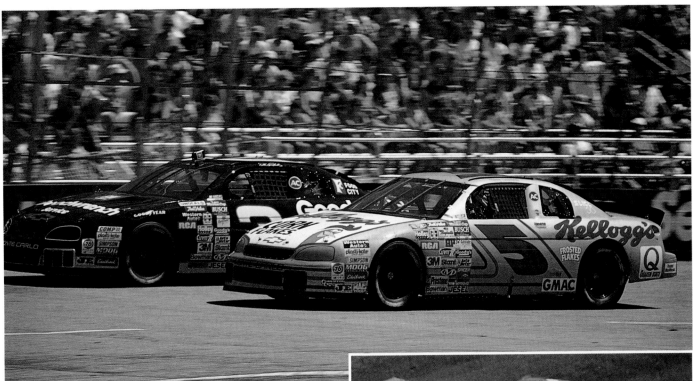

(Above) Terry Labonte and Dale Earnhardt battle side by side to the delight of the fans who filled North Wilkesboro's grandstands. Despite not leading a lap in the race, Earnhardt secured the third finishing spot and collected enough points to trail leader Jarrett by just two markers at the end of the day. *(Right)* Robert Pressley (33) is hounded by Bobby Hamilton as the two young drivers fight through the corners. Pressley had an outstanding day, finishing fourth on the lead lap, while Hamilton continued his impressive season with an eighth-place finish.

ries — a record all expect to stand forever.

As a tribute to Labonte and to call attention to his record-tying feat, the Hendrick Motorsports effort painted his car iron-gray in recognition of the streak that began when Terry went to the line in Billy Hagan's Chevrolet way back at Riverside in January of his 1979 rookie season.

The color of the car made little difference to Labonte when it came to qualifying. During the opening events of the year, he had been one of the fastest during the first session at track after track, scoring a pair of pole positions in the first half-dozen events. His second lap in the silver-gray car was the best, and again he emerged with the fastest time

Mark Martin's Valvoline team, heartened by their Bristol pole and solid run to third place, was fast enough to claim the inside of the second row, and Bobby Hamilton turned in another fine short-track qualifying performance in Richard Petty's STP Pontiac to start fourth. Ken Schrader and Ted Musgrave made up the third row, and Ricky Craven continued to impress, notching the seventh-fastest lap, just a tick faster than Sterling Marlin. Jeff Burton and

MacDonald, Dave Marcis and Bobby Hillin all were unable to start the race.

Earlier in his career, Labonte chalked up thousands of test laps at North Wilkesboro when he drove for Junior Johnson. Drawing from that vast storehouse of experience once the green flag fell on the First Union 400, Labonte streaked away from the field to lead the first 56 laps of the event. After he finally yielded the point, he ran in the top handful of cars during the middle portion of the race, ready to strike if the opportunity presented itself.

Just after half-distance, Rusty Wallace moved his Miller Ford into the lead, and for the longest time, it looked as though Wallace was headed for his first victory of the season. During a green-flag run that lasted more

(Left) Jeff Gordon defends the inside against Bobby Labonte (18) and Ricky Rudd (10) as Terry Labonte dispenses with Kyle Petty (42) on his way to the front. Although Gordon failed to lead a lap, he battled Terry Labonte in the final laps and finished two car-lengths behind in second place to continue his romp through the point standings. (Above) Kim and Ernie Irvan share some light conversation with Michael Waltrip as they await driver introductions prior to the event.

than 220 laps, Wallace dominated the event.

As the race moved toward its conclusion, the Miller team began to plan its victory celebration. On lap 374, with just 26 laps remaining, however, Lady Luck changed her seat, abandoning the black Ford when John Andretti and Geoff Bodine collided. Andretti careened into the outside wall, and Andretti's Blue Light Special ricocheted back across the track, was hit by Joe Nemechek's Chevrolet, and smashed into the water barrels protecting the concrete pit wall in the third turn. Rusty, who went low when he saw Andretti sliding high, had no options when John's Ford came back across the track. Hitting the purple-and-orange Thunderbird, Wallace's hopes for the elusive first win of the season were gone. Rusty returned to the track after repairs,

Jeremy Mayfield made up the fifth row, with Robert Pressley and Rusty Wallace starting 11th and 12th.

In the second round of qualifying, seven drivers ran again, but none of them were fast enough to crack through the top 32 times, which was the number of cars entered in the field by speed. For the second straight race, Bill Elliott took a former champion's provisional, allowing Joe Nemechek to join Hut Stricklin, Michael Waltrip and Ricky Rudd as provisional starters. That meant that Ward Burton (the Darlington pole-sitter), Mike Wallace, Randy

It was Terry Labonte's day at North Wilkesboro. He dominated the race, leading the most laps on his way to a victory celebration with wife Kim, and collected an additional $129,200 from Unocal for winning from the pole.

but with all but two cars running at the finish, the 10 lost laps left Wallace in 33rd place at the end of the day.

The accident brought out the red flag for 11 minutes while the barrels were replaced and filled with water. When the race resumed under caution on lap 377, the lead-lap cars headed for pit road for tires and fuel for a sprint to the finish.

The Kellogg's team knew when Terry slid into his pit stall, that it was time to either win or lose. The Gary DeHart-led crew responded, turning Terry back onto the track after a 19.2-second stop. Pressing as hard as he could while keeping the speed limit in mind, Terry headed up pit road, knowing that this pit stop would go a long way toward determining the winner of the race. At the end of pit road, Gordon's Rainbow Warriors were cranking out a fine stop of their own, getting Gordon serviced in 19.5 seconds. But as the jack dropped under the DuPont Chevrolet and Jeff hit the go pedal, Terry inched past, beating the defending champion to the timing line to take the lead.

The green came out on lap 386, with just 14 laps to go, and the two Hendrick Motorsports drivers were left to battle for the victory. Gordon tried every way he could — other than wrecking Labonte — to wrest the lead from the Texan, but Terry, with the victory in sight, didn't make a slip. Keeping Gordon at bay, Labonte went on to record a two-car-lengths victory.

Labonte's win was his first since the August Bristol race last season, and it provided the biggest payday in his long and storied career. The Unocal Challenge bonus, awarded to any driver who wins from pole, had rolled over to $129,200. Added to the race winner's purse, the bonus brought Labonte's check to a whopping $229,025 — nearly $100,000 more than his previous best payday of $138,475 for his 1994 Daytona 500 third-place finish. More importantly, it moved him to third place in the point standings, a mere 57 points behind Jarrett.

Earnhardt also moved closer to Jarrett, despite not leading a lap for only the third time this year. The Goodwrench Chevrolet driver finished a fighting third at North Wilkesboro, ahead of sparkling performances by Robert Pressley and Marlin, the final drivers on the lead lap. Irvan grabbed sixth after leading early in the race, ahead of yet another strong performance from Craven. Hamilton was a solid eighth. Ken Schrader made it three Hendrick cars in the top nine positions, and Bobby Labonte claimed 10th place.

Jarrett finished 11th after suffering a cut tire in a collision with a lapped car, losing two laps while having the tire changed under green. He was never able to make up the lost laps. When he looked at the point sheet following the race, he found his name at the top of the list, but just barely. The combination of finishes had moved Earnhardt to within two points of the leader.

First Union 400

Fin. Pos.	Str. Pos.	Car #	Driver	Team
1	1	5	Terry Labonte	Kellogg's Corn Flakes Chevrolet
2	17	24	Jeff Gordon	DuPont Refinishes Chevrolet
3	26	3	Dale Earnhardt	GM Goodwrench Service Chevrolet
4	11	33	Robert Pressley	Skoal Bandit Chevrolet
5	8	4	Sterling Marlin	Kodak Film Chevrolet
6	22	28	Ernie Irvan	Texaco Havoline Ford
7	7	41	Ricky Craven	Kodiak Chevrolet
8	4	43	Bobby Hamilton	STP Pontiac
9	5	25	Ken Schrader	Budweiser Chevrolet
10	28	18	Bobby Labonte	Interstate Batteries Chevrolet
11	29	88	Dale Jarrett	Quality Care / Ford Credit Ford
12	6	16	Ted Musgrave	Family Channel / PRIMESTAR Ford
13	15	12	Derrike Cope	Mane 'N Tail Ford
14	31	1	Rick Mast	Hooters Pontiac
15	33	10	Ricky Rudd	Tide Ford
16	35	8	Hut Stricklin	Circuit City Ford
17	34	21	Michael Waltrip	Citgo Ford
18	16	81	Kenny Wallace	Square D / T.I.C. Ford
19	27	7	Geoff Bodine	QVC Ford
20	10	98	Jeremy Mayfield	RCA Ford
21	37	94	Bill Elliott	McDonald's Ford
22	32	19	Dick Trickle	Healthsource Ford
23	19	11	Brett Bodine	Lowe's Ford
24	24	30	Johnny Benson	Pennzoil Pontiac
25	30	17	Darrell Waltrip	Parts America Chevrolet
26	25	29	Steve Grissom	Cartoon Network Chevrolet
27	21	75	Morgan Shepherd	Remington Arms Ford
28	23	15	Wally Dallenbach	Hayes Modems Ford
29	9	99	Jeff Burton	Exide Batteries Ford
30	13	42	Kyle Petty	Coors Light Pontiac
31	18	23	Jimmy Spencer	Camel Cigarettes Ford
32	2	27	Elton Sawyer	David Blair Motorsports Ford
33	12	2	Rusty Wallace	Miller Ford
34	20	37	John Andretti	Kmart / Little Caesars Ford
35	14	9	Lake Speed	Spam Ford
36	36	87	Joe Nemechek	Burger King Chevrolet
37	3	6	Mark Martin	Valvoline Ford

Goody's Headache Powder 500

Front-row starters Ricky Craven (41) and Kyle Petty race at the point in the early going of the Goody's Headache Powder 500. Petty finds room on the inside to scoot past Craven to take the lead on lap 28. Craven took the pole in just his 40th career NASCAR Winston Cup start, the first of his big league career.
***(Right)** Before the 100-lap mark, Rusty Wallace had once again asserted himself as the Master of Martinsville. Rusty went on to win his fourth consecutive spring event at Martinsville – his fifth win in the last seven starts at the Virginia half-mile.*

Two days after his rich victory at North Wilkesboro, Terry Labonte — about to become racing's "Ironman" by starting at Martinsville — met another sportsman with the same nickname. Attending a Baltimore Orioles game at Camden Yards, Labonte spent time with "Ironman" Cal Ripken Jr., who set a new Major League Baseball record with his own streak of consecutive games. At the ballpark, Terry tossed out the first pitch, signed hundreds of autographs and made a clubhouse visit to meet the rest of the Orioles.

Labonte then headed for Martinsville and the iron-gray Chevrolet prepared by crew chief Gary DeHart, who promised Terry that the new car would be even better than the Monte Carlo he had driven to victory the previous week at North Wilkesboro.

The Goody's Headache Powders 500 would be the long-awaited 514th-consecutive start for Labonte, moving him into sole possession of the NASCAR record. Although Labonte would break The King's record of consecutive starts, the Texan nonetheless went about the business of practice and qualifying in his normal, unassuming manner.

Although Terry was the "Ironman" on the track, the Speedway was secretly planning another celebration of career longevity that garnered far fewer headlines. Friday evening, Dick Thompson, the only full-time public relations director in the track's history, was escorted to Martinsville's hospitality area where he was honored with a surprise dinner to celebrate his 30th anniversary with Martinsville Speedway. Thompson was roasted and toasted by three decades' worth of media members, as well as a variety of NASCAR officials, team owners and drivers.

It was a touching celebration and an opportunity for the many people he helped through the years to share their appreciation for his selfless career contributions to the sport he loves. After the "war stories" and roasting were completed, track owner Clay Earles and Martinsville president Clay Campbell presented Thompson with a diamond ring and painted portrait to be hung in the newly-named Dick Thompson Press Box at the track.

The festivities honoring Thompson weren't the only celebrations held in southern Virginia Friday night. While the toasting went on in the hospitality area at the track, the crew of the Kodiak Chevrolet driven by Ricky Craven was doing some serious partying of its own!

mary Bud Chevy suffered a broken bolt during practice, which allowed the lead weights in a frame rail to tumble onto the track, causing Schrader to careen into the concrete wall. The car was so badly damaged that the Budweiser team went right to the spare Monte Carlo.

Labonte and Dale Earnhardt made up the fourth row. Newcomer Stacy Compton and Bobby Labonte completed the top 10, just ahead of Dave Marcis and Dale Jarrett. Jeff Gordon, the hottest driver on the tour, qualified 13th, and Derrike Cope put Bobby Allison's car safely into the field alongside the DuPont Chevrolet.

Like Craven, Compton was the surprise of the first timed session. A regular on the North Carolina and Virginia NASCAR Winston Racing Series Late Model Stock circuit, Compton was behind the wheel of a Chevrolet formerly owned by the A.G. Dillard team and driven by Ward Burton. Dillard sold his team earlier this year to Dean Monroe of Lynchburg, Va., and the new group spent several days testing at Martinsville prior to the event, trying to make the team's debut a success. It worked.

Saturday's qualifying was even more dramatic than Friday's. A total of 18 cars had yet to make the race, and only seven spots remained in the field before teams could

The Maine native, making just his 40th career NASCAR Winston Cup start, knew his Chevrolet was fast following the day's practice sessions. Craven drew an early number and, of the first five who ran, put the fastest lap on the clocks. Ricky knew, however, that most of the strong runners had yet to post their times.

Waiting as driver after driver failed to better his mark, Ricky began to wonder if he had, indeed, claimed a spot in next year's Busch Clash. Then, Labonte and Mark Martin, both of whom posted quick practice times, ambled down the line for their runs. When neither driver bettered Ricky's time, the celebration began.

Kyle Petty's lap was 0.014 seconds slower than Craven's, but good enough to grab the outside of the front row, the best starting position for the Coors Light Pontiac so far this season, and his first front-row start since 1993. Bill Elliott, after using a former champion's provisional to start the races at Richmond and North Wilkesboro, turned his short-track program around with a strong third-place starting position, with Martin on his right to fill the second row. Rusty Wallace, with his wounded North Wilkesboro mount repaired, claimed the fifth-fastest lap, and Ken Schrader took a backup Budweiser Chevrolet to the outside of the third row. The pri-

Newcomer Stacy Compton (46) gives ground to Jeff Gordon, who would lead the most laps before finishing third. Compton had a stellar qualifying performance in his NASCAR Winston Cup debut, driving to the ninth-fastest time. During the race, however, he suffered brake problems and was listed 33rd in the final rundown.

ous week), Randy MacDonald, Steve Grissom, Dick Trickle, Bobby Hillin and Ward Burton out in the cold.

The biggest news, however, was that Wally Dallenbach had not made the field either. Too far down in the point standings to use a provisional,

(Left) Hut Stricklin (8), Ernie Irvan (28) and Joe Nemechek (87) look for an opening to get past Michael Waltrip (21) and Robert Pressley (33), who got turned around in the race's early going.
(Below) A hallmark of Martinsville is tight, side-by-side racing, as vividly demonstrated by Irvan, Geoff Bodine (7), Rudd (10), Spencer (23), Musgrave (16) and Stricklin (8). Morgan Shepherd (75) bides his time, waiting for an opening to occur.

use provisionals. Of the 18 drivers, 12 prepared to make runs, with Rick Mast the fastest of the dozen to claim the Busch Clash "wild card" slot. When all the spots were filled, the difference between the pole position and 32nd place was a mere 0.251 seconds, the closest qualifying field in the history of NASCAR Winston Cup racing at Martinsville.

Ted Musgrave, Ernie Irvan, Robert Pressley and Hut Stricklin were forced to use provisionals to make the field, leaving Elton Sawyer (the second-fastest qualifier the previ-

Dallenbach and car owner Bud Moore were forced to load the Hayes Modems Thunderbird onto the transporter and head for the Spartanburg, S.C., shop. After 605 straight races, the longest consecutive race streak by a NASCAR Winston Cup stock car owner, Bud Moore's team would not start an event in which it had made a qualifying attempt. The last race that Moore's team missed was at Martinsville in 1964 when Billy Wade's car was disqualified before the race began for having disc brakes installed.

Wallace and Gordon swapped the lead back and forth, depending on the cycling of pit stops during the green periods. Earnhardt, Terry Labonte and Ernie Irvan all spent time at the front as well. Midway in the race, Wallace fell a half of a lap behind after suffering problems during a pit stop and receiving a mismatched set of tires that sent him slipping and sliding around the half-mile. When the fifth caution flew for oil on the track on lap 414, Wallace breathed a huge sigh of relief and headed for pit road, making up his deficit and getting a new set of Goodyear "stickers" that he hoped would enable him to contend for the victory.

(Above) Kenny Wallace loops his Square D Ford as Jeff Burton gives himself enough room to drive by. Wallace recovered, and managed a 14th-place finish at the end of the day. (Right) Jeremy Mayfield (98) blows past Derrike Cope as he charges toward the lead pack. Mayfield continued to demonstrate early-season strength in Cale Yarborough's Fords by finishing a career-best fourth at Martinsville.

While Moore was overseeing the loading of his Thunderbird, NASCAR inspectors were confiscating an ineligible clutch from the Pennzoil team after Johnny Benson qualified 18th. Crew chief Doug Hewitt was later fined $5,000 and handed a two-race suspension for using the part during qualifying.

As the pace car led the field around the manicured half-mile in preparation for the start of the Goody's event, an unfamiliar driver was behind the wheel. Marlin Wright, the pace car driver for NASCAR Busch Series events not held in conjunction with NASCAR Winston Cup events, had replaced regular driver Elmo Langley, who missed the race after undergoing a procedure to clear a blocked artery. The Martinsville race was the first event Elmo had missed in a decade, and as he watched the race unfold on television in his home, he saw a humdinger.

When the green flag dropped, Craven held the point for the first 28 laps, giving a good account of himself and his Chevrolet. On lap 29, Petty forced his way to the point and put his Pontiac in the breeze, leading until Rusty Wallace's Miller mates put him in front following the third caution flag of the event. For more than 250 laps, the race ran under green-flag conditions — a huge surprise at Martinsville where the flat short-track action usually produces a considerable number of caution periods.

Midway through the race, Jeff Gordon (24) and Rusty Wallace began a classic Martinsville duel, swapping the lead back and forth until the fourth caution flew on lap 262. Dale Jarrett (88) had a great view of the action, but could not catch the front-runners.

When the final yellow waved for debris on the track with just over 50 laps to go, Wallace again headed for pit road, where his crew dropped the track bar slightly and changed the air pressure in the new tires that they slapped on the black Ford. Earnhardt and Irvan remained on the track, and when the field formed again, Wallace trailed the two black

Dale Jarrett needed his crew's assistance to get stopped at the end of pit road after suffering a faulty brake caliper. Parrott and company made repairs and returned Jarrett to action, but the time lost on pit road ultimately dropped Dale from first to third in the point standings.

cars and Gordon, whose Rainbow Warriors had turned him out of the pits ahead of the Miller Ford. Labonte, a threat to win throughout the day, began struggling with brake problems, and when the field took the green flag for the final time with 52 laps left in the race, Terry remained on pit road with DeHart and the rest of the Kellogg's crew frantically trying to solve the problem.

Gordon and Wallace had new Goodyears on their cars, and Earnhardt and Irvan hoped to hold off their challengers long enough for their tires to wear slightly, making all four cars equal for the sprint to the green flag. The strategy up front didn't work as Gordon and Wallace blasted past Irvan four laps after the green, then needed just one more lap to put a slowing Earnhardt behind them.

Jeff's car was strong, and Rusty challenged repeatedly, but he could not find the lane to move past the multicolored Chevrolet. Finally, Wallace backed off a little to cool his brakes and tires, readying the Ford for one last run at Gordon. With 11 laps to go, Wallace nosed under the rainbow Chevrolet in the fourth turn, raced side by side with Jeff down the frontstretch and completed the pass by pinning the DuPont car behind Hendrick teammate Labonte, who had returned to the track. As Rusty began to pull away over the next four laps, Irvan also moved past Gordon to claim second place.

Wallace held on for his first 1996 victory and his first win since September of 1995, making him the first driver to win four straight spring races at Martinsville. Rusty's victory margin over the Texaco Ford was more than two seconds, but Irvan and his team had their own reasons to celebrate. Forced to use a provisional to make the race, they had fought all the way up to second place despite pitting on the backstretch.

Gordon took third place, ahead of a superb performance by Jeremy Mayfield, who edged past Earnhardt as Dale's tires faded during the final 50 laps. A lap behind the winner, Bobby Hamilton claimed sixth place, while Ken Schrader beat Bobby Labonte, Ted Musgrave and Sterling Marlin in their battle of twice-lapped cars.

Earnhardt may have drifted from the point in the rush to the finish, but one look at the point standings at the end of the race brought a big grin to the seven-time champion's face. Jarrett had struggled throughout the event with brake caliper problems, falling 42 laps behind to a 29th-place finish. The combination of the two finishes moved Earnhardt into the point lead and dropped Jarrett into third behind the red-hot Gordon, who continued to rocket up the standings sheet. Earnhardt now held an 76-point lead over the defending champion, and many thought another battle to Atlanta was in the offing for the same two drivers who had contested the 1995 crown.

Goody's Headache Powder 500

Fin. Pos.	Str. Pos.	Car #	Driver	Team
1	5	2	Rusty Wallace	Miller Ford
2	34	28	Ernie Irvan	Texaco Havoline Ford
3	13	24	Jeff Gordon	DuPont Refinishes Chevrolet
4	16	98	Jeremy Mayfield	RCA Ford
5	8	3	Dale Earnhardt	GM Goodwrench Service Chevrolet
6	21	43	Bobby Hamilton	STP Pontiac
7	6	25	Ken Schrader	Budweiser Chevrolet
8	10	18	Bobby Labonte	Interstate Batteries Chevrolet
9	33	16	Ted Musgrave	Family Channel / PRIMESTAR Ford
10	15	4	Sterling Marlin	Kodak Film Chevrolet
11	24	9	Lake Speed	Spam Ford
12	1	41	Ricky Craven	Kodiak Chevrolet
13	3	94	Bill Elliott	McDonald's Ford
14	28	81	Kenny Wallace	Square D / T.I.C. Ford
15	26	1	Rick Mast	Hooters Pontiac
16	23	17	Darrell Waltrip	Parts America Chevrolet
17	27	21	Michael Waltrip	Citgo Ford
18	31	11	Brett Bodine	Lowe's Ford
19	32	23	Jimmy Spencer	Camel Cigarettes Ford
20	20	75	Morgan Shepherd	Remington Arms Ford
21	4	6	Mark Martin	Valvoline Ford
22	25	99	Jeff Burton	Exide Batteries Ford
23	30	10	Ricky Rudd	Tide Ford
24	7	5	Terry Labonte	Kellogg's Corn Flakes Chevrolet
25	18	30	Johnny Benson	Pennzoil Pontiac
26	29	87	Joe Nemechek	Burger King Chevrolet
27	19	7	Geoff Bodine	QVC Ford
28	14	12	Derrike Cope	Mane 'N Tail Ford
29	12	88	Dale Jarrett	Quality Care / Ford Credit Ford
30	2	42	Kyle Petty	Coors Light Pontiac
31	36	8	Hut Stricklin	Circuit City Ford
32	22	90	Mike Wallace	Heilig-Meyers Ford
33	9	46	Stacy Compton	IHC Chevrolet
34	35	33	Robert Pressley	Skoal Bandit Chevrolet
35	11	71	Dave Marcis	Prodigy Chevrolet
36	17	37	John Andretti	Kmart / Little Caesars Ford

Winston Select 500

*Ernie Irvan (28), Dale Jarrett (88) and Sterling Marlin (4) vie for the lead on Talladega's expansive frontstretch. Third-place starter Jeremy Mayfield (98), Ted Musgrave (16) and Mike Skinner (31) pull up behind the leaders as the field begins to take shape in the early going of the Winston Select 500. **(Right)** Terry Labonte contemplates his car's setup during a pre-race practice session, knowing his ride with Hendrick Motorsports is secure. Earlier in the week, Terry, crew chief Gary DeHart, and sponsor Kellogg's inked contract extensions that would keep the team together though the year 2000.*

With grim looks on their faces, the red-white-and-blue-clad Quality Care/Ford Credit crew from the Robert Yates stable unloaded its Ford Thunderbird from the transporter in the garage area at the massive Talladega Superspeedway and began preparations for the weekend's Winston Select 500.

There was reason for the unusual lack of frivolity among Dale Jarrett's team. A cut tire at North Wilkesboro had cost the team two laps and resulted in an 11th-place finish. Then, at Martinsville the following weekend, Jarrett struggled with brake caliper problems, finishing 42 laps behind and falling from first to third in the NASCAR Winston Cup point standings.

Now, the team arrived at the fastest track on the tour without its best superspeedway car — the Thunderbird that claimed the checkered flag in the Daytona 500 last February. That Ford, still equipped with the engine that powered Jarrett to his second Daytona 500 victory, was installed in the new Daytona USA attraction scheduled to open during the Pepsi 400 weekend.

Despite the fact that the new Ford they brought for this weekend had been massaged with track and wind-tunnel tests, it wasn't quite as good as the Daytona-winning machine. Jarrett knew he had his work cut out for him if he hoped to take another step toward becoming only the second driver in history to win the Winston Select Million.

R.J. Reynolds' rich $1 million bonus, available to competitors since 1985, has only been won once since its inception. Bill Elliott won the million during that magical season when it was posted for the first time. Others have tried to win the coveted prize, but no one has found the same answer that Elliott did with his red-and-white Coors rocket ship.

Jarrett and the Yates team knew that if they won the Winston Select 500, it would not only put them in the driver's seat for the bonus, but it would also eliminate any other team from contention for the money. A Talladega victory would mean that the team needed to win either at Charlotte in May or Darlington in September to cash the huge check. A win would also guarantee the "consolation" bonus of $100,000 from Reynolds, available to the first driver to win two of the four events comprising the program if the Winston Select Million was not claimed.

While Jarrett and his mates were keeping a close eye on the practice times posted by their competition, Hendrick

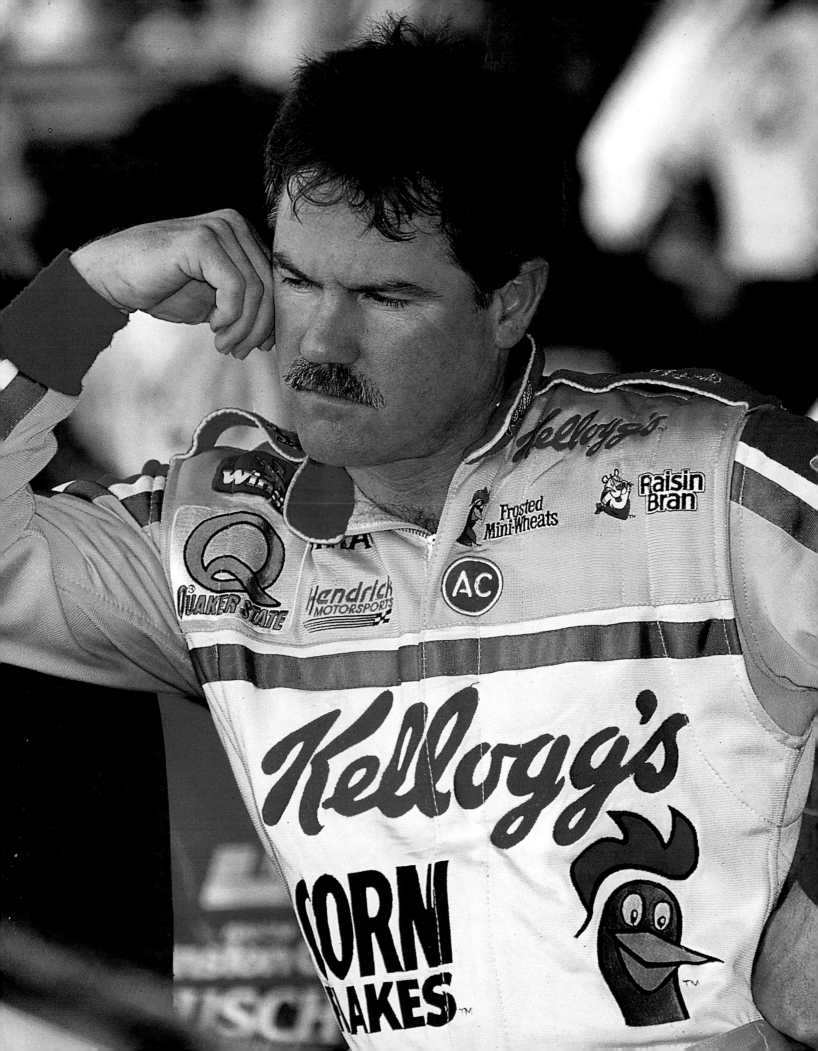

raised their eyebrows. Jeremy Mayfield's red-and-white Ford was near the top of the list — just as it had been at Daytona. After a career-best fourth-place finish the previous weekend at Martinsville, Mayfield and the Cale Yarborough-owned team were pumped. With the RCA Ford humming, morale was at an all-time high. After Mayfield made his qualifying run, there was even more reason for the high-fiving that ensued among the crew mem-

(Left) The Kodak crew was superfast on pit road, complimenting Marlin's Kodak Chevrolet, which was superfast on the track. The combination allowed Sterling to lead the most laps in the race on the way to his first win of the season. (Below) Ernie Irvan grabbed the pole, and Dale Jarrett would start second to make it an all-Robert Yates-owned front row, but neither driver was completely satisfied with his mount for the race.

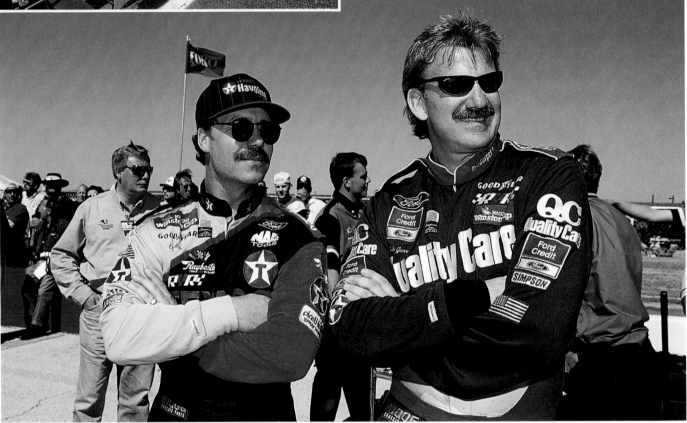

Motorsports announced that the Kellogg's/Terry Labonte/Gary DeHart combination would remain together through the year 2000. The contract extensions, signed by all involved, were a huge vote of confidence for the job done by Labonte and the Kellogg's crew headed by DeHart. Terry's smile told the entire story. He had said repeatedly throughout the past 15 months that the team was the best he had ever driven for. While Labonte was accepting the congratulations of many in the garage area, Chuck Bown had his own grin pasted on his face. Car owners Check and Earl Sadler announced that Shoney's Restaurants had signed to sponsor their Ford for 15 of the remaining races in the season.

As the qualifying line formed for the first timed sessions, crews took a look at the list of final practice times and

bers — Jeremy posted the fastest time and it held up as driver after driver made their runs.

That is until a black-yellow-and-red Thunderbird fired up on pit road and driver Ernie Irvan took the checkered flag following his laps. Mayfield's time became secondary as Irvan was nearly a mile per hour faster. After withstanding a challenge from Yates teammate Jarrett, Ernie won his fourth Talladega pole, his first since his comeback began. He pipped Jarrett for the inside of the front row, with just .076 second separating the two Thunderbirds.

Mayfield's run held up for the inside of the second row, while Sterling Marlin qualified fourth with his Kodak Chevrolet, the only Monte Carlo to qualify in the top five. Ted Musgrave was fifth-fastest with his Family Channel

Ford, barely beating Mike Skinner's outstanding performance in Richard Childress' research and development Chevrolet. Jeff Purvis backed up his strong Daytona efforts with the seventh-fastest lap in the Phoenix Racing Chevrolet, while Robert Pressley claimed the outside of the fourth row, ahead of the Exide Ford of Jeff Burton and Johnny Benson's highest-qualifying Pontiac. Jeff Gordon and Derrike Cope barely missed the top 10, while Terry and

ately repaired. Saturday night, the team took parts and pieces from the damaged engine and two backups to build Sunday's race motor.

Joe Nemechek's Burger King Chevrolet was the fastest of the cars that ran during Saturday's second round of qualifying, but a large shadow hung over the entire day's activities. ARCA President Bob Loga was critically injured in an automobile accident while leaving the track Friday afternoon and succumbed to his injuries Saturday afternoon. Loga had been president of the sanctioning body since 1990 and was instrumental in the growth of the series for the last two decades. He was well-liked and respected by everyone in the sport, and his infectious enthusiasm for his series will be missed by everyone in the ARCA and NASCAR garage areas.

(Above) Michael Waltrip (21) pulls Bobby Hamilton along-side Terry Labonte (5) as Michael charges all the way from his 31st starting spot to the lead pack in the first fifty laps. Waltrip stayed with the leaders throughout the race and finished a strong fifth in the Wood Brothers' Ford.
(Right) Dale Earnhardt's Goodwrench Chevrolet was strong enough to pull this train around the 2.66-mile superspeedway. He carved up the field, moving from his 16th starting position to the top five in the first four laps, taking the point on lap 15 and finishing third to maintain his lead in the points.

Bobby Labonte qualified side by side for row seven, ahead of Rusty Wallace and Earnhardt.

While Irvan was celebrating his first pole position since the New Hampshire race in 1994, his crew was pushing the Texaco Havoline Thunderbird to a secured area of the garage. NASCAR officials, responding to requests from several car owners to determine horsepower differences between the Ford and General Motors machines, obtained use of a mobile chassis dyno test bed and planned to test both Irvan's and Marlin's cars immediately after qualifying. Irvan's Ford was rolled onto the chassis dyno to be tested. Unfortunately, the clutch slipped and damaged the Ford's engine. Then, the computer malfunctioned and the car was rolled off the dyno. Both Irvan's and Marlin's cars ultimately went untested.

Irvan's crew chief, Larry McReynolds, immediately huddled with car owner Yates as the team began tearing down the Ford engine to determine the damage. This engine was not only the qualifying motor, but also the race motor, and they found that the damage was too extensive to be immedi-

With Pontiac-driving Bobby Hamilton and Kyle Petty and Ford-driving Mike Wallace and Brett Bodine forced to use provisionals to make the field, and with Darrell Waltrip choosing to use a former champion's provisional, the 43-car field was set. Those left off the grid included Phil Barkdoll, Chad Little, Steve Seligman and Bobby Hillin, who was missing his fourth consecutive event in the Jasper Motorsports Ford.

Everyone expected a thriller when the green flag fell on the field Sunday — and no one was disappointed. Earnhardt fans had plenty to cheer about when the seven-time champion set sail and ripped his way through the field from his 16th starting position to claim a place among the top five in just four laps! Michael Waltrip was giving Citgo guests plenty to wave their hats about as well, hauling his red-and-white Wood Brothers Ford from 31st to the top six in just 50 laps.

While Earnhardt and Waltrip, among others, were delighting the huge throng, Sterling Marlin took one look at the water temperature gauge in his Kodak Chevrolet and gulped. One of the fastest drivers in Saturday afternoon's "Happy Hour," and after more than 1,000 miles of pre-event testing to eliminate

(Right) *Rusty Wallace, who put his Miller Ford at the point for 16 laps before mid-distance, holds the inside line as nearly half the field fans out behind him.*
(Below) *The Quality Care crew reloads Dale Jarrett's Thunderbird with tires and fuel during one of the race's six caution periods. Jarrett, shooting for the second leg of the Winston Select Million, challenged Marlin in the closing laps, but came up two-tenths of a second short and finished second.*

the engine problems that thwarted a "three-peat" in the Daytona 500, Marlin watched the needle on the gauge rocket to more than 230 degrees. Fortunately, the first caution of the day allowed him to head for pit road on lap seven. When the yellow Monte Carlo came to a stop, crew chief Tony Glover and other team members immediately removed some of the tape blocking the radiator. Marlin restarted the race in 36th place. With the water temperature steadying at approximately 210 degrees, Marlin began carving his way through the field. Within 30 laps, he had moved to the point, underscoring the power and speed at his disposal with the Kodak car.

Shortly after Sterling moved to the front, Mayfield's promising day ended in a collision with

After an early-race overheating problem, Sterling Marlin asserted himself as the class of the field by leading the most laps during the race (48) and capturing his second straight victory at Talladega.

Lake Speed, sending the field to pit road on lap 63. Bill Elliott, who had moved into the top 10, pitted under the yellow but a miscue on pit road put him back in the field for the restart on lap 67. Ten laps later, Elliott lost control in the fourth turn and his McDonald's Ford slammed the pavement with enough force to break his left leg near the hip.

For the next 30 laps, the battle for the lead was furious. Rusty Wallace, Earnhardt, Gordon, Terry Labonte and Michael Waltrip rocketed around the track, trading the point back and forth until the fourth yellow flag of the day flew when Dave Marcis spun exiting the second turn. With the field racing side by side, and with the Wood Brothers Ford at the point, the green dropped on lap 119. Less than 10 laps later, Gordon and Mark Martin touched, sending Mark into the wall and then back into the path of Ward Burton. With nowhere to go, the pack behind them tangled in a chain-reaction accident that involved some 14 cars, with Ricky Craven's Kodiak Chevrolet taking the worst licking.

When the tire smoke cleared and the damaged cars were towed toward the garage area, a 52-minute red-flag period ensued while maintenance crews went to work. When the race restarted, the lead pack soon split into two groups: Jarrett, Michael Waltrip, Earnhardt, Bobby Hamilton, Terry Labonte and Steve Grissom comprised the first and Marlin headed a pack of five that was charging hard to catch the front-runners.

Sterling's Chevrolet was so strong that it took him less than 10 laps to pull his group up to the lead pack, and then Marlin began snipping away. He moved to the lead for the final time on lap 167 and looked in his mirror to see Jarrett, Earnhardt and Terry Labonte fighting for second place. The Kodak Chevrolet had more than enough to hold the point, and when Jarrett finally broke away from the three-way battle for second place and tried to run down Marlin, Sterling knew he was home free. Marlin knew that none of the cars had enough juice to pass him on its own, and unless Earnhardt and Labonte got into line and came to help Jarrett, there was no way the Ford could pass the Chevrolet.

Earnhardt and Labonte were stubbornly fighting each other for third place, and Jarrett received no assistance. His valiant try to win the Winston Select 500, the second leg of the Winston Select Million, came up just a car-length short as Marlin posted his first victory of the season. It made Sterling eligible for the huge Reynolds bonus, and now either Jarrett or Marlin would have to win both the Coca-Cola 600 and the Mountain Dew Southern 500 to claim the $1 million prize.

Labonte lost his third-place battle to Earnhardt, and Michael Waltrip came home fifth, his best showing since joining the Wood Brothers. Grissom was sixth, ahead of Pressley and Musgrave, while John Andretti and Benson completed the top 10.

Winston Select 500

Fin. Pos.	Str. Pos.	Car #	Driver	Team
1	4	4	Sterling Marlin	Kodak Film Chevrolet
2	2	88	Dale Jarrett	Quality Care / Ford Credit Ford
3	16	3	Dale Earnhardt	GM Goodwrench Service Chevrolet
4	13	5	Terry Labonte	Kellogg's Corn Flakes Chevrolet
5	31	21	Michael Waltrip	Citgo Ford
6	23	29	Steve Grissom	Cartoon Network Chevrolet
7	8	33	Robert Pressley	Skoal Bandit Chevrolet
8	5	16	Ted Musgrave	Family Channel / PRIMESTAR Ford
9	34	37	John Andretti	Kmart / Little Caesars Ford
10	10	30	Johnny Benson	Pennzoil Pontiac
11	39	43	Bobby Hamilton	STP Pontiac
12	35	15	Wally Dallenbach	Hayes Modems Ford
13	26	87	Joe Nemechek	Burger King Chevrolet
14	30	81	Kenny Wallace	Square D / T.I.C. Ford
15	24	1	Rick Mast	Hooters Pontiac
16	9	99	Jeff Burton	Exide Batteries Ford
17	6	31	Mike Skinner	RealTree Camouflage Chevrolet
18	40	42	Kyle Petty	Coors Light Pontiac
19	32	19	Dick Trickle	Healthsource Ford
20	17	25	Ken Schrader	Budweiser Chevrolet
21	43	17	Darrell Waltrip	Parts America Chevrolet
22	36	8	Hut Stricklin	Circuit City Ford
23	41	11	Brett Bodine	Lowe's Ford
24	14	18	Bobby Labonte	Interstate Batteries Chevrolet
25	28	95	Chuck Bown	Shoney's Restaurants Ford
26	29	7	Geoff Bodine	QVC Ford
27	19	22	Ward Burton	MBNA America Pontiac
28	18	10	Ricky Rudd	Tide Ford
29	12	12	Derrike Cope	Straight Arrow Ford
30	15	2	Rusty Wallace	Miller Ford
31	1	28	Ernie Irvan	Texaco Havoline Ford
32	3	98	Jeremy Mayfield	RCA Ford
33	11	24	Jeff Gordon	DuPont Refinishes Chevrolet
34	37	6	Mark Martin	Valvoline Ford
35	7	44	Jeff Purvis	MCA Records Chevrolet
36	22	41	Ricky Craven	Kodiak Chevrolet
37	33	27	Elton Sawyer	David Blair Motorsports Ford
38	42	90	Mike Wallace	Heilig-Meyers Ford
39	21	71	Dave Marcis	Prodigy Chevrolet
40	38	23	Jimmy Spencer	Camel Cigarettes Ford
41	20	94	Bill Elliott	McDonald's Ford
42	27	9	Lake Speed	Spam Ford
43	25	75	Morgan Shepherd	Remington Arms Ford

Save Mart Supermarkets 300

*Dale Earnhardt (3), Terry Labonte (5) and Jeff Gordon (24) each led at some point during the Save Mart Supermarkets 300. Each driver also yielded his lead to Rusty Wallace, who led 36 of 74 laps and returned to victory lane at a road course for the first time since winning here in 1990. **(Right)** Crew members are the picture of intensity as they prepare to service Joe Nemechek's Burger King Chevrolet.*

The haste with which teams packed up their gear, loaded the transporters and exited the expanse of Talladega Superspeedway was understandable. They had only a narrow time window in which to head for their shops and exchange cars, spares and other equipment for the cross-country haul to the Northern California wine country.

Within a matter of hours after arriving at the shops, the transporters were back on the interstate, headed west on the southern route to the Bay Area. Drivers and crew members had a short respite, but by Wednesday, most were headed for the twisting Sears Point Raceway to prepare for the first road course event of the year.

The visit to Sears Point is a vacation of sorts for all the drivers and car owners. The days leading to the event provide a great opportunity to experience the beauty of the Bay Area, from the redwood forests to the lovely rolling hills of the Napa and Sonoma Valleys. There are cable cars to ride in San Francisco, great restaurants to visit near Fisherman's Wharf, a different culture to see in Chinatown and great shopping for those who wish to sample the city's haute couture. Spectacular vistas are also part of the San Francisco/Bay Area experience for the NASCAR Winston

Cup teams and everybody looks forward to it.

Most importantly, the knowledgeable crowds that pack the raceway throughout the weekend give drivers even more incentive to perform well on the road course. Since the tour began visiting the Bay Area in 1989, the crowds have increased annually, quickly making the Save Mart Supermarkets 300 the largest-attended sporting event in the state.

Before heading for the track, Rusty Wallace spent part of Thursday participating in a promotion for United Cerebral Palsy, one of his favorite charities. He arrived at the top of Lombard Street, the steep, winding street often featured in chase scenes in movies filmed in San Francisco. His ride? A San Francisco taxi cab! He buckled into the cab, gave everyone a "thumbs-up," and with that familiar grin creasing his face, released the parking brake and began the descent. The sound of camera shutters whirring disappeared in the squeal of the cab's tires as Rusty plummeted down the serpentine street. He emerged at the bottom, grin still in place, and commented that the ride had given him all the practice he needed for the upcoming race!

After Friday's first round of qualifying, Wallace was right

times and has never qualified out of the top four. His best effort came up four-tenths of a second short of Labonte's fast lap, but Ricky was pleased to have his Tide Ford on the front row for the 74-lap race.

The biggest surprise of the first session of qualifying was the lap of Ron Hornaday Jr. in Ricky Craven's Kodiak Chevrolet. Although Ricky planned to start the race, he was so bruised and sore following the previous weekend's tumbling act at Talladega that he planned to get out of the car at the first opportunity. Hornaday, driver for Dale and Teresa Earnhardt's NASCAR Craftsman Truck Series team, was enlisted to relief drive for Craven and spent the weekend shuttling back and forth between Sears Point

(Above) Road-course specialist Tom Kendall (inset) took the wheel for an injured Bill Elliott at Sears Point. After a practice accident, the primary car was unusable and Tom was forced to qualify the backup car. Kendall led briefly in the latter stages of the race, but transmission problems dropped him to 28th for the day.
(Right) Ricky Craven hired west-coaster and NASCAR Craftsman Truck Series driver Ron Hornaday Jr. to qualify his Kodiak Monte Carlo, and Ron promptly plunked it on the inside of row two for the start of the race.

in the hunt, putting his Miller Ford on the inside of the fourth row. Nothing Rusty — or any other driver — could do, however, was enough to keep Terry Labonte from claiming his fourth Busch Pole of the season and the first of his career at Sears Point. It was the eighth time in his career that Labonte had taken a car to the fastest lap during qualifying on a road course.

He had needed everything in his formidable war chest of experience to wrest this one away from Ricky Rudd. In eight tries at Sears Point, Rudd has claimed the pole four

and Portland, Ore., the site of the truck series race. Hornaday justified Craven's driver choice by putting the green-and-white Chevrolet on the inside of the second row, ahead of Mark Martin and Earnhardt.

Defending NASCAR Winston Cup Champion Jeff Gordon was alongside Earnhardt on the third row, while Kyle Petty surprised many with his eighth-fastest time in the Coors Light Pontiac to secure the fourth-row spot next to Rusty Wallace. Joe Nemechek was just as surprising, claiming the inside of the fifth row. Wally Dallenbach turned in a rock-solid run in Bud Moore's Hayes Modems Ford to beat Ted Musgrave and Ken Schrader for the final slot in the top 10.

Robert Pressley was forced to try to make the field with a backup car after he crashed his Skoal Bandit during practice and emerged from qualifying safely in the field in 30th

Wally Dallenbach prepares to begin the race in Bud Moore's Ford. Wally started the race from the 10th position and was charging toward the point in the closing laps before coming home third, his best finish of the season so far.

place. Tommy Kendall, nominated to drive Bill Elliott's McDonald's Ford, also crashed in practice, but eventually put the team's backup Thunderbird in the field in 32nd place. West Coaster Ken Pederson was installed in the TriStar Motorsports Ford for qualifying, and he put the Healthsource Ford in 36th place for Dick Trickle, who started the race.

Lake Speed claimed the Busch Pole "wild card" slot as the fastest second-round qualifier, while Jeff Burton, Steve Grissom, Dave Marcis and Mike Wallace all used provisionals to make the grid. Winston West regulars Larry Gunselman and Rich Woodland also used their series' provisionals.

Missing from the garage area was David Blair's Ford team and driver Elton Sawyer. The unsponsored team decided to skip Sears Point and remain in North Carolina to concentrate on the upcoming Winston Select Open and Winston Select all-star weekend at Charlotte. Bobby Hillin's team, after failing to make the field at four consecutive races, arrived at Sears Point with Mike Hillman in charge of the crew, and Hillin qualified 34th.

The only way to pick a favorite to win at Sears Point is to put a dozen or so names in a hat and

(Above) Bobby Labonte bears down on Dale Jarrett (88) as Jimmy Spencer and Geoff Bodine crest the hill in hot pursuit. Bobby had a good run in the Interstate Batteries machine to finish ninth, while Dale came home 12th and maintained second place in the point standings. (Left) Ricky Rudd's crew fits the Tide Ford with fresh rubber to keep the outside pole-winner among the leaders. Rudd was competitive all day, but fell to seventh in the closing laps.

draw one out. Rudd and Wallace would be in, as would Earnhardt and Martin. Dallenbach and Kendall would rate, particularly based on their road racing backgrounds. Terry Labonte also would be in. Ernie Irvan has won at Sears Point, and John Andretti, Darrell Waltrip, Geoff Bodine and Gordon all have run well at road racing circuits in the past, with Darrell and Geoff scoring victories at Riverside and Sears Point, respectively. Kyle Petty's Glen win in 1992 would have to be considered, also.

When the field fired on pit road and began moving off for the pace laps, there was suddenly a flurry of activity

around Martin's Valvoline Thunderbird. Crew chief Steve Hmiel and car owner Jack Roush raised the hood of the red-white-and-blue car to diagnose a misfiring engine. One spark plug wire was loose, and when tightened, the Ford motor settled into its familiar throaty growl. The hood went down, and Mark moved away, headed for his fourth-place starting position. However, because the hood had gone up, NASCAR officials determined that it had been a pit stop. The radio in Mark's ear came to life and Hmiel told him to fall in at the end of the field for the start. It was a nightmare for Martin. He knew that he had one of the best cars in the field, but now he would have to fight all the way to the front. Hitting the radio button on his steering wheel, he told his crew chief to get all the heads together and think of a pit strategy to help him move through the pack.

Once the race began, Labonte claimed the early lead but, by the end of the first 10 laps, saw a charging Wallace in his

Steve Grissom, driving the Cartoon Network Chevrolet, and Morgan Shepherd, in the Remington Arms Ford, demonstrate their techniques through turn 11. One of the more popular places to complete a pass on the California road course, the 180-degree hairpin turn is commonly the site of such fender-to-fender action.

rearview mirror. Rusty put the hammer down and moved to the point on lap 14 before yielding it to Earnhardt. Wallace reclaimed it on the 33rd lap following the second caution period of the race, then continued to pace the field.

As the race cycled through a series of green-flag pit stops with less than 25 laps to go, it looked as though Wallace's hopes for a second career Sears Point victory suddenly had come to an early end. Gordon's Rainbow Warriors had beaten the Miller team on pit road to send Gordon back to the track in front of Wallace. However, both trailed Kendall in Elliott's McDonald's Ford. Tommy and the Mike Beam-led team had played their cards perfectly, and the veteran road racing champion was solidly in command as the race headed into its final third.

But, on lap 56, Kendall lost all but fourth gear when he downshifted heading into turn 12 and yielded the lead. Suddenly, the pit stop that enabled Gordon to beat Wallace off pit road looked like the key moment of the race. Rusty was ripping and snorting his way around the track, gamely trying to close in on Gordon, but just as he moved to within striking distance, a lapped car caused Wallace to make an

off-road excursion with just 10 laps left. He recovered, but everything he had gained chasing Gordon was lost. Jeff appeared headed for victory at the track located just 30 miles from where he was born.

But with less than 10 laps left in the race, Wallace received the break he needed when the fourth yellow flag flew for an accident that included Dave Marcis. Rusty closed on Gordon's bumper.

With 27 cars on the lead lap, there was no stopping for fresh tires and a top-off of fuel. To pit meant losing track position that could not be made up in the remaining laps, and both Gordon and Wallace, along with the majority of the leaders, remained on the track.

When the green flew for the restart, Wallace hit the afterburners. He had carefully cleaned off his tires during the yellow-flag laps in an effort to get every bit of bite from his Goodyears when he mashed the pedal. Gordon hadn't done as good a job of cleaning his tires, and Rusty got all of his engine's power to the asphalt, while Gordon spun his wheels just a bit.

It was all Wallace needed. He jumped past Gordon and eased away to the point when the green flag flew on lap 69. Gordon began to fall back, with Martin, Dallenbach and Earnhardt all moving past the DuPont Chevrolet. When the field was slowed by another yellow on lap 70, Wallace again did his tire-cleaning act, making sure he was ready for

Joe Nemechek had high hopes for a strong run after qualifying in the top 10, but wound up on this bank of tires after being forced off turn two in the late going.

the final restart that came with two laps to go. He led the field under the waving green and, despite brave efforts from Martin, held the point to claim the victory.

Mark Martin? The same one who started last because of the loose spark plug wire? Yep. The feisty Arkansas native, with some brilliant work on pit road by his team, worked his way into the top 10 by the one-third mark of the race and was fourth at the two-thirds mark. His car was faster than Wallace's at the end of the race, Mark said, but there was no way to get past the black Ford. His last-to-second-place performance was one of the highlights of the beautiful Northern California afternoon.

Dallenbach fought his way past Earnhardt to finish third in his brand-spanking-new Hayes Modems road-course Ford from Bud Moore's shop, while Terry Labonte and Gordon finished behind Earnhardt but ahead of Rudd. Ken Schrader, Bobby Labonte and Ward Burton took the final positions in the top 10, with Burton finishing just in front of Andretti.

Rusty's second victory of the season brought a huge celebration in victory lane. His infectious enthusiasm, however, was tempered by the time he arrived to face the media for his post-race interview. The Miller Ford was found to be a half-inch too low during the postrace inspection, and after examination, the reason was found. Wallace's off-course excursion flat-spotted the tires and bent a jack-bolt, allowing the car to sag on its suspension. Rusty's team was fined $25,000 for the infractions, but the victory was allowed to stand because there had been no intentional rule-bending by the team.

Mark Martin tackles the Carousel during his charge to the front, followed by Steve Grissom (29), Mike Wallace (90) and Rick Mast. Mark qualified fourth, but dropped to the rear of the field before the initial green flag after pitting during the warm-up laps. He spent his race slicing through the field to finish a close second.

Save Mart Supermarkets 300

Fin. Pos.	Str. Pos.	Car #	Driver	Team
1	7	2	Rusty Wallace	Miller Ford
2	4	6	Mark Martin	Valvoline Ford
3	10	15	Wally Dallenbach	Hayes Modems Ford
4	5	3	Dale Earnhardt	GM Goodwrench Service Chevrolet
5	1	5	Terry Labonte	Kellogg's Corn Flakes Chevrolet
6	6	24	Jeff Gordon	DuPont Refinishes Chevrolet
7	2	10	Ricky Rudd	Tide Ford
8	12	25	Ken Schrader	Budweiser Chevrolet
9	21	18	Bobby Labonte	Interstate Batteries Chevrolet
10	15	22	Ward Burton	MBNA America Pontiac
11	25	37	John Andretti	Kmart / Little Caesars Ford
12	20	88	Dale Jarrett	Quality Care / Ford Credit Ford
13	35	8	Hut Stricklin	Circuit City Ford
14	27	17	Darrell Waltrip	Parts America Chevrolet
15	14	4	Sterling Marlin	Kodak Film Chevrolet
16	26	9	Lake Speed	Spam Ford
17	19	43	Bobby Hamilton	STP Pontiac
18	31	30	Johnny Benson	Pennzoil Pontiac
19	38	1	Rick Mast	Hooters Pontiac
20	13	11	Brett Bodine	Lowe's Ford
21	22	23	Jimmy Spencer	Camel Cigarettes Ford
22	16	21	Michael Waltrip	Citgo Ford
23	11	16	Ted Musgrave	Family Channel / PRIMESTAR Ford
24	24	75	Morgan Shepherd	Remington Arms Ford
25	40	29	Steve Grissom	Cartoon Network Chevrolet
26	39	99	Jeff Burton	Exide Batteries Ford
27	33	81	Kenny Wallace	Square D / T.I.C. Ford
28	32	94	Tommy Kendall	McDonald's Ford
29	36	19	Dick Trickle	Healthsource Ford
30	8	42	Kyle Petty	Coors Light Pontiac
31	3	41	Ricky Craven	Kodiak Chevrolet
32	37	98	Jeremy Mayfield	RCA Ford
33	41	71	Dave Marcis	Prodigy Chevrolet
34	30	33	Robert Pressley	Skoal Bandit Chevrolet
35	28	14	Jeffrey Krogh	Clearwater Forest Industries Chevrolet
36	43	35	Larry Gunselman	Race Stuff / Olson Technology Ford
37	44	38	Rich Woodland	Bill Stroppe Motorsports Chevrolet
38	29	00	Scott Gaylord	Oliver Gravity Separators Chevrolet
39	17	12	Derrike Cope	Straight Arrow Ford
40	23	7	Geoff Bodine	QVC Ford
41	9	87	Joe Nemechek	Burger King Chevrolet
42	18	28	Ernie Irvan	Texaco Havoline Ford
43	34	77	Bobby Hillin	Jasper Engines Ford
44	42	90	Mike Wallace	Heilig-Meyers Ford

The Winston Select

&

The Winston Select Open

*All-star action under the lights at Charlotte Motor Speedway. Robert Yates' drivers Ernie Irvan (28) and Dale Jarrett (88) duel off turn four with Geoff Bodine (7), Jeff Gordon (24) and Kyle Petty (42) in chase. **(Right)** Michael and Elizabeth "Buffy" Waltrip commanded the spotlight in Charlotte's winner's circle following what many felt was a most unlikely victory in The Winston Select. Michael transferred into the main event in the 20th and final position, then piloted the Wood Brothers Ford to victory for his first big-time win on the NASCAR Winston Cup tour.*

With a weekend off following the Sears Point event, a group of hardy souls gathered Monday morning at 8:30 a.m. at Harley-Davidson of Sacramento, ready for a cross-country ride that organizers Kyle Petty and Geoff Bodine hoped would raise in excess of $750,000 for the Winston Cup Racing Wives Auxiliary (WAXX) and the National Make-A-Wish Foundation.

The cast of characters numbered well over 100, counting those who would ride motorcycles across the country and the support troops, and when the Harleys rumbled to life, the second great adventure had begun. Petty had staged the trip last year, aiming to replenish the WAXX trust fund that is used to help those in the NASCAR Winston Cup family in times of need. The first trip raised more than $600,000 for the fund. This year, the pledges and other monies would be split between WAXX and the Make-A-Wish Foundation, of which Bodine is a member of the national board of directors.

By the time the group arrived in Atlanta six days later, the riders had crossed the Hoover Dam, ridden through Yosemite National Park, and literally sold the shirts, pants and boots off their bodies during evening auctions to raise additional dollars for the charities.

Arriving at Atlanta, the entourage rolled into Gwinnett Mall to help open the first NASCAR Thunder store, then mounted up again for the final leg of the cross-country ride to Charlotte.

Harry Gant was one of the participants in the cross-country ride, and he took a lot of ribbing along the way that the 3,012-mile journey was his chance to "get back into shape" for his upcoming date behind the wheel of Bill Elliott's McDonald's Ford. Gant agreed to return from NASCAR Winston Cup retirement to pilot the red-white-and-yellow Thunderbird on a one-race basis for The Winston Select all-star race while Elliott recovered from the broken femur he suffered in the Talladega accident.

Two days after Gant and his fellow travelers stopped in Atlanta, the NASCAR Winston Cup family was saddened by the news that veteran crew chief Harry Hyde had succumbed to a fatal heart attack. Hyde was a legendary figure in the sport, and longtime NASCAR Winston Cup fans remembered him from the K&K Dodge days, when he pre-

spots remained in the rich, non-points winner's-only finale. A total of 38 cars had been entered for The Winston Select Open, and the top-five finishers in the preliminary event would fill the available spaces in The Winston Select.

For all the teams in the garage area, the weekend would be watched and evaluated thoroughly because it was the first race for the Ford teams following NASCAR's rule change that allowed them to lower their rear roof lines by a half-inch. The change was to help the Thunderbirds obtain the downforce needed to compete on equal terms with the Monte Carlos. Chevrolets had won seven of the first 10 races of the season.

From the appearance of the starting grid for The Winston Select Open, the rule change helped considerably. Lake Speed led a charge of the Blue Oval teams that saw

(Top) Lake Speed and his wife Rice display the pole-winner's trophy following qualifying for The Winston Select Open. Lake finished second in The Open, which qualified him for The Winston Select, in which he finished 12th. (Above) The only incident in The Open occurred early in the event when defending ARCA Champion Andy Hillenburg, driving the No. 33 Skoal Bandit for injured Robert Pressley, spun in turn four and collected Greg Sacks (35) and Ted Musgrave (16). John Andretti (37) and Jay Sauter (40) avoided the mishap and were able to continue. (Right) For The Winston Select, Dale Earnhardt's Monte Carlo donned this special paint scheme honoring the athletes of the Olympic Games to be held in Atlanta.

pared some of the fastest cars on the circuit for Bobby Isaac, Buddy Baker and Dave Marcis. More recent fans will remember him for his association with Bobby Hillin, Geoff Bodine and Tim Richmond. Casual observers often took a look at Harry and saw a crusty old codger. The truth is, he was a warm-hearted soul who stood up for what he felt was right, and he was a masterful storyteller. He will be greatly missed by his peers.

When the garage area opened at Charlotte Motor Speedway in preparation for the sport's all-star weekend, The Winston Select and The Winston Select Open, five

(Above) Pole-winner Jeff Gordon leads the all-star field under the green flag and down the frontstretch to begin one of the most exciting spectacles of the season. (Left) Jimmy Spencer's Smokin' Joe's machine gets sandwiched between Hut Stricklin's Circuit City Ford and Michael Waltrip's Citgo Thunderbird, illustrating once again, why he's called "Mr. Excitement." Spencer transferred to the all-star race by charging through The Open field from his 15th starting spot. He took the lead on lap 31 of the 50-lap event and never looked back, taking the win.

14 Fords in the first 17 positions. Only the Pontiacs of Johnny Benson and Bobby Hamilton, and the Chevrolet of Robby Faggart were able to claim a position in the top 17. Steve Grissom slotted the Cartoon Network's Monte Carlo into 18th, while other strong Chevrolets like those of Joe Nemechek (19th) and Ken Schrader (28th) struggled with poor qualifying laps.

Robert Pressley's bad luck continued at Charlotte. He crashed hard during practice (despite a four-leaf clover taped to his dashboard for good luck) and after a broken rib was diagnosed, the Skoal Bandit team turned its backup car over to driver Andy Hillenburg. Stacy Compton and Gary Bradberry also had accidents during their qualifying laps and failed to make the race.

The Open field rolled into action, and although Speed commanded the spotlight early in the event, it was clear to see who was coming from the middle of the field and who appeared to have the best car on the track. Jimmy Spencer,

starting in 15th place, planned to have his Smokin' Joe's Ford in the field when The Winston Select took the green flag later in the evening.

Spencer blasted his way into the top five by the 17th lap and kept the pressure on. He moved past Speed's Spam Ford with 19 laps remaining in the event and rolled to a three-car-length victory, the first win for a Travis Carter-owned machine since he began fielding cars in 1989. Behind Spencer and Speed came Hut Stricklin, Jeff Burton and Michael Waltrip, who held off a late-race charge from Benson to claim the final transfer slot.

When the five Fords from The Winston Select Open were moved onto the frontstretch to complete the field for the all-star race, few in the huge crowd gave any of The Open competitors more than a fleeting chance to emerge victorious in The Winston Select. The event had been staged since 1985, and no driver had ever come out of The Open to collect the trophy and the huge paycheck awaiting the winner.

The big dogs were waiting, led by pole-sitter Jeff Gordon, who had completed the unique qualifying system for The Winston Select with a new record speed. Qualifying for The Winston Select encompasses three laps, with a right-side, two-tire stop in the middle of the run which brings the entire team into play, rather than simply pitting driver and machine against the clock. Gordon's pole-winning average was 142.001 mph, beating the mark of 139.817 mph set last year by Bobby Labonte.

Dale Earnhardt was on Gordon's right, with the Goodwrench Monte Carlo sporting a special red-white-and-blue paint scheme honoring the upcoming Centennial Olympic Games in Atlanta. Ford-driving Mark Martin and Dale Jarrett made up the second row, ahead of Sterling Marlin and Ward Burton. Terry Labonte and Ricky Rudd comprised the fourth row, with Darrell Waltrip and Kyle Petty right behind. Geoff Bodine and Bobby Labonte headed Ernie Irvan and Gant, while Rusty Wallace was the 15th starter, shotgun on the field of winners after he missed his pit stall during his banzai qualifying effort.

The Winston Select was designed to provide great drama for the fans, and with no points awarded, the event brings out some of the best, no-holds-barred racing seen during the season. Divided into three segments of 30, 30 and 10 laps, the race encourages sprint racing, and the final 10-lap shoot-out for the big dollars has provided the setting for dramatic endings in the past.

In the first segment, Jarrett ran to the front and brought home a three-second margin over Bobby Labonte, while Ward Burton finished third. For Jeff Burton, the evening ended early when he failed to complete a lap after the

engine died in his Exide Ford. Earnhardt, who most thought would be the man to beat in the first segment with his front-row start, instead faded toward the back of the field. He ultimately finished 12th in the first 30 laps, and when the teams went to work on the cars between segments, the Goodwrench crew made several adjustments that included inserting a rubber in the right-front spring, raising the panhard bar and adjusting the wedge in the Chevrolet.

The huge crowd voted before the race to invert the field for the start of the second segment, but to Michael Waltrip, the lineup made no difference. He had started from the 20th spot and worked his way to 10th at the end of the first portion of the race. He was in the middle of the pack no matter which end started first.

Gant, who could not find the handle on the McDonald's Ford during the early going and finished last, led the field away for the second 30-lap segment. Darrell Waltrip and Terry Labonte were right behind the McDonald's Ford entering the first turn, but the Kellogg's Chevrolet, with Ricky Rudd's Tide Ford on its bumper, took less than two laps to blast past the Mac Attack. Earnhardt mounted a charge and took the lead for the first time with five laps left in the segment. He beat Terry to the line to claim the honors at the end of the second segment and set up what many considered to be a dog-eat-dog battle for the final 10-lap sprint.

The lineup for the final dash for the cash had Rusty Wallace right behind Earnhardt, with Michael Waltrip lined up in the fourth starting spot behind Labonte. With no points on the line and the big check waiting, the immense crowd stood and waited for the start of what has become the most unpredictable 10 laps of the NASCAR Winston Cup season.

(Left) Terry Labonte jumps out to a short lead over Dale Earnhardt after starting the final 10-lap dash side by side at the front of the field. The duo was well-matched, and as they fought each other for the big prize, Michael Waltrip slipped underneath both of them to assume the point. *(Below)* Once in front, Waltrip stuck the Citgo Ford on the bottom of the track and held it there for the final eight laps to flash across the finish line barely a second ahead of second-place Rusty Wallace.

The champagne was flying in victory lane as the Wood Brothers Racing team celebrated with their driver, Michael Waltrip. This was the first such celebration for the famed "21" team since March 20, 1993, when Morgan Shepherd drove to victory at Atlanta.

The green flew and immediately the yellow flag came out when it was obvious that several drivers had tried to jump the start. The field reformed, and the green flag flew again. This time, the sprint was on.

Earnhardt and Labonte rocketed around the track side by side, with Labonte crossing the start/finish line with the barest of leads. On the second lap, as the two Monte Carlos headed into the first turn, they collided, and as Earnhardt and Labonte fought to regain control of their cars, Michael flat-footed the go pedal and yanked the steering wheel to the left, finding the opening underneath the yawing Chevrolets. Wallace followed the Citgo Ford through the opening, and many in the crowd quickly remembered 1989, when Rusty tangled with Darrell Waltrip in the waning laps, sending Darrell spinning from the lead as Rusty drove to victory in the event.

Could Rusty get a fender under the Citgo Ford in the remaining seven laps?

The answer was no. All Wallace could do was stare at the "CITGO" on the television panel above the rear bumper of the Wood Brothers Ford for the remainder of the event, as Michael protected his lead and out-ran everyone to claim the biggest victory of his career.

The win was most improbable. Michael had barely made it into The Winston Select by gaining the final transfer slot. He had fought and cussed his Ford for the first 60 laps of the all-star event and the Wood Brothers had made adjustment after adjustment, and change after change to the car throughout the evening. Finally, they had hit the right combination during the break before the final 10 laps. The car was perfect when it needed to be, and Michael had driven it with the voracity needed to secure the victory.

The win was worth $211,200, and after doing a victory jig on top of the car in victory lane, Michael shared congratulatory hugs with everyone in sight, including the Woods and older brother Darrell, who came to the winner's circle to help Michael celebrate the huge victory.

"Man, I knew something was going to happen," Michael cracked when asked about the pass for the win. "The '3' and the '5' were racing side by side and I gave them room. Heck, I've seen this show before on TV. I waited for it to happen. I knew neither one of them was going to give an inch and I figured I was either going to wreck with them, or I was going to pass them. For once, it worked out right for me. Most other times, I'd have been in it with them!"

The upset victory made Michael and Darrell the first brothers to win The Winston Select in history. Darrell claimed the inaugural running of the event in 1985, crossing the line in Junior Johnson's Chevrolet just before the hand-grenade engine in the car erupted some 100 yards past the flag stand.

The Winston Select

Fin. Pos.	Str. Pos.	Car #	Driver	Team
1	20	21	Michael Waltrip	Citgo Ford
2	15	2	Rusty Wallace	Miller Ford
3	2	3	Dale Earnhardt	GM Goodwrench Service Chevrolet
4	3	6	Mark Martin	Valvoline Ford
5	7	5	Terry Labonte	Kellogg's Corn Flakes Chevrolet
6	8	10	Ricky Rudd	Tide Ford
7	13	28	Ernie Irvan	Texaco Havoline Ford
8	1	24	Jeff Gordon	DuPont Refinishes Chevrolet
9	4	88	Dale Jarrett	Quality Care / Ford Credit Ford
10	5	4	Sterling Marlin	Kodak Film Chevrolet
11	10	42	Kyle Petty	Coors Light Pontiac
12	17	9	Lake Speed	Spam Ford
13	12	18	Bobby Labonte	Interstate Batteries Chevrolet
14	16	23	Jimmy Spencer	Camel Cigarettes Ford
15	14	94	Harry Gant	McDonald's Ford
16	18	8	Hut Stricklin	Circuit City Ford
17	11	7	Geoff Bodine	QVC Ford
18	9	17	Darrell Waltrip	Parts America Chevrolet
19	6	22	Ward Burton	MBNA America Pontiac
20	19	99	Jeff Burton	Exide Batteries Ford

Segment 1

1	Dale Jarrett	11	Jimmy Spencer
2	Bobby Labonte	12	Dale Earnhardt
3	Ward Burton	13	Geoff Bodine
4	Mark Martin	14	Lake Speed
5	Jeff Gordon	15	Ricky Rudd
6	Sterling Marlin	16	Kyle Petty
7	Rusty Wallace	17	Terry Labonte
8	Ernie Irvan	18	Darrell Waltrip
9	Hut Stricklin	19	Harry Gant
10	Michael Waltrip	20	Jeff Burton

Segment 2

1	Dale Earnhardt	11	Ernie Irvan
2	Terry Labonte	12	Jeff Gordon
3	Rusty Wallace	13	Hut Stricklin
4	Michael Waltrip	14	Kyle Petty
5	Lake Speed	15	Jimmy Spencer
6	Mark Martin	16	Harry Gant
7	Sterling Marlin	17	Darrell Waltrip
8	Bobby Labonte	18	Geoff Bodine
9	Dale Jarrett	19	Ward Burton
10	Ricky Rudd	20	Jeff Burton

Coca-Cola 600

As the Charlotte Motor Speedway went from twilight to darkness, Dale Jarrett emerged at the front of the field and drove on to dominate the final third of the Coca-Cola 600 to take his second win of the season.
(Right) *Ken Schrader sits patiently in his "office" as he waits for the command to "start your engines" that begins the Coca-Cola 600. Typically fast at Charlotte, Ken worked his way to a fifth-place finish, and climbed from tenth to seventh in the championship point standings.*

The morning after Michael Waltrip emerged victorious in the closing laps of The Winston Select, it was business as usual. An appearance was already on the schedule, and Michael found in the days between The Winston Select and the opening of practice for the Coca-Cola 600 that there was precious little time to spend savoring the biggest victory of his career.

There were a couple of unfamiliar faces in the garage area at Charlotte when the gates opened for practice for the longest race of the season. Robert Pressley's broken rib would prevent him from running the full 600 miles, and car owner Leo Jackson and crew chief Andy Petree chose Greg Sacks to be the relief driver in the Skoal Bandit. Harry Gant's one-time drive in the Elliott-Hardy Racing McDonald's Ford was completed, and Bill Elliott selected Todd Bodine as his "permanent" replacement driver until the redhead was able to return to competition.

While Sacks and Bodine were fitting themselves into the team activities of the "33" and the "94," several teams made announcements regarding their futures. Hendrick Motorsports said that sponsors DuPont and Budweiser had exercised the options in their contracts and had signed on

to sponsor the Jeff Gordon and Ken Schrader Chevrolets through the year 2000. Team owner Rick Hendrick said Gordon and Schrader also had re-signed — moves that would give his operation stability. Kellogg's and driver Terry Labonte had already signed through 2000.

Team owner Larry Hedrick had an announcement of his own, saying that Kodiak had signed its contract to renew sponsorship of his team through 1998 and that he expected Ricky Craven to be part of the effort for "at least that long."

Then car owner Joe Gibbs stepped to the microphone to say that Interstate Batteries also had inked on the dotted line, extending its sponsorship of his team and driver Bobby Labonte through the year 2000. While all this was happening, Kyle Petty stood at the end of the Coors Light transporter and tried to set the record straight with reporters. Rumors had swirled around the SABCO team that Petty was dissatisfied with the performance of the team and was looking for another ride for the coming season. Not true, Kyle said, pointing out that he felt the team had made considerable progress and that he had been the driver for the team since it began. He said he expected to continue to drive the Pontiacs for the remainder of this year and into the future.

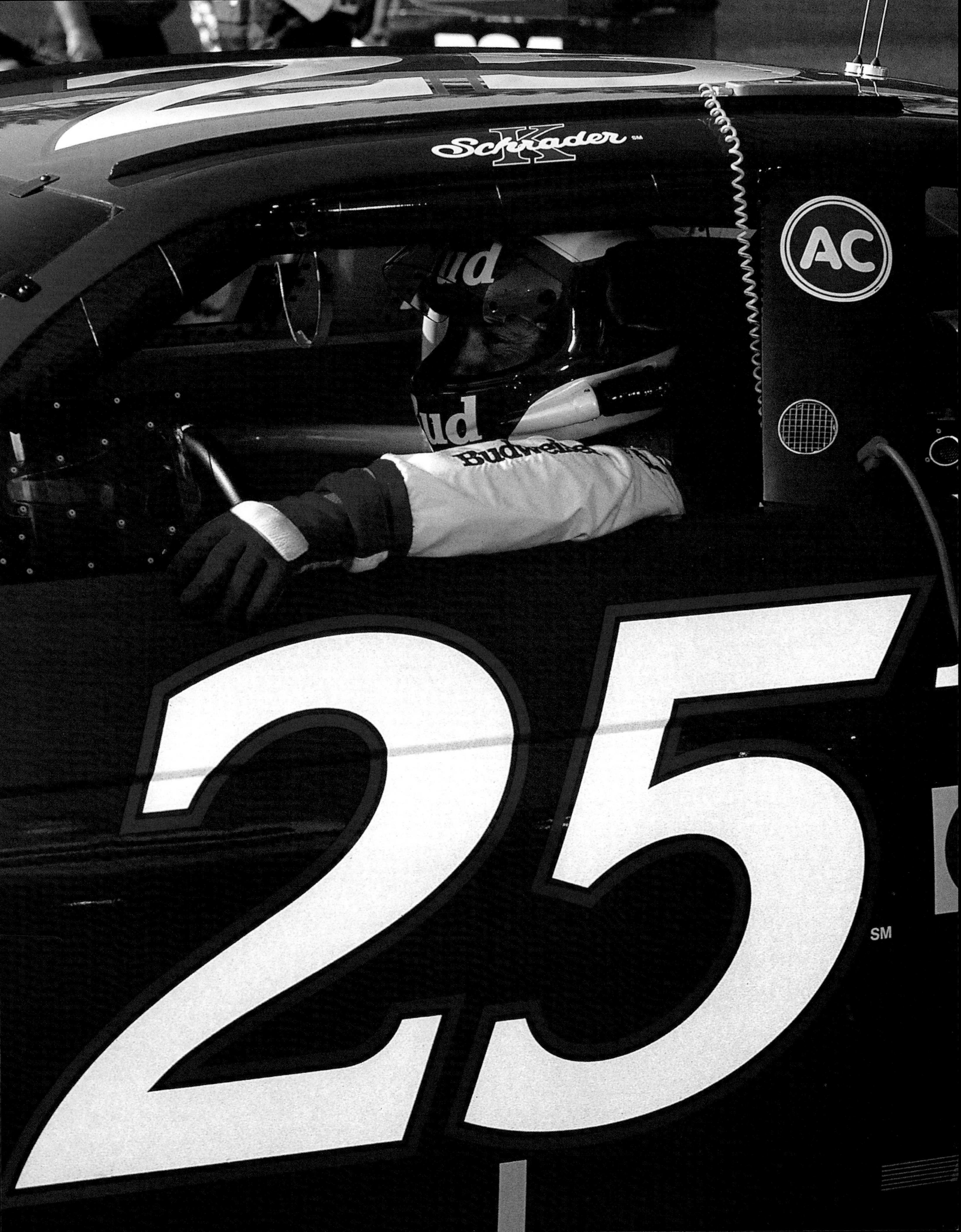
Schrader
AC
Bud
Bud
25
SM

The jury was out on whether the changes made by NASCAR to the rear roof lines of the Fords had made much difference during The Winston Select weekend at Charlotte. Chevrolet forces were quick to point out that Fords swept the top five positions in The Winston Select Open to advance to the all-star race, but Ford followers argued that most of the really good Chevrolets were already in the feature event.

tires), and you have to wait until those tires get some laps on them before you really see the difference," Evernham explained. "The Chevrolets are going to get beat just like we did the other night. Qualifying is a one-lap deal, and Jeff Gordon can hold his breath for one lap."

Whether he did or not, Gordon rolled to his third consecutive Coca-Cola 600 pole with a lap in excess of 183 mph. He was the only driver to crack the mark. Ricky Craven, apparently fit following his Talladega incident, celebrated his sponsor's renewal of its contract by putting the

(Left) The Tide team affects repairs after Ricky Rudd's Thunderbird sustained right-side damage in an on-track skirmish. Rudd continued in the race and managed a 15th-place finish, four laps off the pace. (Below) Outside front-row starter Ricky Craven rockets into the lead around pole-sitter Jeff Gordon on the first lap of the race. Third-place starter John Andretti (37) falls in line ahead of Terry and Bobby Labonte, who started fourth and fifth, respectively.

Then the Chevrolet folks reminded the Blue Oval troops that a Ford had won the race. Ford backers conceded the fact that Michael had won in the Citgo Ford fielded by the Wood Brothers but added that Chevrolet drivers Dale Earnhardt and Terry Labonte all but took themselves out of contention with their contretemps just two laps after the drop of the green flag in the final race segment.

Many thought that qualifying for the Coca-Cola 600 would be more of a true indication of whether a model had an advantage — until DuPont crew chief Ray Evernham pooh-poohed the idea. "A car that doesn't make a lot of downforce is going to go fast for one lap on stickers (new

the Kodiak Chevrolet on the outside of the front row with a lap of more than 182.8 mph.

The first Ford driver to crack the field was John Andretti. The Kranefuss/Haas team had built and tested a Lincoln Mark VIII prior to the Charlotte activities. Although the car never was raced, the hot rod Lincoln showed exciting promise. Andretti's third-fastest lap came in his regular Kmart/Little Caesars Thunderbird.

Terry and Bobby Labonte completed the top-five qualifiers, both in Chevrolets, and Chad Little surprised the regulars in the NASCAR Winston Cup garage by taking the outside of the third row with his Pontiac. Mark Martin,

Todd Bodine, behind the wheel of Bill Elliott's McDonald's Ford, gives ground to Ernie Irvan (28) and Dale Earnhardt (3), who teamed up early in the race from mid-pack and carved through the field.

who had one of the fastest cars on the track during practice, drew a low number and ran his qualifying lap early in the session. He could only turn the seventh-fastest lap, one matched by Michael Waltrip. Because Jack Roush, Mark's car owner, was higher in the owner points than the Wood Brothers, Martin started on the inside of the row.

Dick Trickle gave the Healthsource Ford a strong ride to ninth on the grid, and Lake Speed had the key turned in the Spam Ford hard enough to grab the final berth in the top 10. Johnny Benson's Pennzoil Pontiac and the McDonald's Ford with Todd Bodine at the reins occupied the sixth row, while Jeff Burton and Derrike Cope were right behind them.

Dale Earnhardt and Sterling Marlin, both expected to figure high in the results of the race, would start from 20th and 36th place, respectively, while Brett Bodine (debuting a new Ford painted gold to celebrate the 50th anniversary of Lowe's stores) was in a qualifying lap crash that necessitated bringing another car from the team's shop. Brett took a provisional to get into the field, as did Ted Musgrave and Dave Marcis. Rusty Wallace, unable to make the field the first day, opted to use a champion's provisional, allowing Elton Sawyer to make the field.

For Randy MacDonald, Ed Berrier, Hermie Sadler, Mark Gibbon, Robby Faggart, Delma Cowart and Steve Seligman, the news wasn't pleasant following the final qualifying session. All were forced to load their machines back onto their transporters after not making the grid.

When the drivers slid through the windows of their mounts for the day-into-night running of the Coca-Cola 600, more than a victory in one of the most prestigious races of the season was at stake. Earnhardt hoped to build on his 115-point lead over Jarrett, and Jarrett was looking over his shoulder at the consistently-running Terry Labonte, who was only 16 points behind him. Gordon, seeking to defend his

Jeff Gordon (24) and Terry Labonte (5) swapped the lead several times in the early stages of the race, then found themselves running together as the event drew to a close. Here, Labonte looks for room on Gordon's outside with the laps winding down. Labonte eventually completed the pass to beat Jeff for third place.

paid to the first driver to win two of the four events if there was no Winston Select Million winner that season.

During the first quarter of the race, however, it didn't appear that Jarrett would do much to accomplish either of his goals. Gordon and Hendrick Motorsports teammate Terry Labonte led at will almost to the 100-lap mark on the 1.5-mile oval. Jarrett finally forced his way to the lead on

(Left) Drivers scramble for room at the exit of turn four after Bobby Hillin spun following a restart. On the low side, Ricky Rudd jumps on the binders to avoid a spinning Geoff Bodine. Bodine recovered and continued on to score his first top-10 finish of the year. (Below) Front-runners Gordon (24), Jarrett (88) and Bobby Labonte slow as they enter pit road during one of the race's six caution periods.

NASCAR Winston Cup title, was fourth in the standings, 187 points behind Earnhardt. Behind them, Marlin and Ricky Rudd were separated by a mere four points. Wallace, seventh in the standings, was only 11 points ahead of Craven, and Ted Musgrave trailed Craven by 14 points as a total of only 25 points separated the seventh, eighth and ninth places. Martin, stranded in 13th place, hoped the magic that worked the previous day, when he streaked to the Red Dog 300 NASCAR Busch Series victory, would settle over his Valvoline Ford for the upcoming 600 miles.

Jarrett's quest was twofold. He hoped to gain ground in the point race, but he was also very aware that a victory in the Coca-Cola 600 would send him to Darlington in September with a chance to become only the second winner of the Winston Select Million since it was first offered in 1985. He had won at Daytona and had nearly won the Winston Select 500 at Talladega. Three victories in four races would give him the huge bonus, a prize that has been won only by Bill Elliott. Even if he failed to win Darlington's Mountain Dew Southern 500, a Charlotte win would guarantee him the program's "consolation" prize of $100,000,

lap 130, but green-flag pit stops shuffled the field until Marcis (with help from Andretti) spun in the infield grass.

Eight laps later, Petty collided with Musgrave while trying to get a lap back on a restart, and a 13-car accident ensued at the front of the pack, collecting Wallace, Martin, Bobby Labonte, Benson, Speed and Michael Waltrip, among others. Kyle drew a five-lap stop in the penalty box, and when car owner Felix Sabates' protests were judged a little more vocal than appropriate, NASCAR officials tacked another pair of laps onto Kyle's penalty for "rough talking."

Gordon was still the dominant player in the race until lap 228, when Jarrett once again blazed past the DuPont Chevrolet. From that point on, it became more clear with every passing lap that Jarrett and the Robert Yates Racing team had the Quality Care Thunderbird dialed in.

Earnhardt fought his way through the field to second place, but he had nothing to challenge Jarrett with on this May evening. The Ford simply eased away from the field and led 166 of the final 174 laps of the event in dominant form. At the end, he was nearly 12 seconds ahead of Earnhardt. Labonte battled to third place, just ahead of

Dale Jarrett and crew chief Todd Parrott proudly display their Coca-Cola 600 trophy following their second win of the season. By winning and leading the most laps, Jarrett not only picked up 10 points on Dale Earnhardt, but also qualified to win the Winston Select Million.

Gordon. Those four cars were the only ones on the lead lap at the end and, by leading the most laps, Jarrett managed to pick up 10 points on Earnhardt in the point battle to close the gap to 105.

Schrader came in fifth, the first driver a lap in arrears, and gave his team a 3-4-5 finish. Marlin was sixth, ahead of Martin. Michael Waltrip backed up his Winston Select victory with an eighth place, while Ernie Irvan was ninth and Geoff Bodine finished 10th, both two laps behind.

The second victory of the season for Jarrett came in another of the year's biggest races, and he had assured himself of the $100,000 bonus from the Winston Select Million pool. He had put the red-white-and-blue Ford in the position to claim the big bucks at Darlington, and the second generation driver was jubilant after the win.

"This race is a really important one for any team to win because it is here at Charlotte, where most of the teams work and live," D.J. explained. "It's a big money race and all that, but it's also important because it gives a team 'bragging rights' in its hometown — at least for a few days, until we get to Dover next weekend.

"It makes us eligible to win the Million from the Winston folks, and we're going to really try to do that in September. But right now, this win is very important to our team because it enabled us to clip a few points from Earnhardt's lead, and the championship is the reason we're all competing.

"It's a big win — and one I'll treasure — but the big picture is the title at the end of the year."

Crew chief David Smith observes his Goodwrench team from behind pit wall as they service driver Dale Earnhardt's Chevrolet. Dale led seven laps in the race, but could do nothing with Dale Jarrett and finished second, nearly 12 seconds behind the winner.

Coca-Cola 600

Fin. Pos.	Str. Pos.	Car #	Driver	Team
1	15	88	Dale Jarrett	Quality Care / Ford Credit Ford
2	20	3	Dale Earnhardt	GM Goodwrench Service Chevrolet
3	4	5	Terry Labonte	Kellogg's Corn Flakes Chevrolet
4	1	24	Jeff Gordon	DuPont Refinishes Chevrolet
5	23	25	Ken Schrader	Budweiser Chevrolet
6	36	4	Sterling Marlin	Kodak Film Chevrolet
7	7	6	Mark Martin	Valvoline Ford
8	8	21	Michael Waltrip	Citgo Ford
9	22	28	Ernie Irvan	Texaco Havoline Ford
10	31	7	Geoff Bodine	QVC Ford
11	35	22	Ward Burton	MBNA America Pontiac
12	26	1	Rick Mast	Hooters Pontiac
13	28	17	Darrell Waltrip	Parts America Chevrolet
14	14	12	Derrike Cope	Badcock Ford
15	30	10	Ricky Rudd	Tide Ford
16	21	29	Steve Grissom	Cartoon Network Chevrolet
17	18	23	Jimmy Spencer	Camel Cigarettes Ford
18	13	99	Jeff Burton	Exide Batteries Ford
19	19	15	Wally Dallenbach	Hayes Modems Ford
20	9	19	Dick Trickle	Healthsource Ford
21	42	27	Elton Sawyer	David Blair Motorsports Ford
22	5	18	Bobby Labonte	Interstate Batteries Chevrolet
23	32	42	Kyle Petty	Coors Light Pontiac
24	40	11	Brett Bodine	Lowe's Ford
25	33	87	Joe Nemechek	Burger King Chevrolet
26	17	77	Bobby Hillin	Jasper Engines / Federal-Mogul Ford
27	3	37	John Andretti	Kmart / Little Caesars Ford
28	25	8	Hut Stricklin	Circuit City Ford
29	38	75	Morgan Shepherd	Remington Arms Ford
30	39	16	Ted Musgrave	Family Channel / PRIMESTAR Ford
31	37	43	Bobby Hamilton	STP Pontiac
32	16	81	Kenny Wallace	Square D / T.I.C. Ford
33	29	33	Robert Pressley	Skoal Bandit Chevrolet
34	43	2	Rusty Wallace	Miller Ford
35	10	9	Lake Speed	Spam Ford
36	12	94	Todd Bodine	McDonald's Ford
37	2	41	Ricky Craven	Kodiak Chevrolet
38	11	30	Johnny Benson	Pennzoil Pontiac
39	27	90	Mike Wallace	Heilig-Meyers Ford
40	41	71	Dave Marcis	Prodigy Chevrolet
41	24	98	Jeremy Mayfield	RCA Ford
42	34	95	Chuck Bown	Shoney's Restaurants Ford
43	6	97	Chad Little	Sterling Cowboy Pontiac

Miller 500

It must have been Jeff Gordon Day at Dover. Seen here flashing under the checkered flag to complete a nearly perfect weekend, Jeff started from the pole (his second of the year), led 307 of 500 laps, including the final 129, and took his series-leading fourth win of the season, all at the track just down the road from sponsor DuPont's headquarters.
(Right) *TriStar crew members hustle around the Healthsource Ford while driver Dick Trickle waits to return to the action. Trickle, sitting in for injured Loy Allen, surprised everyone during qualifying by turning the second-fastest lap to take the outside front-row position. Ward Burton, who qualified third, pits directly behind Trickle.*

Anyone who questioned how serious Dale Earnhardt was about making a run for his eighth NASCAR Winston Cup championship needed only to look at the results of the first third of the season.

Dale had finished 31st at Richmond in the third race of the season and had taken 14th in the TranSouth 400 at Darlington, but the black Chevrolet also had been a factor in every race, from the lid-lifting Busch Clash to the Coca-Cola 600 at Charlotte.

He posted his first victory of the season at Rockingham and won again at Atlanta. He chalked up seconds at Charlotte and in the Daytona 500, and was third at North Wilkesboro and in the Winston Select 500 at Talladega. At Sears Point, he came home fourth, which was the same position he finished in at Bristol, and he posted a fifth place at Martinsville. That's a pair of wins and nine top-fives in the first 11 races of the year.

It was no wonder he was at the top of the point ladder when the teams arrived at Denis McGlynn's one mile concrete oval in Delaware's capital city. Dale had been at or near the top of the point heap throughout the first third of the season, and after taking over the top rung following

Martinsville, he remained there. Although plenty of racing remained in the season and Earnhardt's lead over "the other Dale" (Jarrett) was just 105 points at Dover, most observers felt that the long-sought-after eighth title would fall to the Earnhardt/Richard Childress juggernaut this season.

There were, however, a few who still needed some convincing. Jarrett was one of them, and he was rapidly becoming a believer that his Robert Yates Racing team had the goods to keep him in the championship hunt for the rest of the season. His finishes hadn't been quite as consistent as Earnhardt's, but here he was in second place in the standings, within shouting distance of the black Chevrolet.

Other than three blemishes on his record — including a 24th and a 34th in the first two events of the season, and a 24th at Martinsville — Terry Labonte was having almost as strong a start to the season as Earnhardt. Labonte had triumphed at North Wilkesboro and was second at Atlanta and Bristol. The season's beginning was rather unusual for Terry because he usually started slowly and then finished the season with a charge. The run had begun early this year.

And then there was the defending NASCAR Winston Cup champion. After a 42nd-place finish in the Daytona

500, Gordon finished 40th at Rockingham due to engine problems. He answered that with a victory at Richmond in the third race, and then ran off a stint that included two more victories (at Darlington and Bristol) in the three events following his initial win of the season. He was third at Atlanta and Martinsville and second at North Wilkesboro. In the span of those half-dozen races, he had rocketed from 43rd position in the point standings to second place following the Goody's 500 at Clay Earles' half-mile in Virginia.

At Talladega, he was 33rd after being involved in Ricky Craven's multicar accident and fell to fourth in the stand-ings. In his next two outings, he was sixth at Sears Point and fourth in the Coca-Cola 600. Gordon remained fourth in the standings, but clearly was in the hunt to defend his title, and his team of Rainbow Warriors was grinning again.

If the Hendrick Motorsports team needed any additional boost in confidence, it would come as a result of the venue for this event. Last fall, the DuPont-sponsored team came to Dover and whipped the field in front of its sponsor's executives at their "home track," some 45 miles south of the DuPont corporate headquarters. It was Gordon's first Dover victory, and it became one of the linchpins of his drive to the NASCAR Winston Cup championship. No one on the team had forgotten that special September afternoon — especially the corporate representatives.

In the week between Charlotte and Dover, several items of note had occurred with teams in the garage area. Chuck Bown was out and Gary Bradberry in as the driver for the Sadler/Shoney's team, and Steve Grissom had been

from its transporter and was pushed to the inspection line, heads turned and eyes blinked in astonishment.

Instead of the usual colorful paint job, the Pontiac was painted black with white numbers and letters and had a silver band around the bottom of the Grand Prix. Car owner Felix Sabates, who was miffed at the penalty box call on Petty the previous week at Charlotte, was not at the Dover race (he turned in his annual credential after the Coca-Cola 600) and said he would not attend any more races this year. He had ordered the car painted to look like Dale Earnhardt's Monte Carlo as a further protest of the Charlotte incident. Petty was caught in the middle of the fray, saying only that "it was Felix's decision."

By the time everyone finished pointing and chuckling at Petty's ride, Friday's qualifying session was about to begin. Dover's concrete track and banked turns demand a combination of strong engines and excellent chassis preparation, and when the first timed session was complete, there was yet another reason for the Rainbow Warriors to high-five their way to the garage area.

For the second straight race (or third, if you count The Winston Select) the DuPont team and driver Gordon had

informed by the owners of the Diamond Ridge team that his contract would not be renewed for the coming season. David Blair, struggling to find a sponsor since purchasing Junior Johnson's "27" team at the end of the 1995 season, decided that running out of his own pocket wasn't the most economical thing to do. He executed what he called a "strategic retreat," releasing driver Elton Sawyer and planning to run a limited number of events in the second half of the season. He told media members that his concentration was on finding a sponsor for the coming season. He expected the team to run at Indianapolis, Charlotte and Atlanta in the second half of the season, although he left room for additional races if warranted.

The garage-dwellers were surprised to hear that R.J. Reynolds' CEO Jim Johnston, a friend of the racers, had decided to leave the company "to spend some time with my family while I'm still young enough to appreciate the experience." He had spent 12 years of his professional career with RJR and had been chairman and CEO of the domestic tobacco company before becoming chairman of the worldwide tobacco company in 1993. His resignation was effective June 30.

Johnston's decision wasn't the only surprise of the weekend. When Kyle Petty's Coors Light Pontiac emerged

claimed the second-round Busch bonus and the year-end "wild card" slot, and NASCAR Busch Series regular Hermie Sadler, who had failed to make the field at Charlotte, qualified 30th to make his NASCAR Winston Cup debut. Jeremy Mayfield, Darrell Waltrip and Dave Marcis used provisionals to join the field, as did the Skoal Bandit Chevrolet, which would be driven the entire weekend by Greg Sacks while Robert Pressley continued to recover from the injuries he suffered in the Charlotte practice accident.

There was little doubt early in the race who had the fastest car. Gordon rolled into the first corner ahead of the pack, and the rear bumper of the DuPont Chevrolet was all the field would see for 174 of the first 190 laps. He was shuffled from the lead in the middle of the race after a cau-

(Left) Jeff Gordon is chased down the backstretch by (in order) Bobby Labonte, Terry Labonte, John Andretti and Wally Dallenbach. All would try to catch the DuPont driver, but none would succeed this day. (Below) Ted Musgrave (16) attempts to overtake Mike Wallace by using the outside lane on Dover's concrete banks. The preferred groove is clearly evidenced by the black rubber worn into the bright racing surface, and few drivers care to venture too far from the safety of its grip.

tion flag interrupted the action for Mast's accident on lap 194. Green-flag pit stops had just been completed, and the only contenders who headed for pit road under the yellow flag were Gordon and Rusty Wallace. They returned to the track in 14th and 15th place for the restart, and Gordon was left to fight his way back to the front.

He climbed to the top five, and when another caution flew on lap 362, the Rainbow Warriors worked their magic. They sent Gordon off pit road with the lead, and after Jeff won a spirited five-lap battle for the point with Earnhardt, Gordon was gone.

His lead at the end of the race was more than three seconds over Terry Labonte, who had beaten Earnhardt in their battle for second place, and Ernie Irvan brought his Texaco Havoline Ford home in fourth place. Irvan had the highest finishing Thunderbird and was the final car on the lead lap.

Bobby Labonte beat Jimmy Spencer for fifth place, with Spencer posting his best finish of the season so far. Rusty

posted the fastest lap to claim the pole. This one came with a lap time that set a new track record and was more than a tenth of a second faster than his surprising front-row mate, Dick Trickle, who logged his second consecutive top-10 starting position with the TriStar Healthsource Ford. Trickle was filling in for the injured Loy Allen and his second-fastest time had breathed new life into the Ford team.

In the second row were Ward Burton and Terry Labonte, while Hut Stricklin and Dale Jarrett posted the fifth- and sixth-fastest laps. Bobby Labonte and Rusty Wallace claimed the fourth row, and Kenny Wallace and Rick Mast logged strong runs to claim the final spots in the top 10, barely beating Brett Bodine and Mark Martin. Gary Bradberry, making his first run in the Sadler/Shoney's Ford,

Jeff Gordon, shown accompanied by wife Brooke, coasted to the win and then to victory lane to pick up his Miller 500 trophy.

Wallace, Ricky Rudd, Jeff Burton and Ken Schrader completed the top 10, all just a single lap behind.

Gordon was beaming after the victory. It was his second-straight triumph at Dover, and it sent the DuPont executives home with another trophy to display in Monday morning's management meetings. More importantly, it moved Gordon into third place in the point standings, behind Earnhardt and Labonte.

Where was Jarrett? After leading in the middle portion of the race and appearing to have a car capable of posting a top-five finish, if not challenging for the victory, Jarrett slipped in some oil left on the track from Bradberry's blown engine and smacked the concrete wall. It sent him to a 36th-place finish and dropped him to fourth place in the point standings, 215 points behind Earnhardt.

Others had similar days to Jarrett's. Mark Martin lost the timing chain in his engine and was sidelined for the third time this year with motor problems. He finished 40th, while Sterling Marlin also had engine problems and finished one position behind Martin.

Kyle Petty's paint job didn't help his situation. The black Pontiac handled poorly throughout the afternoon, and he was four laps behind at the conclusion of the race, in 18th place.

Crew chief Paul Andrews checks the suspension on Geoff Bodine's QVC Thunderbird before returning Geoff to action in the Miller 500. Bodine, who was running at the finish, was disappointed with 30th place. He had felt his team had turned the corner last week with a top 10 at Charlotte.

Miller 500

Fin. Pos.	Str. Pos.	Car #	Driver	Team
1	1	24	Jeff Gordon	DuPont Refinishes Chevrolet
2	4	5	Terry Labonte	Kellogg's Corn Flakes Chevrolet
3	14	3	Dale Earnhardt	GM Goodwrench Service Chevrolet
4	21	28	Ernie Irvan	Texaco Havoline Ford
5	7	18	Bobby Labonte	Interstate Batteries Chevrolet
6	24	23	Jimmy Spencer	Camel Cigarettes Ford
7	8	2	Rusty Wallace	Miller Ford
8	16	10	Ricky Rudd	Tide Ford
9	18	99	Jeff Burton	Exide Batteries Ford
10	31	25	Ken Schrader	Budweiser Chevrolet
11	27	21	Michael Waltrip	Citgo Ford
12	39	98	Jeremy Mayfield	RCA Ford
13	20	16	Ted Musgrave	Family Channel / PRIMESTAR Ford
14	29	41	Ricky Craven	Kodiak Chevrolet
15	33	94	Todd Bodine	McDonald's Ford
16	3	22	Ward Burton	MBNA America Pontiac
17	23	30	Johnny Benson	Pennzoil Pontiac
18	15	42	Kyle Petty	Coors Light Pontiac
19	28	90	Mike Wallace	Heilig-Meyers Ford
20	9	81	Kenny Wallace	Square D / T.I.C. Ford
21	38	43	Bobby Hamilton	STP Pontiac
22	34	15	Wally Dallenbach	Hayes Modems Ford
23	17	12	Derrike Cope	Badcock Ford
24	11	11	Brett Bodine	Lowe's Ford
25	36	87	Joe Nemechek	Burger King Chevrolet
26	32	9	Lake Speed	Spam Ford
27	40	33	Greg Sacks	Skoal Bandit Chevrolet
28	2	19	Dick Trickle	Healthsource Ford
29	22	77	Bobby Hillin	Jasper Engines / Federal-Mogul Ford
30	13	7	Geoff Bodine	QVC Ford
31	42	71	Dave Marcis	Prodigy Chevrolet
32	37	75	Morgan Shepherd	Remington Arms Ford
33	25	37	John Andretti	Kmart / Little Caesars Ford
34	5	8	Hut Stricklin	Circuit City Ford
35	10	1	Rick Mast	Hooters Pontiac
36	6	88	Dale Jarrett	Quality Care / Ford Credit Ford
37	30	26	Hermie Sadler	Peebles Chevrolet
38	26	95	Gary Bradberry	Shoney's Restaurants Ford
39	41	17	Darrell Waltrip	Parts America Chevrolet
40	12	6	Mark Martin	Valvoline Ford
41	19	4	Sterling Marlin	Kodak Film Chevrolet
42	35	29	Steve Grissom	Cartoon Network Chevrolet

UAW-GM Teamwork 500

Crew members swarm around the Bobby Allison-owned Badcock Ford as Derrike Cope brings the car in for tires and fuel. Derrike qualified a season-best second and ran with the leaders for most of the race. After damaging the car's nose, however, Cope fell off the pace and finished a disappointing 27th.
***(Right)** Two-time Pocono winner Dale Earnhardt offers some friendly advice to Jeff Gordon and Ray Evernham. Dale may have regretted this visit after the race: Jeff won from the pole for the second straight week and gained 118 points on Dale, who left the race early with engine problems.*

After a weekend off, NASCAR's Winston Cup teams arrived in the scenic Pocono Mountains rested and ready to wage battle at Drs. Rose and Joe Mattioli's triangular superspeedway. Since the last time the Cuppers visited the Poconos in August 1995, the Mattiolis had overseen a repaving of the entire racing surface. There was little doubt that the new asphalt would produce record speeds on the huge track.

The trip to Pocono marked the beginning — and the end — of associations within some teams, unusual this early in the season. Four days before the opening of practice at Pocono, Junie Donlavey's Heilig-Meyers Ford team and driver Mike Wallace parted ways. Mike immediately slotted himself back into his ARCA car and promptly won the Pocono event on Saturday!

Loy Allen returned to the TriStar Healthsource Ford after recovering from injuries suffered in an accident at Rockingham in the second race of the season. Dick Trickle, who filled in for Allen with aplomb during his recovery, became available for "temporary" duty and immediately his phone rang. Trickle agreed to drive Donlavey's Ford on a "let's see what happens" basis.

Making its first appearance in the garage area at Pocono was a Chevrolet owned by Dale Earnhardt, carrying No. 14 with sponsorship from Racing for Kids magazine, the publication purchased earlier in the year by a group of investors that included the seven-time champion Earnhardt and current title-holder Jeff Gordon. Earnhardt's regular NASCAR Busch Series driver, Jeff Green, was behind the wheel and hoped to make the team's NASCAR Winston Cup debut a sparkling one.

Robert Pressley returned to the wheel of the Skoal Bandit Chevrolet nearly recovered from his rib injuries suffered during a practice accident at Charlotte. Meanwhile, in the stall of the Remington Arms Ford owned by Butch Mock, new crew chief Gere Kennon was making his presence felt. Kennon had come to the team from his previous role as the chassis specialist for Ted Musgrave's Family Channel/PRIMESTAR team to replace Troy Selberg. Mock and driver Morgan Shepherd were frustrated with their lack of progress together, having just a single top 10 (eighth at Darlington) to show for the first third of the season.

Earnhardt seemed well in control of the point fight and held a margin of 136 over Terry Labonte as the teams pre-

Jeff Gordon leads the field at the start as second-place qualifier Derrike Cope (12) takes a peek on the outside. Hut Stricklin (8), who started from the third position, stuck low through the turn and emerged the leader at the end of lap one. Hut led four times for 19 laps, but transmission problems ultimately relegated him to a 29th-place finish.

pared for the first round of qualifying. Gordon had moved to third place in the standings after his Dover win, but still trailed by 182 markers. Dale Jarrett held fourth place, and Ricky Rudd was fifth in the standings but was well off the pace at 352 behind.

Practice times indicated that most of the field would qualify faster than the track record held by Rusty Wallace. When the first session was complete, no one was surprised to see the DuPont Chevrolet at the top of the time sheet. Gordon was clearly on a roll, notching his fourth straight pole (including The Winston Select) by more than a tenth of a second over his closest competitor.

The fastest Ford in the field sat alongside Gordon's Monte Carlo — and it wasn't the usual rocket ship entry from either Penske South or Yates Racing. Instead, the car carried orange and navy colors and the name Badcock Furniture on the side. Derrike Cope, the fastest driver during pre-event testing, had carried that speed through qualifying and claimed the second-fastest time of the session with the new chassis turned out by Bobby Allison Motorsports.

Right behind Cope on the qualifying results list was Hut Stricklin, who recorded his second consecutive strong performance during time trials. The Circuit City Ford beat the times turned by Chevrolet drivers Ricky Craven and Ken Schrader, while Mark Martin's Valvoline Ford would line up on Schrader's right in the third row.

Bobby Labonte and Joe Nemechek posted the seventh- and eighth-fastest laps, and Rudd and Earnhardt earned the final positions in the top 10, just ahead of Terry Labonte and Ward Burton. Allen made his return to the wheel a successful one and claimed the final position available on the first day. Geoff Bodine turned the fastest second-round qualifying lap, good for the Busch bonus and the "wild card" entry for the Busch Clash in February 1997.

Green made the field in 33rd place with Earnhardt's blue Monte Carlo, while Pontiac drivers Kyle Petty (back in his familiar colors) and Johnny Benson took provisionals. Mike Wallace drove Kyle's Pontiac during the second round of qualifying after Kyle went home for his maternal grandmother's funeral. Trickle was also forced to use a provisional, making Donlavey's Ford the final car in the field. Dave Marcis, with no provisionals left to use, loaded his Monte Carlo into the transporter after he failed to run fast enough to qualify.

Dale Jarrett's weekend began on the wrong track when he crashed during his qualifying lap, writing off the primary Quality Care Ford and sending the team scurrying to the transporter to unload the spare. Worse yet, a subsequent examination determined that Jarrett had broken a bone in his right knee and one of his left-side ribs in the accident. He hobbled through the garage area on crutches, assuring Robert Yates he could go the distance during the race. As a backup plan, however, Mike Wallace was asked to stand by as a

Dale Jarrett suffered another blow to his championship bid at Pocono. In qualifying, he crashed the primary Quality Care Ford (above) and was forced to revert to his backup ride. In the race, a broken crankshaft sent him to the garage after only 37 laps, dropping him to 38th place in the final results.

relief driver if D.J. needed one during the race.

The new pavement at Pocono was as smooth as a billiard table. Between the grip from the new asphalt and the Eagles that Goodyear brought to the track, 37 drivers smashed Wallace's two-year-old track record, with 14 of them surpassing it by more than a second. Gordon's new mark was more than five miles per hour faster than the former record.

With a string of seven consecutive top-five finishes this season and a history of success at Pocono (16 top 10s in 29 starts, a pair of wins and nine top-five finishes), most expected Earnhardt to charge to the front and be a player in the victory battle at Pocono.

Instead, Dale suffered problems with the engine in the Goodwrench Chevrolet, an unusual occurrence for the team, and eventually dropped from the race, finishing 32nd in the rundown. It cost him a pile of points, and what had appeared to be a comfortable lead entering the race shriveled to just 52 points by the end of the event.

The battle at the front for the Pocono victory raged back and forth

NASCAR Busch Series standout Jeff Green drives the Racing For Kids Monte Carlo in the team's NASCAR Winston Cup debut at Pocono. The car, owned by Dale Earnhardt, developed engine woes and was listed in 36th place at the end of the day.

engine problems, Wallace's Miller Ford lost its chance to win when Rusty burned out the clutch while leaving a green-flag pit stop.

Bodine became Gordon's only challenger, but he also fell from the victory hunt when a lug-nut problem during his

(Left) Joe Nemechek takes a shortcut across the grass near turn three after getting together with Bobby Labonte in the opening laps. Joe returned to the asphalt and completed the race. Bobby (on the track behind Marlin's "4" car) did not return and was credited with last place.
(Below) Rusty Wallace (left) and Jimmy Spencer discuss the matters at hand as they await the start of the race at Pocono.

between Gordon, Cope, Stricklin, Rudd and Rusty Wallace for the first 130 laps before Geoff Bodine also joined the fray with his QVC Ford. Geoff had struggled through the early part of the season but finally had his ducks in order at Pocono — and he took full advantage of the situation.

Stricklin fell from contention when the gearshift knob came off in his hand while he was shifting from third to fourth, and the transmission decided it had been punished enough. Cope, after his best run of the season, bumped into the rear of Robert Pressley's Skoal Bandit on a restart, damaging the nose of the Ford and spoiling the aerodynamics. Overheating resulted from the damage and Cope's chance for the win was gone. After Earnhardt went out with

Ricky Rudd (10) takes his turn at the front of the field as he leads Cope (12) and Gordon through Pocono's sweeping turn three. Although Rudd ran well throughout the race, he could do nothing with Gordon and eventually finished second, maintaining fifth place in the point standings.

final pit stop put him in third place at the conclusion of the event. Still, third was a huge accomplishment for the team, and Bodine said afterward that the finish "was like a transfusion to us."

The demise of the contenders left Gordon alone at the front of the pack, and for the second straight race, he whistled home the winner by more than three seconds. Rudd

Jeff Gordon with wife Brooke on his left, collects his fifth trophy of the season. He maintained third place in the points, but had now closed to within striking distance of point leader Dale Earnhardt.

fought his way to second with a spanking-new Tide Ford, and Martin finished fourth, behind Bodine. Bobby Hamilton's fifth place gained Pontiac its first top-five finish of the year, while Shepherd and his new crew chief combined for a sixth place, the best finish for the Remington Arms Ford this season.

Terry Labonte continued his stellar season with a seventh place, and Jimmy Spencer climbed further through the point standings by logging his second-straight top-10 finish, bringing Travis Carter's Smokin' Joe's Ford home eighth to the delight of Spencer's fellow Pennsylvanians. Jeff Burton was ninth, and Todd Bodine 10th in Bill Elliott's McDonald's Ford.

A total of 16 cars finished on the lead lap of the race, which had 26 lead changes among a dozen drivers before it was completed.

For Robert Yates and his crews, the Pocono event turned out to be a nightmare of huge proportions. Ernie Irvan lost control of the Havoline Ford while exiting the third turn just 27 laps into the race and collected Brett Bodine in the ensuing accident. Just 10 laps later, Jarrett's day ended when a crankshaft bolt on the front of the engine in his Quality Care Ford broke, damaging it beyond repair. Mike Wallace's help wasn't needed behind the wheel, and for the second consecutive race, Jarrett lost points in his battle for the championship.

Gordon was thrilled with his fifth victory of the season. However, the most important aspect of the win was that Earnhardt had finished 32nd, allowing Jeff to pick up 118 points in a single race and close to within 64 of Earnhardt. With Labonte in second place, just 52 points behind Earnhardt, the point battle had suddenly become a real contest among the three drivers.

Jarrett remained in fourth place in the standings, but now trailed Earnhardt by 233 markers. He knew something had to happen quickly if he was to get back into the heat of the battle. In addition, it took just a single look at the point standings following the first visit to Pocono for Jarrett to realize that Rudd's strong finish had yanked him into a position to challenge Jarrett for fourth place. Ricky was now just 11 points behind the red-white-and-blue Ford driver, and Rudd has long been one of the most tenacious drivers on the circuit. "We certainly didn't need something like this to happen," Jarrett said after the event.

Martin ended his string of poor racing luck with a solid fourth place and commented that it felt good to finally run well at a superspeedway — he had posted just three top-seven finishes on the big tracks so far this season.

"It wasn't quite good enough," Mark analyzed after the race, "but we did a good job with what we had to work with. We need to make it better, and maybe we'll be able to do that next week at Michigan."

UAW-GM Teamwork 500

Fin. Pos.	Str. Pos.	Car #	Driver	Team
1	1	24	Jeff Gordon	DuPont Refinishes Chevrolet
2	9	10	Ricky Rudd	Tide Ford
3	26	7	Geoff Bodine	QVC Ford
4	6	6	Mark Martin	Valvoline Ford
5	15	43	Bobby Hamilton	STP Pontiac
6	27	75	Morgan Shepherd	Remington Arms Ford
7	11	5	Terry Labonte	Kellogg's Corn Flakes Chevrolet
8	18	23	Jimmy Spencer	Camel Cigarettes Ford
9	16	99	Jeff Burton	Exide Batteries Ford
10	24	94	Todd Bodine	McDonald's Ford
11	23	4	Sterling Marlin	Kodak Film Chevrolet
12	29	15	Wally Dallenbach	Hayes Modems Ford
13	31	77	Bobby Hillin	Jasper Engines / Federal-Mogul Ford
14	14	21	Michael Waltrip	Citgo Ford
15	34	98	Jeremy Mayfield	RCA Ford
16	20	37	John Andretti	Kmart / Little Caesars Ford
17	4	41	Ricky Craven	Kodiak Chevrolet
18	5	25	Ken Schrader	Budweiser Chevrolet
19	30	16	Ted Musgrave	Family Channel / PRIMESTAR Ford
20	39	42	Kyle Petty	Coors Light Pontiac
21	8	87	Joe Nemechek	Burger King Chevrolet
22	37	29	Steve Grissom	Cartoon Network Chevrolet
23	25	19	Loy Allen	Healthsource Ford
24	36	78	Randy MacDonald	Diamond Rio Ford
25	40	30	Johnny Benson	Pennzoil Pontiac
26	41	90	Dick Trickle	Heilig-Meyers Ford
27	2	12	Derrike Cope	Badcock Ford
28	13	1	Rick Mast	Hooters Pontiac
29	3	8	Hut Stricklin	Circuit City Ford
30	32	17	Darrell Waltrip	Parts America Chevrolet
31	19	2	Rusty Wallace	Miller Ford
32	10	3	Dale Earnhardt	GM Goodwrench Service Chevrolet
33	35	33	Robert Pressley	Skoal Bandit Chevrolet
34	21	9	Lake Speed	Spam Ford
35	12	22	Ward Burton	MBNA America Pontiac
36	33	14	Jeff Green	Racing for Kids Chevrolet
37	38	81	Kenny Wallace	Square D / T.I.C. Ford
38	28	88	Dale Jarrett	Quality Care / Ford Credit Ford
39	17	28	Ernie Irvan	Texaco Havoline Ford
40	22	11	Brett Bodine	Lowe's Ford
41	7	18	Bobby Labonte	Interstate Batteries Chevrolet

Miller 400

Bobby Hamilton (43) turned the fastest lap in qualifying and started on the pole for the first time in his NASCAR Winston Cup career. It was also the first pole for Petty Enterprises in more than 16 years. Derrike Cope (12) started from the front row for the second consecutive week, but experienced engine problems during the race.
(Right) *Rusty Wallace and his Miller mates put their practice time to good use, testing the fuel mileage on the Miller Ford. In the end, the knowledge they gained helped them win in the race sponsored by their car sponsor, and on the track owned by their car owner.*

It had been a long and difficult two years for Ernie Irvan and his fans. He had overcome every obstacle placed in his way — from beating the one-in-10 odds of surviving his practice crash in July 1994 at Michigan International Speedway, to recovering his equilibrium and vision, to returning to the wheel of a race car to display his considerable talent.

Now it was time to return to the site of the accident. All that had passed during those two years — the tears, the pain, the frustration, the doubts and the rehabilitation — was part of the past. Ernie Irvan was ready to battle for victory.

It was time to stand in front of the huge crowd assembled for the spring event at Roger Penske's splendid two-mile oval and acknowledge the rolling thunder of cheers from fans paying tribute to Ernie's single-minded and unswerving dedication to return to the sport he loves.

When Ernie got behind the wheel of the Havoline Ford at Daytona, many wondered if he could still compete with the upper-echelon drivers. Three finishes in the 30s in the first five races of the season offset a strong run to fourth at Atlanta, and speculation centered around whether Irvan could get the job done.

What was forgotten in those ill-founded rumblings was the fact that during Ernie's time away from the sport, considerable changes had taken place in tire technology and in the aerodynamic influences on the Robert Yates Racing Thunderbirds prepared by Larry McReynolds. There was also the "rust factor." Like it or not, it took a while for Ernie to get back into the groove after being out of a race car for some 18 months, and he and his teammates had to re-learn how to communicate with each other. The chassis packages Dale Jarrett preferred last season while driving the "28" cars provided a much different feel than Ernie wanted in his cars, and that issue took a while to sort out.

After his sixth place at North Wilkesboro and his runner-up position at Martinsville, Irvan had finishes of seventh in The Winston Select, ninth in Charlotte's Coca-Cola 600 and fourth at Dover. He had moved from 34th in the point standings following Richmond to 16th after Pocono, and both he and his team firmly believed he could make a run to the top 10 by the end of the season.

For now, however, the most important item on Irvan's Michigan agenda was winning the race.

Bobby Labonte and his Interstate Batteries team were also

glad to return to Michigan. The green-and-black Chevrolet had been first to the line at both Michigan races in 1995, and Labonte and crew chief Jimmy Makar were primed to extend the string to three consecutive MIS victories.

The Pontiac teams had small, tight smiles on their faces as they prepared for competition at Michigan. The new Grand Prix had been less competitive than expected when it made its debut this season. The lack of downforce on the nose made the cars push up the track in the corners, slowing lap times around the track. Teams had worked hard trying to massage the new body shape into a week-to-week contender. Now that NASCAR had approved a new nose for the Grand Prix, they hoped their problems would be solved.

After the first session of qualifying, the small smiles on the Pontiac teams had widened into full-scale grins. The new nose was working — at least for the qualifying sessions — and Bobby Hamilton had put car owner Richard Petty in a strange position by turning the fastest lap of the session and claiming the Busch Pole for the Miller 400.

Uh, well, sort of.

(Right) Sterling Marlin (left) pumps Bobby Labonte – the driver who swept both Michigan events last season – for some Michigan secrets. Labonte's setup was not quite as strong this year, and he finished 12th. Sterling must have learned something new: He led the most laps in the event and finished a very strong third.
(Below) With the capacity crowd on their feet, Bobby Hamilton leads 39 other competitors under the green flag on a beautiful day in Michigan's Irish Hills.

Hamilton had notched the fastest lap, but there was no Busch contingency sticker on the car. "We're not very noted for sittin' on the pole," Richard explained after Hamilton's lap. Another thing is my mother (Elizabeth Petty) would probably shoot me if she seen a beer sticker on my car. She can't have a whole lot of control with Kyle, but she's still got control of me."

Therefore, the $5,000 bonus went to Derrike Cope who, for the second straight race, put Bobby Ailison's Badcock Ford on the outside of the front row.

The bonus money issue was one thing. The other question that remained was: Who would receive the invitation to compete in the February Busch Clash that went with the pole position bonus?

Morgan Shepherd, working his second race with crew chief Gere Kennon, was delighted with his green-and-gold Remington Arms Ford and rocketed to the inside of the second row, nipping Mark Martin for the spot by just .005 mph. Bobby Labonte proved he was a contender for a third straight Michigan victory by beating brother Terry for fifth place on the grid, while Jeff Gordon and Sterling Marlin locked up the fourth row, just ahead of Lake Speed and Brett Bodine.

Speed's lap came in his Spam Ford that carried a new paint scheme for the event. The Ford was painted red (instead of its usual blue) in celebration of the 50th anniversary of Melling Tools and to commemorate car owner Harry Melling's success during the '80s with driver Bill Elliott.

Earnhardt finished just outside the top 10,

(Above) Morgan Shepherd, bolstered by his season-best sixth-place finish at Pocono, qualified the Remington Ford third at Michigan and led three times for 44 laps. He just missed a top-10 finish, falling to 11th, but was still on the lead lap. *(Left)* Returning to the site of his 1994 accident could be considered nothing but a victory for Ernie Irvan. He ran well for the entire event and brought the Havoline Ford home in fifth place.

and Jeff Burton was the final qualifier the first day, beating Darrell Waltrip for the 25th spot. With only 40 cars in the garage area for the race, not a single team chose to run in the second qualifying session for the first time in memory. Everyone was in the field, with Todd Bodine and Jimmy Spencer using provisionals for 39th and 40th place, respectively.

Part of every crew chief's strategy for a Michigan race is to try to figure out how to get the most laps from a full fuel load, because time and again, fuel mileage had played a significant role in the final outcome of races there. Everyone spent some time during the final day of practice doing fuel runs on the track, trying to calculate just how far a full tank would go under race conditions. Rusty Wallace and crew chief Robin Pemberton took it a step further Saturday and ran until the tank was completely dry. Those calculations went into the computer and, on Sunday, played a pivotal role in the race.

With the first 53 laps of the race run under green-flag conditions, teams made their first stops of the day when the yellow came out after Cope's hopes for victory went up in a plume of blue smoke behind his Ford. The second yellow came on lap 96, and an unusual mistake by the Rainbow Warriors took Jeff Gordon from contention. He was called back to the pits to have a missing lug nut placed on a wheel. When he returned to action, he was in 32nd place. He eventually worked his way back to the point but then was forced to make a stop late in the race for fuel, dropping him to sixth at the conclusion of the race.

The final 101 laps were run under green-flag conditions, and as the laps wound down, it became a guessing game of

(Above) When it's time to perform those crucial late-race pit stops, no team is better than Rusty Wallace's Penske South crew. And once again, the last round of green-flag stops became "Miller Time." Rusty received four tires and every available drop of fuel in what would ultimately be the race-winning pit stop. (Left) Sterling Marlin (4) drops low, making it three-wide on Michigan's roomy frontstretch, as he charges past Terry Labonte (5) and Bobby Hamilton while trying to build his lead in the late going.

and Labonte returned to full speed, Sterling Marlin seemed well on his way to victory.

The yellow Kodak Chevrolet stretched its lead, and Marlin appeared ready to notch his second victory of the season. For 37 laps, Sterling dug the spurs into the sides of the Monte Carlo, hoping he could build a large enough lead so he would still be a contender when he made his final dash for a splash. Crew chief Tony Glover and the remainder of the Kodak team hoped Sterling could work a miracle but knew in their hearts that the race was lost. With 13 laps left and a nine-second lead, Marlin headed for the pits. He was nearly out of fuel and could not complete the distance without a stop.

That handed the lead to Gordon, who also needed to make a final quick stop for fuel. Behind him, Wallace and Labonte paced themselves, running nose to tail and knowing that if one of the two ran out of fuel, the other probably would make the trip to victory lane.

Then, with just 10 laps left in the race, Gordon slowed and headed for his pit. He could go no further.

Wallace became the race leader, and his team knew that he had run 52 laps earlier in the event on a full load of fuel.

who could make the final run to the flag without stopping for fuel. Jarrett wasn't in the mix, having run out of fuel three-quarters of the way through the race while trying to stretch a green-flag run and get into the window to make just a single stop. The Quality Care Ford wouldn't start after he coasted to his pit for fuel, and when the crew finally got it re-fired, he was out of contention.

The race was ultimately decided on the final green-flag stop, although at the time the teams didn't realize it. Rusty Wallace's Penske South team turned the Miller Ford back out after a superb stop just in front of the effort executed by Terry Labonte's Kellogg's Corn Flakes crew. When Wallace

"Holy race car driver, Batman, it's Wally Dallenbach – and he's wearing your Bat Hat!"

He only needed to repeat the task, and his team could celebrate its third victory of the season.

Rusty rolled into and out of the throttle, trying to ease his way to the win. A single mistake, or a little burp in the motor, and Labonte would be past him. Wallace held his line, worked the throttle like there was an egg between the sole of his shoe and the pedal and eased to a one-second victory over Labonte. It had taken every smidgen of fuel in the cell — and the hoses — to get him to the line. How close was Rusty to running out of fuel? At the fuel pumps after the victory, the Unocal folks pumped 22.2 gallons of fuel into the 22-gallon cell, with the additional 0.2 going into the fuel filler hoses.

Labonte's second place kept his strong string of performances alive and he moved to just 15 points behind Earnhardt in the standings after Dale's ninth-place finish. Marlin recovered to claim third place after his late stop, while Jimmy Spencer reveled in his outstanding run that brought him from 40th place at the start of the race all the way to fourth.

Ernie Irvan's return to Michigan had been a triumphant one. Although he never led, he was a contender throughout the day and finished fifth in the race, ahead of Gordon. Martin was seventh, ahead of teammate Ted Musgrave, and Dale Jarrett fought his way back from the mid-race fuel problem to finish 10th. Morgan Shepherd, after leading early in the race, finished just outside the top 10, while Bobby Labonte's 12th-place finish ended his string of Michigan victories at two.

Dale Jarrett, anticipating the importance of fuel mileage, tried to stretch a green-flag run long enough to make just one final stop. His strategy backfired, however, and Dale coasted into his pit after running the tank dry. He needed this push to get him running again.

Miller 400

Fin. Pos.	Str. Pos.	Car #	Driver	Team
1	18	2	Rusty Wallace	Miller Ford
2	6	5	Terry Labonte	Kellogg's Corn Flakes Chevrolet
3	8	4	Sterling Marlin	Kodak Film Chevrolet
4	40	23	Jimmy Spencer	Camel Cigarettes Ford
5	32	28	Ernie Irvan	Texaco Havoline Ford
6	7	24	Jeff Gordon	DuPont Refinishes Chevrolet
7	4	6	Mark Martin	Valvoline Ford
8	12	16	Ted Musgrave	Family Channel / PRIMESTAR Ford
9	11	3	Dale Earnhardt	GM Goodwrench Service Chevrolet
10	30	88	Dale Jarrett	Quality Care / Ford Credit Ford
11	3	75	Morgan Shepherd	Remington Arms Ford
12	5	18	Bobby Labonte	Interstate Batteries Chevrolet
13	31	15	Wally Dallenbach	Hayes Modems Ford
14	28	77	Bobby Hillin	Jasper Engines / Federal-Mogul Ford
15	1	43	Bobby Hamilton	STP Pontiac
16	27	25	Ken Schrader	Budweiser Chevrolet
17	25	99	Jeff Burton	Exide Batteries Ford
18	17	1	Rick Mast	Hooters Pontiac
19	9	9	Lake Speed	Spam Ford
20	39	94	Todd Bodine	McDonald's Ford
21	21	7	Geoff Bodine	QVC Ford
22	10	11	Brett Bodine	Lowe's Ford
23	35	33	Robert Pressley	Skoal Bandit Chevrolet
24	23	37	John Andretti	Kmart / Little Caesars Ford
25	26	17	Darrell Waltrip	Parts America Chevrolet
26	36	71	Dave Marcis	Prodigy Chevrolet
27	33	8	Hut Stricklin	Circuit City Ford
28	38	19	Loy Allen	Healthsource Ford
29	15	41	Ricky Craven	Kodiak Chevrolet
30	13	98	Jeremy Mayfield	RCA Ford
31	14	10	Ricky Rudd	Tide Ford
32	20	21	Michael Waltrip	Citgo Ford
33	16	81	Kenny Wallace	Square D / T.I.C. Ford
34	22	29	Steve Grissom	Cartoon Network Chevrolet
35	34	22	Ward Burton	MBNA America Pontiac
36	24	87	Joe Nemechek	Burger King Chevrolet
37	37	30	Johnny Benson	Pennzoil Pontiac
38	29	42	Kyle Petty	Coors Light Pontiac
39	19	90	Dick Trickle	Heilig-Meyers Ford
40	2	12	Derrike Cope	Badcock Ford

Pepsi 400

Kyle Petty (42), with yet another limited-edition paint scheme, slips past Mark Martin (6) on Daytona's tri-oval. Petty and team owner Felix Sabates rocked the garage area by announcing that they would part company at the end of the '96 season.
(Right) *Sterling Marlin, under the protection of umbrellas in a soggy victory lane at Daytona, celebrates with his family following a convincing run in the Pepsi 400. Sterling started from the outside of the front row, took the lead on lap one, led 88 of 117 laps (including the last 31) in the rain-shortened event, and grabbed the checkered flag for the third time in the last six races at The Beach.*

There were surprises aplenty in store for the NASCAR Winston Cup followers when they lined up to enter the grandstands at Daytona International Speedway for the running of the Pepsi 400.

SABCO Racing owner Felix Sabates, who left the racing scene in protest after the Charlotte penalty box incident, returned to the tracks for the first time at Michigan. Kyle Petty had been the only driver for SABCO since its inception eight years ago, and following the Michigan race, Petty and Sabates flew home together. On the way, Kyle told Felix that it was time for them to part company because, despite a change in crew chiefs, engine builders and crew members, the team was still struggling. Kyle suggested it was time for Felix to find another driver who might help lead the team back to the front, and at the same time, Petty would be able to pursue other opportunities that might help him get his career back on track.

That conversation led to others in the days that followed, and by the time the team arrived at The Beach for the annual mid-season 400-miler, the divorce was all but final and Felix and Petty prepared themselves to meet with the media to discuss their upcoming dissociation.

Kyle would remain with the team for the remainder of the season, fulfilling his obligations to SABCO, Pontiac and Coors Light, and Felix would be free to enlist the services of another driver for the 1997 season. There was no messy contract work to solve. The entire time Kyle had driven for Felix, the two had no paper contract between them. The deal was done on a handshake — a most unusual arrangement in this day and age.

The announcement was a bombshell that rocked the garage area and made Diamond Ridge's dismissal of Steve Grissom pale by comparison. Grissom had been told earlier that his contract would not be renewed for 1997, and now he was out of the car. Greg Sacks was hired as the interim driver, and his first outing would be at the Pepsi 400 — the same race he won in 1986, his only career NASCAR Winston Cup victory.

Over in a corner of the garage, the McDonald's Ford owned by Elliott/Hardy Racing was attended by the usual crew headed by Mike Beam, but Todd Bodine, Bill Elliott's relief driver since Charlotte, was missing. Elliott, gamely walking with the aid of a metal cane, had returned to action a month earlier than expected. He had hoped to be behind

Brooke and Jeff Gordon (left) and Dale Earnhardt (above) didn't let a few raindrops spoil their fun during the Pepsi 400. Jeff, third in the points and the defending race champion, was on a tear and had already captured his fourth pole of the season. Dale, Daytona's winningest driver and the current point leader, finished third in the race, while Jeff finished fourth.

the wheel of the red-white-and-yellow car at The Brickyard, but his broken femur had healed much more quickly than anticipated. He still had some pain in his leg, and the cockpit of the Mac Attack Ford was more heavily padded than usual, but Bill was back after missing five races and ready to start his climb from 36th place in the point standings. He had been 10th when the accident occurred in the Winston Select 500 at Talladega.

Dave Marcis also gathered some of the headlines prior to the race — the wily veteran rolled out a special car and paint scheme to help celebrate his 800th career NASCAR Winston Cup start. In the history of the sport, only Richard Petty had gone to the line more times than Dave.

While media members clustered around Marcis and his Prodigy Chevrolet, others were talking with Richard Childress. Lowe's stores made the announcement that the company would leave Brett Bodine's team at the conclusion of the season and would join Childress as the primary sponsor of his second team, with Mike Skinner as the driver.

In the champion's slot in the garage area, the DuPont Chevrolet team was working its way through practice sessions and preparing for the upcoming first round of qualifying. The press had plenty of other things to mull over, and Jeff Gordon, Ray Evernham and company went about business as usual. The Rainbow Warriors were on a roll. In the races following the Winston Select 500 at Talladega, their worst finish was an eighth place. Included in that six-race string were a pair of back-to-back victories and four consecutive pole positions. Their Monte Carlo was fast during practice for the Pepsi 400, and Gordon knew he had a chance to win yet another pole if everything went right.

Under threatening skies, the cars were pushed to the line for the first round of qualifying. Gordon had drawn the first number for his attempt and rocketed around the track with a "beat-it-if-you-can" lap of 188.869 mph. He then waited as eight other drivers (including Dale Earnhardt and hot-running Derrike Cope) took their shots and failed. As Gary

In his first ride behind the wheel of the Cartoon Network car, Greg Sacks tries for a solid showing as he runs with Rick Mast's Hooters Pontiac. Sacks had just been named as Steve Grissom's replacement in the Diamond Ridge machine after Grissom was suddenly released before the trip to Daytona.

(Above) Jeff Gordon (24), Ken Schrader (25) and Dale Earnhardt (3) use the entire width of Daytona's 31-degree-banked turn as Ted Musgrave (16) chooses to draft with Schrader up the middle. *(Left)* Darrell Waltrip (inset) was elated with his fourth-place qualifying effort and attacked the famous superspeedway with abandon. Despite the best efforts of his crew, the Parts America Chevrolet lacked the handling needed to run up front at Daytona, and Darrell was disappointed with his 26th-place finish.

Bradberry completed his lap, the gray clouds opened, and rain began falling. Qualifying was delayed and then eventually postponed, with the remainder of the field to make their laps the following day.

No one had an answer for Gordon the following day either, and when the first session was completed, Sterling Marlin had grabbed the outside of the front row with a lap that was four-tenths of a second off Gordon's pace.

Dale Jarrett posted the third-fastest lap, and Darrell Waltrip was doing a little jig beside his Parts America Monte Carlo. He was on the outside of the second row, and the accomplishment clearly had been the tonic needed to rejuvenate his beleaguered team. Johnny Benson and Jeff Purvis, in one of his limited outings this year, grabbed the third row while Earnhardt and Ken Schrader were right behind. Lake Speed, back in a blue-and-yellow Spam Ford, was on the inside of the fifth row, with Bobby Labonte alongside. Rusty Wallace barely missed the top 10, as did Terry Labonte and Dick Trickle, driving Junie Donlavey's Heilig-Meyers Ford for the third straight race.

There were only three cautions during the Pepsi 400, and pit crews up and down pit road scrambled to gain track position for their drivers during each. Johnny Benson's Pennzoil crew was particularly excited after their driver qualified his Pontiac an impressive fifth. Benson ran well, but the leading contender for Rookie of the Year faded to 25th by the end of the race.

Mark Martin and Dave Marcis both had engine problems during their first-round qualifying runs, and Steve Seligman's engine blew up, preventing him from making a lap. As a result, he was the only driver that did not make the field — Ricky Rudd, Martin, Geoff Bodine and Loy Allen used provisionals to join the grid. Marcis was the only driver to re-qualify in the second session and he earned the Busch second-round bonus and the "wild card" slot for the Pepsi 400 race.

That Marcis even made the race was a tribute to an outstanding act of sportsmanship from Childress and his team. The Prodigy Chevrolet's oil pump had locked up and Marcis faced missing the field because of the time shortage between the two qualifying sessions. But Childress instructed his crew to yank the engine and transmission from Earnhardt's car and help Marcis' team install it in the Prodigy Chevrolet. Marcis' second-round qualifying lap resulted in a lap that would have put him eighth in the field (alongside Earnhardt) had it come in the first session!

Mother Nature seemed determined to keep the racers at Daytona for an additional day — race time came and went in the middle of a steady rain. Eventually the water stopped falling, and despite the high humidity, track officials were able to dry the pavement enough for the race to begin. The green flag came nearly three hours after the scheduled start, and it was clear that this event needed to run very quickly in

Hendrick Motorsports stablemates Terry Labonte (5), Jeff Gordon (24) and Ken Schrader (25) team up in a draft to track down Sterling Marlin. But not even their combined effort could match the strength of the Kodak Chevrolet. Sterling simply drove away from everyone, displaying the power of his Runt Pittman-built engine.

order to avoid a distant band of showers that, according to NASCAR's radar, was headed toward the track.

Someone must have told that to Marlin and his Kodak team.

When the green flew over the field, Sterling wasted no time in taking command of the race, pulling past pole-sitter Gordon before the end of the first lap. From there on, it was Sterling's race to lose, and for the longest time, he ran

Jeff Purvis (44) impressed many when he placed the MCA Records Chevrolet sixth during first-round qualifying. Here, Jeff dares to make it three-wide on the high side as he tries to blast past Jeremy Mayfield (98) and John Andretti (37).

as though the hounds of Hades were on his tail.

He was at the point for 43 of the first 65 laps, but on the 66th lap, the yellow Chevrolet slowed and Marlin fell from the lead. He smelled burning wires inside the car and thought the engine had blown. Looking frantically around the cockpit, he finally found the backup ignition box, hit the switch and the motor straightened out.

He was back in 17th place, and with the engine now at full song, he began rolling back through the field. Eight laps later, he was up to 10th, and he moved to fifth when the second caution flag of the event flew for a brief shower. On lap 86, after the green flew again, he blew past Michael Waltrip to regain the lead.

The last caution of the event occurred on lap 101, when Trickle and John Andretti tangled and triggered a four-car accident. While the competitors circled the track behind the safety car under the yellow flag, NASCAR inspectors huddled with crew chiefs, telling them that a severe thunder and lightning storm was just 15 minutes away. That announcement made the decision of whether to pit under the yellow flag a simple one.

Pit? Lose track position with just a few laps remaining in the race when the green came out. Stay out? Retain position and hope your driver could gain a few more positions before the rain came. Easy decision.

The leaders remained on the track, and the drivers could see the storm coming on the horizon. When the green waved on lap 104, a mad scramble for positions ensued. Labonte, Gordon and Earnhardt were lined up behind Marlin and hoped to get a run at the Kodak Chevrolet. Marlin, however, had the measure of the field and remained at the point, holding off the combined challenge of the other three Chevrolets.

Rain began falling, hitting the windshields of the cars and making the track slippery. A lap later, it began pelting the cars in earnest, and Marlin looked in his mirror to see the threesome chasing him fall back a little bit. He streaked around the track and took the yellow flag as thunder rolled and lightning cracked. The red flag soon followed and the event halted after 117 of the scheduled 160 laps. Nearly 40 minutes later the race was declared official.

The win was Marlin's second of a season that had been inconsistent and included a 40th in the Daytona 500, a 41st at Dover and six other finishes in the teens. The Pepsi 400 victory, however, moved him to fifth in the point standings.

Ernie Irvan and Dale Jarrett were the first Ford finishers, coming home fifth and sixth, while Michael Waltrip and Ken Schrader took seventh and eighth, ahead of Brett Bodine and Jimmy Spencer, who had his fourth-straight top-10 finish.

Pepsi 400

Fin. Pos.	Str. Pos.	Car #	Driver	Team
1	2	4	Sterling Marlin	Kodak Film Chevrolet
2	12	5	Terry Labonte	Kellogg's Corn Flakes Chevrolet
3	1	24	Jeff Gordon	DuPont Refinishes Chevrolet
4	7	3	Dale Earnhardt	GM Goodwrench Service Chevrolet
5	14	28	Ernie Irvan	Texaco Havoline Ford
6	3	88	Dale Jarrett	Quality Care / Ford Credit Ford
7	23	21	Michael Waltrip	Citgo Ford
8	8	25	Ken Schrader	Budweiser Chevrolet
9	36	11	Brett Bodine	Lowe's Ford
10	27	23	Jimmy Spencer	Camel Cigarettes Ford
11	40	6	Mark Martin	Valvoline Ford
12	35	15	Wally Dallenbach	Hayes Modems Ford
13	38	16	Ted Musgrave	Family Channel / PRIMESTAR Ford
14	33	99	Jeff Burton	Exide Batteries Ford
15	18	75	Morgan Shepherd	Remington Arms / Stren Ford
16	19	43	Bobby Hamilton	STP Pontiac
17	16	33	Robert Pressley	Skoal Bandit Chevrolet
18	20	87	Joe Nemechek	Burger King Chevrolet
19	15	8	Hut Stricklin	Circuit City Ford
20	32	1	Rick Mast	Hooters Pontiac
21	6	44	Jeff Purvis	MCA Records Chevrolet
22	25	41	Ricky Craven	Kodiak Chevrolet
23	22	37	John Andretti	Kmart / Little Caesars Ford
24	37	42	Kyle Petty	Coors Light Pontiac
25	5	30	Johnny Benson	Pennzoil Pontiac
26	4	17	Darrell Waltrip	Parts America Chevrolet
27	24	98	Jeremy Mayfield	RCA Ford
28	13	90	Dick Trickle	Heilig-Meyers Ford
29	9	9	Lake Speed	Spam Ford
30	42	19	Loy Allen	Healthsource Ford
31	11	2	Rusty Wallace	Miller Ford
32	31	77	Bobby Hillin	Jasper Engines / Federal-Mogul Ford
33	39	10	Ricky Rudd	Tide Ford
34	41	7	Geoff Bodine	QVC Ford
35	29	95	Gary Bradberry	Shoney's Restaurants Ford
36	26	71	Dave Marcis	Prodigy Chevrolet
37	28	94	Bill Elliott	McDonald's Ford
38	21	81	Kenny Wallace	Square D / T.I.C. Ford
39	30	29	Greg Sacks	Cartoon Network Chevrolet
40	10	18	Bobby Labonte	Interstate Batteries Chevrolet
41	34	22	Ward Burton	MBNA America Pontiac
42	17	12	Derrike Cope	Badcock Ford

Jiffy Lube 300

*New Englander Ricky Craven used his home turf to announce his newly-formed partnership with team owner Larry Hedrick, then promptly rewarded himself with his second Busch Pole of the season. Starting on the outside of the front row is Bobby Hamilton, continuing to post strong performances in Richard Petty's STP Pontiac. **(Right)** Crew chief Larry McReynolds hoists the winner's trophy with driver Ernie Irvan and team owner Robert Yates alongside. They had not been to victory lane together since before Ernie's accident at Michigan in August 1994, and finally, Ernie's comeback seemed complete.*

The combination of finishes in the rain-shortened Pepsi 400 at Daytona had Dale Earnhardt leading the battle for the title by only five points as the teams unloaded in New Hampshire's garage area to prepare for the Jiffy Lube 300 at the Bahre family's superb speedplant. Defending champion Jeff Gordon now found himself third on the point ladder, only 37 points behind.

The fight for this year's championship appeared to be sorting itself out, with three Chevrolet drivers — Dale Earnhardt, Terry Labonte and Jeff Gordon — set to battle amongst themselves for the NASCAR Winston Cup title. Dale Jarrett, fourth in the standings, was 237 points behind the leader, and if the Quality Care Ford driver was to make a run for the title, he needed to get moving right now. It was mid-season and there was plenty of racing left — but he simply could not afford to leave any points on the table from this point on.

He also needed some help from the three drivers ahead of him. If Jarrett had trailed just a single driver by 237 points, life would have been much simpler. A blown engine here or a mechanical problem there could help pull the Ford driver back into the hunt. Jarrett's problem, however, was that he needed that kind of racing luck to happen to all three of the drivers at the top of the point table, and the odds on that happening were steadily dropping.

Sterling Marlin's victory in the Pepsi 400 had pulled him to fifth in the point standings, but he was nearly 300 points behind Earnhardt. The Kodak team's inconsistency in the first half of the season had kept Marlin from mounting the championship drive he and the team had envisioned in January and February. Ken Schrader, Ricky Rudd, Mark Martin, Ted Musgrave and Rusty Wallace were locked in a tight battle for positions in the rest of the top 10. The point difference between those five was so small that most positions changed after almost every race.

Bob and Gary Bahre were grinning from ear to ear when practice opened at the oval, and the reason was evident. The Bahres had purchased half of North Wilkesboro Speedway earlier in the year, and had been able to move one of the two 1997 dates from the five-eighths-mile track in North Carolina's Brushy Mountains to the scenic New Hampshire countryside. Next year, the track would host a pair of NASCAR Winston Cup events, with the second race falling on the September 14 weekend, near-perfect timing

Crew members survey the damage to the Interstate Batteries Monte Carlo after Bobby Labonte shortened it against the outside wall in the morning practice session before first-round qualifying. The team quickly pulled the backup Chevrolet off the transporter, and Bobby drove it to the third-fastest lap to start the race from the second row.

for the tens of thousands of visitors to share in the beauty of New England's autumn.

A simultaneous announcement was being made in Texas: An April 6 date had been given to Texas Motor Speedway, Bruton Smith and Speedway Motorsports, Inc. Smith had purchased the other half of North Wilkesboro and had successfully lobbied to move the spring NASCAR Winston Cup date to his new track under construction in the Ft. Worth area. The move meant that North Wilkesboro would lose both its NASCAR Winston Cup events for the coming year, bringing an end to competition at the track that had been one of the pioneer speedways on the circuit,

dating back to 1949. The race at North Wilkesboro on the last Sunday in September would be a poignant one.

There were other items to keep teams talking. TriStar Motorsports announced it would cut back to a very limited schedule for the remainder of the season, and Kodiak Chevrolet team owner Larry Hedrick announced that he and driver Ricky Craven had agreed to become partners in Hedrick-Craven Motorsports. The partnership basically would turn the running of the team over to Craven, while Hedrick took over the responsibility of sponsor relations and team management.

The day before the announcement by Craven and Hedrick, Ricky had underscored the fact that he was all the way back from his May Winston Select 500 accident at Talladega. He ran early during the first qualifying session for the Jiffy Lube 300 and recorded a new track record with his lap of over 129 mph. Then he and car owner Hedrick were forced to sit, watch and wait as the others in the field made their efforts to unseat Craven from the pole.

Craven had won the first Busch Pole of his career earlier this season at Martinsville, but this one was much bigger to him. It came at what he often called his "home" track, the nearest NASCAR Winston Cup stop to Bangor, Maine, where he grew up. He had lived for several years in the

Ricky Rudd, who won in New Hampshire in 1994, waits patiently for the Jiffy Lube 300 to begin. After starting 20th, Rudd worked his way through the field, led briefly in the final stages of the race, and finished a very strong third in his Tide Thunderbird. In the four NASCAR Winston Cup events run here, Rudd has never finished out of the top five.

Concord, N.H., area while he was running the NASCAR Busch North tour, and to come "home" to win the pole for the Jiffy Lube 300 was an accomplishment that delighted the soft-spoken New Englander.

To capture the pole the day after the announcement of a second NASCAR Winston Cup date for New Hampshire, and the day before he and Hedrick made their statement regarding the future of their team, was even sweeter.

Bobby Hamilton plunked his STP Pontiac on the outside of the front row, just over a tenth of a second off Craven's record mark, and Bobby Labonte's third-fastest lap was pure testimony to his team's talents. He had found the wall during the morning practice session, and his Interstate Batteries team hurriedly yanked the team's backup Monte Carlo from the transporter and hustled around the green-and-black car, referring to clipboards and notebooks to set the chassis the same way it had for the first car. Labonte's lap just beat Kyle Petty, who turned in one of his better qualifying performances of the season in the Coors Light Pontiac.

The third row belonged to Dale Earnhardt and Ernie Irvan, ahead of Geoff Bodine and Ken Schrader. Dick Trickle had a solid run to ninth place for the start of the race, while Dale Jarrett was 10th, just ahead of Joe

(Right) Michael Waltrip (21) leads Rusty Wallace (2) and Jeff Burton (99) off pit road after a round of pit stops under caution. Pit work played an important role early on as five of the race's eight yellow flags fell before the halfway mark. (Below) Dale Earnhardt (3) tests the pavement on the outside groove as Rusty Wallace protects the inside line by closing the gap behind Ernie Irvan (28). Earnhardt was a strong contender, but ran out of gas on the last lap and dropped to 12th in the final rundown. His misfortune also cost him the lead in the point standings.

Nemechek and Robert Pressley.

Among the others having problems during their qualifying laps were Jeremy Mayfield, who stuffed his RCA Ford into the fourth-turn wall and was forced to go to a backup car, and Wally Dallenbach, who spun exiting the second turn. Johnny Benson stumbled and was forced to slow dramatically to save his Pennzoil Pontiac during his lap. With the second round of qualifying rained out, the rest of the field was determined by the first-round times, and Mayfield and Dallenbach were forced to use provisionals to make the field. All of the cars in the garage area made the race.

The Jiffy Lube 300 had the appearance of a dogfight right from the beginning, with 11 lead changes during the first third of the race. By the halfway point, five of the race's eight cautions were already in the books, and the event still looked like it could be anybody's race. The track was tearing up slightly, and track position became more and more criti-

cal as the race wore on. Nearly every car on the lead lap had a chance to win the event, depending on team and pit strategy, and two-tire stops had become the order of the day as crew chiefs sought to move their drivers to the front of the pack.

The last caution of the afternoon fell just after the two-thirds mark of the race, leaving teams with a battle to make it to the end of the event without stopping for fuel, particularly because the final caution came just five laps after a caution that sent drivers to pit road for fuel and tires. Most remained on the track for the final yellow flag, and that set the stage for the finish of the race.

(Above) The Texaco Havoline crew gives Ernie Irvan two tires and fuel in a lightning-fast final pit stop. Larry McReynolds' gutsy call late in the race proved to be a winning one. When the round of green-flag stops was complete, Ernie had regained the lead and drove all the way to victory lane. (Left) A bobble during qualifying put Johnny Benson in 38th place for the start of the event. Once the green flag flew, however, the Rookie-of-the-Year contender drove the race of his life, leading 17 laps and finishing a career-best ninth.

None of the leaders could make it to the end without refueling, and it became a chess game on pit road. Irvan, a contender throughout the day, headed for pit road on lap 244, giving up the lead he held but gambling that when all of the others cycled through their green-flag stops, he would be back at the front and in position to claim his first victory since his return to the seat of the Havoline Ford. Crew chief Larry McReynolds called for right-side tires and fuel, and Irvan was back on the track without losing a lap to the leaders.

The remaining leaders cycled through their stops, and when everyone had emerged back on the track, Irvan was in command of the race, taking the point again on lap 277. From that point on, both Ernie and crew chief McReynolds

prayed for no more cautions. A late stop would leave Irvan at a huge disadvantage because he had older right-side tires and lefts that had gone more than 140 laps. The cars behind him would be on fresher tires with more adhesion and grip, and Ernie would probably be beaten.

Providence answered Ernie and Larry. The yellow flag remained furled between starter Carl Simmons' knees (regular starter Doyle Ford missed the race due to illness) and Irvan continued to lead the pack around the 1.04-mile oval. At the finish, he was more than five seconds ahead of teammate Jarrett, with Ricky Rudd fighting his way to third ahead of Jeff Burton and Robert Pressley. Terry Labonte beat Rusty Wallace for sixth place, while Ken Schrader came home eighth, just ahead of Johnny Benson, who posted the best finish of his brief NASCAR Winston Cup career. Michael Waltrip claimed the final position in the top 10, ahead of Ted Musgrave and Dale Earnhardt.

During the middle portion of the event, it looked as though Jeff Gordon was headed for yet another victory, but a rare problem with the DuPont Chevrolet dropped him well off the pace. There was a mysterious ignition problem within the Monte Carlo's innards. Gordon slowed on lap 238 and hit the switch for the backup ignition system, but

Dale Jarrett and crew chief Todd Parrott review their notes after practice, trying to come up with the right setup for the race. They did their homework well. Dale spun in the opening laps and had to rely on his Ford's handling ability to fight back through the field. With the help of great pit work, Jarrett finally finished a commendable second.

when it failed, he was forced to pit. Ray Evernham and the remainder of the Rainbow Warriors fell to work, and sent Gordon back onto the track for a handful of laps, but he brought the car to the garage after completing only 253. He was classified 34th in the field and lost points to Labonte, Earnhardt and Jarrett.

Jarrett's second place was the result of a superb drive through the field and some brilliant work by his crew, led by Todd Parrott, who burned his hands working on Jarrett's car during one of the stops. Dale had spun on the third lap of the race, bringing out the first caution but fortunately not damaging the Quality Care Thunderbird. He worked his way back through the field and his crew performed flawlessly on pit road, helping him gain track position throughout the race.

Earnhardt fell to 12th place after running out of fuel on the final lap of the race, and Terry Labonte's run to sixth place brought him the point lead. When reminded that the last two champions have taken the lead after the New Hampshire race, Terry merely smiled and said he was pleased to be the point leader — but he'd rather have this conversation after the race in November at Atlanta!

Irvan's victory was hugely popular and marked his return to the winner's circle after his battle back from the practice accident at Michigan in 1994. He was all the way back, it appeared, and his victory was a combination of heady driving, strategic work on pit road by his crew chief and his crew, and excellence in the team's motor room, where the right balance between power and fuel mileage had been obtained.

Robert Pressley keeps his Skoal Bandit Chevrolet ahead of Ted Musgrave's Family Channel Ford while negotiating New Hampshire's flat, sweeping corners. Pressley had an eventful day, to say the least. He led three times for 48 laps, slapped the fourth-turn wall and fought a fast but ill-handling car all the way to a top-five finish.

Jiffy Lube 300

Fin. Pos.	Str. Pos.	Car #	Driver	Team
1	6	28	Ernie Irvan	Texaco Havoline Ford
2	10	88	Dale Jarrett	Quality Care / Ford Credit Ford
3	20	10	Ricky Rudd	Tide Ford
4	24	99	Jeff Burton	Exide Batteries Ford
5	12	33	Robert Pressley	Skoal Bandit Chevrolet
6	23	5	Terry Labonte	Kellogg's Corn Flakes Chevrolet
7	17	2	Rusty Wallace	Miller Ford
8	8	25	Ken Schrader	Budweiser Chevrolet
9	38	30	Johnny Benson	Pennzoil Pontiac
10	31	21	Michael Waltrip	Citgo Ford
11	21	16	Ted Musgrave	Family Channel / PRIMESTAR Ford
12	5	3	Dale Earnhardt	GM Goodwrench Service Chevrolet
13	32	1	Rick Mast	Hooters Pontiac
14	37	94	Bill Elliott	McDonald's Ford
15	7	7	Geoff Bodine	QVC Ford
16	26	11	Brett Bodine	Lowe's Ford
17	29	23	Jimmy Spencer	Camel Cigarettes Ford
18	40	15	Wally Dallenbach	Hayes Modems Ford
19	15	81	Kenny Wallace	Square D / T.I.C. Ford
20	2	43	Bobby Hamilton	STP Pontiac
21	33	77	Bobby Hillin	Jasper Engines / Federal-Mogul Ford
22	28	75	Morgan Shepherd	Remington Arms Ford
23	13	8	Hut Stricklin	Circuit City Ford
24	18	9	Lake Speed	Spam Ford
25	30	22	Ward Burton	MBNA America Pontiac
26	1	41	Ricky Craven	Kodiak Chevrolet
27	9	90	Dick Trickle	Heilig-Meyers Ford
28	4	42	Kyle Petty	Coors Light Pontiac
29	14	4	Sterling Marlin	Kodak Film Chevrolet
30	35	29	Greg Sacks	Cartoon Network Chevrolet
31	3	18	Bobby Labonte	Interstate Batteries Chevrolet
32	36	78	Randy MacDonald	Diamond Rio Ford
33	22	6	Mark Martin	Valvoline Ford
34	16	24	Jeff Gordon	DuPont Refinishes Chevrolet
35	11	87	Joe Nemechek	Burger King Chevrolet
36	39	98	Jeremy Mayfield	RCA Ford
37	19	17	Darrell Waltrip	Parts America Chevrolet
38	25	12	Derrike Cope	Badcock Ford
39	34	71	Dave Marcis	Prodigy Chevrolet
40	27	37	John Andretti	Kmart / Little Caesars Ford

Miller 500

*Mark Martin spends some time signing autographs for enthusiastic Pocono fans. Mark's look of confidence is well warranted. He had already taken his third pole at Pocono, the 30th of his career. In the race, he was a dominant force until a miscue in the pits took him out of contention for the win. **(Right)** It's evident that Rusty Wallace loves to win for his team sponsor as he proudly displays the winner's trophy, presented by Miller Beer.*

The majority of the NASCAR Winston Cup drivers and teams journey to and from events via private and chartered aircraft, enabling them to avoid the long waits often associated with commercial aircraft travel. Usually, teams exit the track, head for smaller airports, board KingAirs and Twin Beechcrafts and are home within a couple of hours.

Usually.

Every once in a while, however, there's a glitch in the plan and when that happens, it makes a good story. That's what occurred with several crew members of Roush Racing following the New England race. The chartered plane that was originally scheduled to take them home was delayed by severe thunderstorms, and then the takeoff was scratched due to electrical problems within the plane. The crew headed for a motel for the night, but could find only a single room — with one bed — for the five crew members. They hustled up rollaway cots and returned to the airport the next morning, only to find that the replacement plane had clipped a pole during an instrument landing, shearing off the landing gear, and the pilot had been forced to (successfully) crash land the plane at another airport.

A quick huddle among the crew members resulted in the decision to fly home commercial, but the computers went down while issuing the tickets. By the time the crew members left, they had missed their connecting flight in Newark, N.J. Three hours later, they were on their way. When they finally arrived home, it was nearly 8 p.m.

Five days later, the crew members were at Pocono ready to shepherd the Ted Musgrave and Mark Martin Fords for the Miller 500. They had recovered from their adventure — but shared the highlights with anyone who asked. The story went on and on, embellished by each crew member, and left listeners shaking with laughter as they walked away.

This was the second time around at the ol' spinach patch for the teams this season. This particular appearance at Pocono had added meaning because the cars many of the teams had on hand for the Miller 500 were the same mounts slated for the upcoming Brickyard 400 at Indianapolis Motor Speedway. In addition, the Goodyear Eagles for Pocono were the same tires that would be used in a few weeks for the Brickyard event. Many drivers and crew chiefs felt Pocono was the closest thing to The Brickyard, with its long straightaways and the sweeping, flat

NASCAR
MILLER 500
NASCAR WINSTON CUP EVENT
WINNER
July 21, 1996 Pocono
Miller 500 CHAMPION
BOSCH
Miller

third turn that is similar to the Indianapolis banking. This would be a fair trial for the tires and the chassis in preparation for the richest race on the tour.

In the week between New Hampshire and Pocono, Bill Elliott had become the sole owner of his race team. Elliott and partner Charles Hardy, a Georgia car dealer and businessman, had dissolved their package, with Elliott purchasing Hardy's 50 percent of the team. "I didn't have a lot of choice in the matter," Bill said in the garage area. "I had to get on with it if I was going to continue to race. So, here I am, a new car owner."

The session resumed at 9 a.m. Saturday morning, and the weather was considerably colder than Friday afternoon. A chilly 58 degrees with gusting winds greeted the rest of the field as car after car made their timed runs. When the session was finally completed, Mark Martin had hustled his Valvoline Ford to his 30th career NASCAR Winston Cup Busch Pole.

After his run, Mark explained that the wind behind him on the long straights had helped considerably — perhaps by as much as five miles per hour. His tach registered much higher than he expected, and he said he could feel the gusts

(Above) Crew members fight rain and wind as they return the Interstate Batteries Monte Carlo to the garage. When the weather finally cleared, Bobby Labonte blew around the Pocono track and secured the third-fastest qualifying lap. (Right) While Bill Elliott waits for his turn to qualify, wife Cindy and son William Jr. keep him company along pit road. Bill had just announced that he had become sole owner of his race team after dissolving his partnership with Charles Hardy, adding yet another name to the owner/driver ranks.

Bill had plenty of time to do the interviews regarding his new status as a full team owner — a weather front was hanging over Drs. Rose and Joe Mattioli's triangular superspeedway, delaying many activities. Finally, teams began practice Friday at noon. However, practice was soon cut short by more poor weather, and the beginning of the first qualifying session was also moved back. When qualifying began, only five cars were able to make their timed runs, and Johnny Benson's Pennzoil Pontiac was the fastest as rain again swept the circuit.

(Left) Pole-winner Mark Martin sets up for Pocono's turn one on the outside of fourth-place starter Geoff Bodine (7). Morgan Shepherd tucks in behind Martin after starting the race from the second position, his best start of the season so far. Mark led the most laps during the day, but fell to ninth at the finish. (Below) Ricky Rudd (10) is chased by Ken Schrader (25), Ernie Irvan (28) and Greg Sacks (29) through turn three. Rudd, who hung around the leaders all day, took the point on lap 162 after a two-tire stop, but couldn't hang on and finished second.

pushing him down the start/finish straight. The pole was his second of the season, and his career third at Pocono.

Morgan Shepherd had the best qualifying run of the season for the Remington Ford, although it was almost three-tenths of a second slower than Martin's lap, and he claimed the outside of the front row. Bobby Labonte and Geoff Bodine were lined up in the second row for the start of the race. Pontiacs grabbed the third row as Ward Burton claimed the fifth spot and Benson sat alongside him. Ricky Rudd and Dale Earnhardt were paired in the fourth row, while Jeff Burton and Derrike Cope turned in strong runs to take the final spots in the top 10, ahead of Lake Speed and Elliott.

The delayed qualifying session turned out to be the only one of the weekend for the NASCAR Winston Cup teams. With 41 cars in the garage area and four provisionals available, everyone made the field. Robert Pressley and Darrell Waltrip used provisionals, as did Hut Stricklin, who crashed his primary car during the qualifying session and went to a backup Circuit City Ford. Michael Waltrip, who qualified 24th, did so in his backup Citgo Ford after damaging his primary car during Friday's abbreviated practice session.

There are few races Rusty Wallace likes to win more than those sponsored by Miller, the same name he carries on his

Fords. It just seems like it should be that way, Wallace tells people. "We sure don't like it when a Coors or a Bud car takes home the Miller trophy," Wallace said with a grin. "We want to do it ourselves; keep it in the family."

For the longest time during the running of the Miller 500, it appeared that Wallace wouldn't have to worry about toting the trophy to the airport. Martin had blasted away at the drop of the green, and appeared to have the best car in the field for the first three-quarters of the race. He gave up the lead only while shuffling through green-flag pit stops, and it wasn't until the second caution period of the afternoon — on lap 161 — that the field had a chance to catch its breath and see if anyone could challenge the Valvoline Ford.

It took a problem on pit road to breathe new life into the other teams. A lug nut jammed in an air wrench during the Martin pit stop, enabling the crew to change only right-side tires. It meant that Mark was back on pit road a lap later to have the left-sides changed, costing him valuable track position. With three more cautions in the final 40 laps of the race, the field remained bunched and Mark was unable to work his way back to the point.

Martin's problems turned into good fortune for Wallace, whose crew made several adjustments in air pressure in the

to fight his own battle for second with a fast-closing Dale Jarrett. Rudd eased across the line in second, just a half-second ahead of Jarrett, while Ernie Irvan hammered his way home to fourth place, giving Ford a 1-2-3-4 finish and only the seventh victory for the Blue Oval teams in the first 17 races of the season.

Benson made his fine qualifying lap stand up all the way to a fifth place, the best of his young NASCAR Winston Cup career, while Sterling Marlin came home sixth. Jeff Gordon, who entered the race 116 points behind NASCAR Winston Cup point leader Terry Labonte, struggled through an oil leak during the race, but finished seventh, ahead of Lake Speed, Martin and Derrike Cope. Geoff Bodine was 11th, the final car on the lead lap at the conclusion of the event.

four new Goodyears they bolted onto the Miller Ford. Rusty emerged for the restart behind Ricky Rudd, who had taken right-side tires to move into the lead, and it took Wallace only five laps to work his way past Rudd to the point.

The final restart came with just 14 laps remaining, and Rusty nailed the throttle, easing away from Rudd and Jeremy Mayfield, who was fighting to regain a lost lap. Ricky lost touch with Rusty, who was able to roll to his fourth victory of the season. Rudd, in the closing laps, had

Gordon managed to gain some points on point leaders Terry Labonte and Dale Earnhardt. Earnhardt was scheduled to come in for a green-flag stop on lap 140, but he felt the car flutter in the third turn a lap early and headed for pit road. His crew changed tires and fueled the Chevrolet,

Rusty Wallace heads for turn one with Ken Schrader (25) and Jeff Gordon (24) hot on his tail.
Rusty took the lead for the first time on lap 171, then held on for the remaining 30 laps to score his third career win at Pocono.

Dale Jarrett and Ernie Irvan prepare for the famous "tunnel turn" at the end of Long Pond straightaway, while fans enjoy the action from a packed infield on a beautiful July afternoon in Pennsylvania's Pocono Mountains.

but when the jack dropped, the black Monte Carlo stalled on pit road. The crew jumped behind the car and began pushing, later assisted by members of several other crews farther down pit road. Finally, the Goodwrench Chevrolet fired and Dale was on his way, but he had lost a lap, and never was in a position to regain it.

Labonte struggled throughout the day with a car he said the team would never bring back to Pocono. "We just didn't have the right piece for this place this year," Terry said after the event. "This is the same car we had for the first race here and we blamed that performance on the motor.

"I really think this particular car just doesn't like this place, and we just struggled with it all day. I'm glad we don't have to come back here again, and I guarantee when we come back next year, it won't be with this car."

Earnhardt was 14th and Labonte 16th in the final rundown. For the second straight week, Jarrett had managed strong gains in the point standings — exactly what he needed to do if he was to climb back into the battle for the championship.

As the teams loaded the cars into the transporters and crew members prepared for the ride home, everyone was looking at the point standings handed out to the crews following the race.

Labonte was still at the top of the table, despite his problems, but he led Earnhardt by only 12 points. Gordon now trailed by 80 points, while Jarrett was still fourth, but had closed to 157. Rudd's second place pushed him past Sterling Marlin into fifth place in the standings, although he trailed leader Labonte by 323 markers.

The DieHard 500 at Talladega was on the horizon, and what had appeared just two races ago to be a three-horse race now had the look of a four-way free-for-all, if Jarrett could continue his torrid pace.

Pocono allows for three-abreast racing, as demonstrated by Greg Sacks (29), Terry Labonte (middle) and Wally Dallenbach. Up to five drivers can fit side by side across the track's spacious frontstretch. Labonte got the best of this trio, finishing 16th to maintain his point lead in the NASCAR Winston Cup standings.

Miller 500

Fin. Pos.	Str. Pos.	Car #	Driver	Team
1	13	2	Rusty Wallace	Miller Ford
2	7	10	Ricky Rudd	Tide Ford
3	20	88	Dale Jarrett	Quality Care / Ford Credit Ford
4	35	28	Ernie Irvan	Texaco Havoline Ford
5	6	30	Johnny Benson	Pennzoil Pontiac
6	17	4	Sterling Marlin	Kodak Film Chevrolet
7	15	24	Jeff Gordon	DuPont Refinishes Chevrolet
8	11	9	Lake Speed	Spam Ford
9	1	6	Mark Martin	Valvoline Ford
10	10	12	Derrike Cope	Badcock Ford
11	4	7	Geoff Bodine	QVC Ford
12	32	98	Jeremy Mayfield	RCA Ford
13	24	21	Michael Waltrip	Citgo Ford
14	8	3	Dale Earnhardt	GM Goodwrench Service Chevrolet
15	22	25	Ken Schrader	Budweiser Chevrolet
16	21	5	Terry Labonte	Kellogg's Corn Flakes Chevrolet
17	2	75	Morgan Shepherd	Remington Arms Ford
18	33	90	Dick Trickle	Heilig-Meyers Ford
19	28	16	Ted Musgrave	Family Channel / PRIMESTAR Ford
20	34	41	Ricky Craven	Kodiak Chevrolet
21	12	94	Bill Elliott	McDonald's Ford
22	5	22	Ward Burton	MBNA America Pontiac
23	36	37	John Andretti	Kmart / Little Caesars Ford
24	18	23	Jimmy Spencer	Camel Cigarettes Ford
25	39	33	Robert Pressley	Skoal Bandit Chevrolet
26	26	42	Kyle Petty	Coors Light Pontiac
27	16	11	Brett Bodine	Lowe's Ford
28	29	71	Dave Marcis	Prodigy Chevrolet
29	38	29	Greg Sacks	Cartoon Network Chevrolet
30	23	1	Rick Mast	Hooters Pontiac
31	19	78	Randy MacDonald	Diamond Rio Ford
32	40	8	Hut Stricklin	Circuit City Ford
33	27	15	Wally Dallenbach	Hayes Modems Ford
34	14	87	Joe Nemechek	Burger King Chevrolet
35	9	99	Jeff Burton	Exide Batteries Ford
36	25	81	Kenny Wallace	Square D / T.I.C. Ford
37	3	18	Bobby Labonte	Interstate Batteries Chevrolet
38	30	77	Bobby Hillin	Jasper Engines / Federal-Mogul Ford
39	31	43	Bobby Hamilton	STP Pontiac
40	41	17	Darrell Waltrip	Parts America Chevrolet
41	37	14	Jeff Green	Racing For Kids Chevrolet

DieHard 500

*When the NASCAR Winston Cup tour arrived at Talladega, the Interstate Batteries team unveiled this special paint job honoring current team owner and former head coach of the Washington Redskins Joe Gibbs, who was inducted into the NFL Hall of Fame. Driver Bobby Labonte had a strong showing on the superspeedway and finished eighth. **(Right)** As the shadows grow in the late Alabama afternoon, Jeff Gordon leads Dale Earnhardt, Mark Martin and Wally Dallenbach through Talladega's tri-oval. Gordon and Earnhardt diced back and forth in a classic duel throughout most of the race, but when the sun finally set, Gordon had captured his sixth victory of the season and taken over the point lead.*

Despite five victories this season, defending NASCAR Winston Cup Champion Jeff Gordon had been unable to take over the point lead, and as the teams waded through the Centennial Olympic Games traffic in Atlanta on their way to the mammoth Talladega Superspeedway, Gordon was in third place in the standings, 80 points behind Hendrick Motorsports teammate Terry Labonte.

Gordon's victories had come in fits and starts — a win at Richmond, back-to-back wins beginning two races later at Darlington and Bristol, and a Dover win six races later, followed with a triumph in the first Pocono race.

The consistency he and his Rainbow Warriors were looking for seemed to be in Labonte's camp, where Terry had been masterful through the first half of the season. The Texan had won only once — at North Wilkesboro — but was working on a string of 10 top-five finishes in the first 17 races, including five second places. The strength of the Kellogg's Chevrolet was obvious to everyone in the garage area, and more often than not, Labonte was near the front or challenging for the victory at the finish of each race. That's the stuff champions are made of.

If Gordon and Labonte were determined to win their

second NASCAR Winston Cups, then consider Dale Earnhardt and his quest for his eighth title.

It was almost time for the stretch run for the title, when the best prepared teams would come to the front — and Earnhardt was already there. Although he had won just twice this season, early in the year at Rockingham and at Atlanta, the black Monte Carlo was a constant threat for victory, and he was right where he wanted to be — within 12 points of Labonte and ready to pounce like a hungry lion. Earnhardt was the odds-on favorite among those in the garage to claim the championship when it came down to nail-biting time.

He had been there too many times before not to win the championship, some said, while others simply looked into Dale's steely blues and marveled at the focus he had held all season. When it came to the Goodwrench bunch, there was no question about the dedication of either the driver or the team. There was little horseplay around the garage. This group was on a mission.

Not to imply that the Rainbow Warriors and the Kellogg's Crew weren't as focused, or as dedicated. But the hunger for the championship was almost palpable near the stall

where the black Monte Carlo was parked.

Back-to-back strong finishes by Dale Jarrett and his Quality Care Thunderbird had pulled him back into contention for his first championship, but most conceded that he was still a long shot. Although he had made big gains, Jarrett trailed by 157 points, and he needed to continue those gains for the remainder of the season if he wanted a piece of the big pie. One look told observers that he did — but he needed another break or two to get back into a real dogfight for the title.

As teams prepared their mounts for the first qualifying session during the steamy July afternoon in Alabama, garage observers walked by No. 18, looked, and then did a double take. The usual black-and-green livery of Bobby Labonte's Interstate Batteries Chevrolet had a different look this week. The car was painted in the burgundy and gold of the NFL's Washington Redskins, in honor of team owner Joe Gibbs, who would be inducted into the NFL Hall of Fame in Canton, Ohio, the following day.

Further down the garage, the Badcock Furniture team was making its preparations, secure in the knowledge that driver Derrike Cope had returned from an

(Right) The Wood Brothers' Citgo Ford waits for its driver, Michael Waltrip, as the dark gray clouds bringing thunderstorms move in the distance. After a rain delay of more than four hours, Waltrip strapped in for the start of the race but lasted only 16 laps before engine failure put him in last place. (Below) Ken Schrader's Budweiser Chevrolet kept a daily count of the medals won by U.S. athletes in the ongoing Olympic games in nearby Atlanta.

emergency trip to Tacoma, Wash., following his father's heart attack. After subsequent quintuple bypass surgery, his dad, Don, appeared to be doing well, and Derrike had high-tailed it back to Alabama, arriving at 4 a.m. on qualifying day.

Gordon drew one of the earliest numbers in qualifying — three — and headed onto the track, turning in the best time of the session at 191.417 mph. The DuPont Chevrolet coasted back into the garage area, the water temperature nearly pegged, and Gordon emerged from the car to wait and see if anyone in the field of 43 cars would be able to beat his lap.

He waited and waited, and waited some more. One by one, the others ran, and only Dale Jarrett approached Jeff's

Front-row starters Jeff Gordon and Jeremy Mayfield prepare to get the DieHard 500 underway. Gordon, the third driver to vie for the starting position, turned a fine qualifying lap in his DuPont machine that held up for most of the day. But late in the session, Jeremy Mayfield rocketed the RCA Thunderbird around the track to win his first career pole.

lap. Gordon, however, had looked at the practice sheets and knew that there was a red Ford still in line that could beat him, if its driver turned as strong a lap in qualifying as he had in practice.

The RCA Thunderbird rolled off the line, and when it coasted back to the garage area, Jeremy Mayfield had claimed the first Busch Pole of his young NASCAR Winston Cup career. His speed was in excess of 192.3 mph, and he was nearly a half-second faster than Gordon.

He had caught a cloud, he explained to the mass of reporters and photographers who greeted him as he slid through the window of Cale Yarborough's Thunderbird. "It probably cooled the track 10 to 15 degrees," he said, adding that the cooler air probably helped the engine in his car and provided just a tiny bit more grip through the corners.

Mayfield was delighted with the pole, which came in his 66th career attempt. But he also said that the lap had come

with the team's race motor, and he had been very concerned on the second lap (usually even faster than the first as the motors wind to full song) when the temperature gauge moved past the 260 degree mark. He and his crew were worried that the engine might have been damaged with the excessive heat.

Alongside Jarrett on the second row was Earnhardt, driving the same car Mike Skinner had run at Talladega in the

(Left) Crew chief Robbie Loomis seeks advice from two-time Talladega winner Richard Petty regarding the setup on the STP Pontiac. Their driver, Bobby Hamilton, could muster only the 37th-fastest qualifying lap, but fought his way to a 17th-place finish by the end of the race. (Below) Defending race champion Sterling Marlin leads Ward Burton (22) and Mark Martin (6) around the bottom of turn four, while Dale Earnhardt (3) and Ernie Irvan mount a challenge on the outside. Marlin and Burton were collected in Earnhardt's wreck on lap 117. Martin and Irvan continued to finish third and fourth, respectively.

Dale Jarrett ponders his current assault on the point leaders while waiting for the weather to clear. After starting third and running among the lead pack throughout the day, the race came down to a battle between himself and Jeff Gordon. Jeff took the win and Dale came in second for his third straight top-three finish.

Pontiac wheeled by Johnny Benson. It was a pairing everyone noticed — the three-time NASCAR Winston Cup champion and his Parts America Monte Carlo on the inside and the outstanding young Rookie-of-the-Year contender on the outside.

Just missing the top 10 were Dick Trickle, driving Junie Donlavey's Heilig-Meyers Ford, and Kenny Wallace, with a superb run in his Square D Ford.

Terry Labonte was struggling, qualifying 29th fastest, while Joe Nemechek was taking a long, hard look at his Burger King Chevrolet, surveying the damage caused when he cut a right-rear tire, spun and hit the third-turn wall during his second qualifying lap.

Others who struggled during qualifying were Pocono winner Rusty Wallace and Bill Elliott, whose red Ford was once the scourge of Talladega. The event marked Elliott's return to the superspeedway, where he broke his left femur during the Winston Select 500. Ricky Craven, also making a return to the track after being injured during the spring race, was likewise outside the top 25 with his qualifying lap.

Most hoped to improve on their times during the second qualifying session but never got the chance when rain eliminated the second round. The field was set according to the times posted during the first session, and Elliott, Geoff Bodine, Brett Bodine and Joe Nemechek took the four provisional spots, forcing Chad Little to load his Pontiac and head for home.

On Sunday, a steady rain greeted the tens of thousands of fans on hand for the drop of the green flag and the crews,

spring race. Lake Speed posted his best qualifying lap of the season to claim the inside of the third row for the Spam Ford. Ernie Irvan, still glowing from his New Hampshire victory, was on Lake's right, while the fourth row was occupied by Jeff Burton's Exide Ford and Mark Martin's Valvoline Thunderbird.

Darrell Waltrip had a strong qualifying run to ninth place on the grid, and on his right was the Pennzoil

(Right) Ward Burton (22) and his brother Jeff (99) team up on the outside, while Darrell Waltrip (17) drops to the low line with Lake Speed (9) in tow, sandwiching a lonely Jeff Purvis (44) in the middle. Darrell was on form in his Parts America Monte Carlo at Talladega, taking his first top-10 finish of the season.
(Below) Ricky Rudd limps back to pit road after being involved in an accident on lap 103. His crew made repairs and Ricky returned to the action, but finished a distant 37th.

Dale Earnhardt, Jeff Gordon, Dale Jarrett and Sterling Marlin lead the field as they head down the frontstretch. All four drivers took their turn at the point, with Earnhardt leading the most laps during the day.

who were going through their pre-race checklists and making the final adjustments they hoped would make the difference between victory and defeat. The time for the start of the race came and went, and teams stood huddled in the rain, waiting and waiting. So did CBS, with a four-hour window of time frittering away as the rain steadily came down in Alabama. NASCAR's weather radar showed a gap in the bands of thunderstorms, but it was very slow in its approach. It looked like the race would take place, but it would begin long after its appointed time.

Finally, four hours after the scheduled start of the race — and after CBS ran out of air time — the cars fired and headed off the line to begin the DieHard 500. Mayfield held the early lead, but another shower halted the race for 15 minutes. When the event resumed, Gordon flashed to the point and then Earnhardt took over. For the first 100 laps, it looked like Earnhardt, Sterling Marlin and Gordon had the best cars in the field.

Then, the complexion of the race changed as John Andretti lost control of his Kmart Ford and triggered a multicar accident that collected some 15 cars. The caution flag lasted until the 112th lap, and when the green dropped on the field, Earnhardt was at the point but in a pitched battle with Gordon, Irvan, Marlin and a host of others.

On lap 117, Earnhardt and Marlin were fighting for the lead when Irvan tapped Marlin on the left-rear and turned him into Earnhardt. Earnhardt, with no control, was thrown into the wall nearly instantly, and when the conflagration was finished, the Goodwrench Chevrolet had also been hit by Robert Pressley, Derrike Cope and Ken Schrader. Dale was assisted from the car and taken to the infield care facility at the track. A total of 12 cars were involved, and NASCAR officials displayed the red flag to stop the race in order to clear the debris from the track.

When the race restarted on lap 125, teams were informed by NASCAR officials that, because of the approaching darkness, the event would continue for just five more green-flag laps. Gordon was the leader at the time of the restart, but Dale Jarrett made his run at the end of the first green-flag lap, taking the point from Gordon with help from Jimmy Spencer's Ford. Then Gordon got his own boost from Jeff Burton, shot back past Jarrett and successfully blocked Dale's chances for victory.

Gordon won by just over a car-length over Jarrett, while Mark Martin came home third, beating Irvan and Spencer. Geoff Bodine finished sixth, ahead of Jeff Burton and Bobby Labonte, while Darrell Waltrip was ninth and Rusty Wallace 10th.

The victory was the first of Gordon's career at Talladega and moved him into the point lead. Earnhardt was classified 28th, and Terry Labonte, involved in the second multicar accident, was 24th after running over a tire from another car.

DieHard 500

Fin. Pos.	Str. Pos.	Car #	Driver	Team
1	2	24	Jeff Gordon	DuPont Refinishes Chevrolet
2	3	88	Dale Jarrett	Quality Care / Ford Credit Ford
3	8	6	Mark Martin	Valvoline Ford
4	6	28	Ernie Irvan	Texaco Havoline Ford
5	15	23	Jimmy Spencer	Camel Cigarettes Ford
6	40	7	Geoff Bodine	QVC Ford
7	7	99	Jeff Burton	Exide Batteries Ford
8	24	18	Bobby Labonte	Interstate Batteries Chevrolet
9	9	17	Darrell Waltrip	Parts America Chevrolet
10	32	2	Rusty Wallace	Miller Ford
11	21	71	Dave Marcis	Prodigy Chevrolet
12	18	42	Kyle Petty	Coors Light Pontiac
13	39	94	Bill Elliott	McDonald's Ford
14	36	75	Morgan Shepherd	Remington Arms Ford
15	42	87	Joe Nemechek	Burger King Chevrolet
16	1	98	Jeremy Mayfield	RCA Ford
17	37	43	Bobby Hamilton	STP Pontiac
18	10	30	Johnny Benson	Pennzoil Pontiac
19	27	41	Ricky Craven	Kodiak Chevrolet
20	12	81	Kenny Wallace	Square D / T.I.C. Ford
21	31	19	Loy Allen	Healthsource Ford
22	41	11	Brett Bodine	Lowe's Ford
23	38	95	Gary Bradberry	Shoney's Restaurants Ford
24	29	5	Terry Labonte	Kellogg's Corn Flakes Chevrolet
25	34	29	Greg Sacks	Cartoon Network Chevrolet
26	26	25	Ken Schrader	Budweiser Chevrolet
27	23	12	Derrike Cope	Badcock Ford
28	4	3	Dale Earnhardt	GM Goodwrench Service Chevrolet
29	16	4	Sterling Marlin	Kodak Film Chevrolet
30	5	9	Lake Speed	Spam Ford
31	14	33	Robert Pressley	Skoal Bandit Chevrolet
32	35	15	Wally Dallenbach	Hayes Modems Ford
33	33	22	Ward Burton	MBNA America Pontiac
34	25	8	Hut Stricklin	Circuit City Ford
35	30	77	Bobby Hillin	Jasper Engines / Federal-Mogul Ford
36	17	16	Ted Musgrave	Family Channel / PRIMESTAR Ford
37	28	10	Ricky Rudd	Tide Ford
38	11	90	Dick Trickle	Heilig-Meyers Ford
39	19	37	John Andretti	Kmart / Little Caesars Ford
40	20	44	Jeff Purvis	MCA Records Chevrolet
41	13	1	Rick Mast	Hooters Pontiac
42	22	21	Michael Waltrip	Citgo Ford

Brickyard 400

*Defending NASCAR Craftsman Truck Series Champion Mike Skinner stands ready to take the wheel of the Goodwrench Chevrolet in relief of Dale Earnhardt. His mission? To stay on the lead lap and bring home as many championship points as possible to keep Earnhardt's hopes for an unprecedented eighth NASCAR Winston Cup championship alive. At the end of the day, Skinner could honestly say, "Mission accomplished." **(Right)** Dale Jarrett gladly accepts the winner's check from PPG Industries following his come-from-behind victory in the Brickyard 400. By the time the victory lane celebration ended and all of his winnings were totaled, Jarrett had claimed more than $564,000 for his day's work behind the wheel of the Quality Care Ford.*

Three days after the conclusion of the rain-delayed and shortened DieHard 500, the garage area at the famed Indianapolis Motor Speedway echoed the rumble of the NASCAR Winston Cup cars as engine builders tuned the motors for the opening of the first practice session.

A swarm of reporters watched as Dale Earnhardt gamely walked from his motor coach to the Goodwrench Monte Carlo's garage stall. The scene was a familiar one — Earnhardt was wearing his trademark Gargoyles under his Goodwrench cap. But there the familiarity ended. Dale was dressed in street clothes, and he was headed for the garage stall to help Mike Skinner in any way possible.

The damage from the Talladega wreck had not been confined to just the black-and-silver Chevrolet. Earnhardt had a broken collar bone and a fractured sternum, and was in visible pain as he walked to the end of the garage area. Skinner, who had won last year's NASCAR Craftsman Truck Series championship for Richard Childress' team and was locked in a battle to defend that title again this year, had been selected by Childress and Earnhardt as Dale's relief driver for the Brickyard 400.

The walk from the coach to the garage was difficult for

Earnhardt in more than one way. Obviously, the pain of his injuries kept him from his usual stride, but emotionally, Earnhardt was in a lot of pain, as well. He had won the Brickyard event last year, and successfully defending that race victory had been high among the goals of both Dale and the team since the beginning of this season. Now, he would run as few laps as possible, and Skinner would try to bring home as good a finish as he could to help keep Earnhardt in contention for his eighth championship while his injuries healed.

The combination of finishes among Earnhardt, Terry Labonte, Jeff Gordon and Dale Jarrett at Talladega had scrambled the point standings. Gordon moved to the lead for the first time this year, and Labonte fell to second place, nine points behind. Earnhardt had dropped from 12 points to 23 behind Gordon and to third place, and Jarrett had used his third straight top-three finish to close to within 82 points of Jeff.

Suddenly, what had appeared to be a battle between two or three drivers just a few races ago had become a four-way tussle, and with Earnhardt injured, the other three drivers knew it was time to put as much distance as possible

between themselves and the seven-time champion. There was no doubt that when he was back on form, he would be a terror in his quest to make up lost ground.

Almost every team in the garage area had what it considered to be the best "piece" in its arsenal for The Brickyard. The purse was the largest of the season, and the prestige of winning at Indianapolis would make up for many disappointments throughout the season. Many of the teams brought brand-new cars to the track, and nearly every team had spent time testing during the summer at The Brickyard in preparation for this weekend.

Skinner had never driven around the track before, and the only time he had even been inside the track was when he played in a Chevrolet media golf tournament last August and rode his cart to the holes in the infield. Needless to say, Wednesday's practice session was exactly that for Skinner, and he turned more than 80 laps during the session. Earnhardt, trying to help Mike become acclimated to the

(Above) Jeff Gordon and Mark Martin lead the field of 40 cars under the green flag to begin the third annual Brickyard 400. (Left) Four-time Indy 500 winner A.J. Foyt entered the Brickyard 400, but failed to run fast enough to make the field and was forced to watch as the NASCAR Winston Cuppers took the track at "The House that Foyt Built."

tricky track in any way possible, was at the side of the car every time Skinner came back to the garage stall, offering advice, listening to Skinner's comments, and sharing the chassis setup.

Thursday, Earnhardt zipped himself into his driver's suit, and with some help from several doctors, including ESPN's Dr. Jerry Punch, wormed his way into the cockpit for a few practice laps prior to qualifying. Heavily padded, Dale ran no more than he needed to and when the first qualifying session moved onto the track, he responded with a lap that earned him the 12th starting position in the field. It was a remarkable performance and underscored the fierce determination that has marked his career since its beginning.

There was little question who the crowd favorite was when it came to qualifying, and hometown hero Jeff Gordon responded with a lap that blistered his competition. He had not been near the top of the speed charts for either practice session prior to qualifying, but his lap of more than 176.4 mph brought a roaring cheer from the tens of thousands of fans on hand for qualifying. Mark Martin was on the outside of the front row with a very strong lap

(Above) Johnny Benson (30) slips past Joe Nemechek on his way to the front of the field. Nemechek was a pleasant surprise in qualifying when he turned the sixth-fastest time in the first round.
(Left) Benson joins fellow Pontiac driver and seventh-row starter Kyle Petty on a parade lap during driver introductions. Benson had an outstanding race in his first Brickyard start – he led the most laps and finished eighth. *(Below)* Brett Bodine (11) is chased by Bobby Labonte (18), Dale Jarrett (88), Greg Sacks (29) and Jeff Burton (99) as the huge crowd of more than 300,000 looks on.

of more than 175.9 mph, but there was no one who could measure up to Gordon as he won his second straight pole for the Brickyard 400.

Lake Speed turned another sterling qualifying effort, grabbing the inside of the second row away from Ken Schrader's Budweiser Chevrolet, while Bobby Hillin startled the garage-watchers with his fifth-fastest lap, just a tick

quicker than another surprising qualifier, Joe Nemechek. Bill Elliott and Rick Mast, who won the pole for the first Brickyard 400, made up the fourth row, while Terry Labonte and Greg Sacks, in the Cartoon Network Chevrolet, claimed the final positions in the top 10. Then came Sterling Marlin and Earnhardt, just ahead of Kyle Petty and Johnny Benson. Dick Trickle claimed the final qualifying position in the top 25, relieving himself and his team of the worry of having to make the field during the second qualifying session.

With 48 cars on hand, the second session was a long, huge drama, with every lap turned and every split second lost determining who made the field for the richest race of the year — and who went home to watch the event on ABC-TV. Eight of the 24 drivers stood on their times from the first session, and the remainder tried to race their way into the field.

Gary Bradberry became the Busch Pole second-round bonus winner and took the 26th spot on the grid. Ricky Craven was the only driver who stood on his time and failed to make the field, and he was forced to use a provisional — as was Dave Marcis. Ron Barfield, Jason Keller, Randy MacDonald, Jeff Purvis, Stacy Compton, Robby Faggart, A.J. Foyt and Steve Seligman were forced to watch their cars being loaded into the transporters after failing to make the field. Purvis was perhaps the most frustrated. He had

(Above) One of Sterling Marlin's crew members begins to look over the damage to the Kodak Chevrolet as a wrecker delivers it to the garage area after Sterling and Kyle Petty tangled on the frontstretch. The car was beyond repair and Sterling was credited with 39th place. *(Left)* Dale Earnhardt is in good spirits as he jokes with Geoff Bodine before the race (inset). Mike Skinner, who took the wheel in relief for Earnhardt, gets past Bobby Hamilton as he works his way from the back of the pack to a very respectable 15th-place finish.

appeared to be working on a lap that would have easily placed him into the field with his Phoenix Racing Chevrolet, but he slipped and scrubbed the wall, and his disappointment was evident when he climbed from the red-and-white Chevrolet in the garage area.

Hillin, Nemechek and Bobby Hamilton also found the wall, with Hillin and Hamilton forced to go to their backup cars hastily pulled off the trucks. Nemechek's damage was mostly cosmetic, and his crew fell to work, beating out the right side of the Burger King Chevrolet. The new paving added at The Brickyard since last August's race had raised the speed ante some five miles per hour, and several drivers found their cars a handful in the banzai qualifying laps.

Unlike last year, race day for the Brickyard 400 was splendid, just the kind of weather Earnhardt would have enjoyed while fighting for the victory. This time, however, he headed for pit road when Robert Pressley received a tap from Michael Waltrip and spun, and the caution flag flew for the first time in the race. Earnhardt managed to get out of the Chevrolet, and Skinner, after putting the steering

wheel back on and pulling the belts tight, set out to accomplish his team's goal — a top-15 finish. Earnhardt was emotionally wired, having to vacate his office so early in the race — and it took him a couple of minutes to be able to respond to questions for the telecast from longtime friend Jerry Punch.

Gordon and Mark Martin fought for the point, but Jeff's hopes for a second silver brick ended when he cut a right-front tire and drilled the concrete. He limped the DuPont Chevrolet back to the pits, and his crew affected repairs, but Gordon was out of the running.

The scene shifted at the front of the pack, with Kyle Petty running to the point with his Coors Light Pontiac, and then yielding it to a hot-running Johnny Benson, whose Pennzoil team used two-tire stops to push him to the front of the field early in the race. Petty then also cut a tire and smacked the fourth-turn wall, bouncing off into the path of Sterling Marlin. Kyle was taken to Methodist Hospital but, after an examination, returned to the track.

Benson was all alone at the front, the clean air a perfect tonic for his bright yellow Pontiac. His crew worked through the pit stops flawlessly, keeping him at the front with two-tire stops and setting the example for many of the other teams. Track position was critical, and passing was extremely difficult for the equally matched cars in the lead pack. Any advantage gained on pit road meant a great deal.

Finally, Benson and his team made a slight mistake during a late caution-flag pit stop, and he fell back to 13th for the restart. Ernie Irvan and Dale Jarrett had worked their way toward the front, and when the green flag fell, Terry Labonte had his Kellogg's Chevrolet at the point, with Rudd right behind, and Jarrett was leading Irvan. This formation lasted less then 10 laps, and Jarrett moved to the point with Irvan in hot pursuit. Ernie went by his teammate just four laps later, and the two Robert Yates Racing Fords began a brilliant duel that would last the remainder of the race. Ernie appeared headed for the victory, but Jarrett hung less than a car-length behind, worrying the Californian and looking for a single, tiny slip that would open the door.

The door finally opened with just six laps to go, when Ernie dove just a little too hard into the corner. Like a cobra, Jarrett struck, yanking his Ford left and nailing the accelerator. He drew even, and then ahead as Ernie regained control of the Havoline Ford. Once in the clean air at the front, Jarrett was in command. He rolled to the victory and added the silver brick to the Daytona 500 and Coca-Cola 600 trophies he already had gained this year.

Behind Irvan, Labonte beat Martin for third place, and

Dale Jarrett waves to the crowd as he takes the checkered flag (under caution) after slipping past Ernie Irvan in the closing laps of the Brickyard 400. His fourth straight top-three finish moved Dale into third place in the point standings and established the "88" team as a serious contender going into the stretch run for the championship.

Morgan Shepherd turned in a strong run to claim fifth, ahead of Rudd and Rusty Wallace. Benson recovered for eighth place, and led the most laps in the race, making it very clear that he would be a factor in events to come in his young career. Rick Mast and Bill Elliott filled out the top-10 positions.

Gordon was classified 37th in the final rundown, and Skinner ran a steady race to 15th, on the lead lap, in his workmanlike effort to help his Childress teammate.

The victory was a huge one for Jarrett and the Yates team, and Irvan's second place made the finish even sweeter for the entire Yates effort. To finish 1-2 in an event as prestigious as the Brickyard 400 was enormous testimony to the work done throughout the year by the entire organization. Jarrett's win marked the first time a Ford had gone to victory lane in the three years of the Brickyard 400 race.

Brickyard 400

Fin. Pos.	Str. Pos.	Car #	Driver	Team
1	24	88	Dale Jarrett	Quality Care / Ford Credit Ford
2	15	28	Ernie Irvan	Texaco Havoline Ford
3	9	5	Terry Labonte	Kellogg's Corn Flakes Chevrolet
4	2	6	Mark Martin	Valvoline Ford
5	38	75	Morgan Shepherd	Remington Arms Ford
6	35	10	Ricky Rudd	Tide Ford
7	17	2	Rusty Wallace	Miller Ford
8	14	30	Johnny Benson	Pennzoil Pontiac
9	8	1	Rick Mast	Hooters Pontiac
10	7	94	Bill Elliott	McDonald's Ford
11	28	99	Jeff Burton	Exide Batteries Ford
12	20	23	Jimmy Spencer	Camel Cigarettes Ford
13	3	9	Lake Speed	Spam Ford
14	36	12	Derrike Cope	Badcock Ford
15	12	3	Dale Earnhardt	GM Goodwrench Service Chevrolet
16	4	25	Ken Schrader	Budweiser Chevrolet
17	18	15	Wally Dallenbach	Hayes Modems Ford
18	16	8	Hut Stricklin	Circuit City Ford
19	27	37	John Andretti	Kmart / Little Caesars Ford
20	29	7	Geoff Bodine	QVC Ford
21	21	16	Ted Musgrave	Family Channel / PRIMESTAR Ford
22	22	11	Brett Bodine	Lowe's Ford
23	25	90	Dick Trickle	Heilig-Meyers Ford
24	23	18	Bobby Labonte	Interstate Batteries Chevrolet
25	19	98	Jeremy Mayfield	RCA Ford
26	5	77	Bobby Hillin	Jasper Engines / Federal-Mogul Ford
27	6	87	Joe Nemechek	Burger King Chevrolet
28	30	21	Michael Waltrip	Citgo Ford
29	26	95	Gary Bradberry	Shoney's Restaurant Ford
30	34	33	Robert Pressley	Skoal Bandit Chevrolet
31	37	43	Bobby Hamilton	STP Pontiac
32	10	29	Greg Sacks	Cartoon Network Chevrolet
33	31	81	Kenny Wallace	Square D / T.I.C. Ford
34	39	41	Ricky Craven	Kodiak Chevrolet
35	40	71	Dave Marcis	Prodigy Chevrolet
36	32	22	Ward Burton	MBNA America Pontiac
37	1	24	Jeff Gordon	DuPont Refinishes Chevrolet
38	13	42	Kyle Petty	Coors Light Pontiac
39	11	4	Sterling Marlin	Kodak Film Chevrolet
40	33	17	Darrell Waltrip	Parts America Chevrolet

The Bud at The Glen

Terry Labonte attacks the Watkins Glen road course with abandon, bolstered by the fact that, on the strength of his third-place finish at Indy, he had once again topped the point standings. Now the cool Texan was on a hot streak and, with his considerable road racing skills, was poised to extend his lead over a wounded Dale Earnhardt. **(Right)** *Geoff Bodine was both elated and relieved after his victory at the track just a few miles from his boyhood home of Chemung, N.Y. His last win came at North Wilkesboro in October 1994, 55 races ago.*

Jeff Gordon's nightmare 37th-place finish at Indianapolis after a cut tire forced him into the wall had wreaked havoc on the defending NASCAR Winston Cup champion's point lead, and when the teams arrived in beautiful upstate New York for the running of The Bud at The Glen, Gordon found himself on the outside looking in.

He had entered Indianapolis Motor Speedway at the top of the point ladder, won the pole and hoped to have a special birthday celebration by winning his second Brickyard 400 in three years. Instead, he was back to fourth in the standings, 104 points behind new leader (and Hendrick Motorsports teammate) Terry Labonte.

On the strength of his third place at The Brickyard, Terry had moved back into the lead, and held a 61-point margin over Dale Earnhardt. At Indy, relief driver Mike Skinner did exactly what was asked of him behind the wheel of the Goodwrench Chevrolet. Skinner came home in 15th place and kept Earnhardt in the middle of the point race while he recovered from his Talladega injuries.

Dale Jarrett's victory, combined with the finishes of the other three title contenders, had pulled him even closer to

the front of the pack. He now trailed Earnhardt by just two points, and was only 63 behind Labonte. Four consecutive top-three finishes, coupled with problems by the other drivers, brought Jarrett back from near oblivion to a challenging position.

The Glen's annual speed celebration once again extended into the cities surrounding the track in the days prior to the event, and tens of thousands of fans turned out to help celebrate NASCAR Winston Cup racing's return to the Finger Lakes region of the state. Drivers signed autographs for hours, and street dances, Chamber of Commerce breakfasts and other activities made the entire week a special one for fans and competitors.

Earnhardt and Kyle Petty, whose early-race accident at Indianapolis left him bruised and sore, made their way into the garage area. Both drivers had lined up relief help in case they were unable to go the distance at The Glen, which featured right- and left-hand corners, as well as hard acceleration and braking points. NASCAR Busch Series point leader David Green was enlisted to help Earnhardt on the road course, while Todd Bodine signed on to drive Petty's Coors Light Pontiac if the third generation driver was too sore to

Budweiser
NASCAR
Winston Cup
SERIES
QVC
PYROTECT
Ford
Bud
RACING
Watkins Glen International
Bud At The Glen
NASCAR Winston Cup Series
August 11, 1996
WINNER

Johnny Benson's Pennzoil Grand Prix and Ricky Craven's Kodiak Monte Carlo ended up in the tires during pre-qualifying practice on Friday, forcing both drivers to use their backup mounts for the rest of the weekend. Benson qualified 36th and managed to salvage a 15th-place finish in the race. Craven's weekend went from bad to worse when, after starting 37th using a provisional, his engine let go on lap 61 and stranded him in 36th place.

handle driving duties at any point during the weekend.

Kyle was very emphatic about his condition, saying he had every expectation that Todd would see considerable action Sunday. "I've got bruised ribs on both sides of my body, and bruises on my right shoulder blade, my left knee and kneecap, my right knee, my right thigh and the bottom of my foot," Kyle said. "My hips hurt on both sides, my thighs and my calves hurt. I have done absolutely nothing this week. I've tried to stay put in one spot. It's hard to go up and down steps, it's hard to get out of bed. Everything I do is real slow. I just can't move quickly."

Bill Elliott also knew he would have problems at The Glen, particularly with his nearly-healed femur, broken in the May Winston Select 500 at Talladega. The Glen track tosses a driver's body back and forth in the seat no matter how well padded it is, and Bill asked road racing star Dorsey Schroeder to work with him during the weekend.

Butch Leitzinger, another road racing ace from nearby State College, Pa., was slated to drive the Cartoon Network Chevrolet for Diamond Ridge, and Mike McLaughlin hoped to make his NASCAR Winston Cup debut. "Magic Shoes" McLaughlin is from Waterloo, N.Y., just over an hour's ride from The Glen. Along with the three Bodine brothers and Leitzinger, McLaughlin gave the track a total

(Above) Dale Earnhardt discusses team strategy with David Green, who was on hand to drive in relief – if needed.
(Left) After shocking everyone with his track-record qualifying performance, Earnhardt jumped to an early lead and held it for the first third of the race, shocking everyone by refusing to yield to relief driver David Green. When the event was over, Dale had led the most laps and taken fourth in perhaps the most gritty performance in recent memory.

of five local products to promote.

A few steps further into the garage revealed that Remington Arms had renewed its sponsorship program with Butch Mock's team for the coming season, but Mock said his Fords would be driven by a different pilot. Morgan Shepherd's contract would not be renewed, and Mock hoped to name his new driver within a few weeks. Almost next door, Andy Petree said that Skoal would return as the sponsor of the "33" cars next season and that he would take over ownership of the team from Leo Jackson on October 1st. He also said that Robert Pressley's contract would not be renewed and, like

Mock, Petree hoped to be able to announce his new driver within weeks.

Each year, the high speed corners at The Glen lull drivers into a sense of security — until it's too late to recover from a mistake. The result usually is a bent machine, and during the practice session prior to the first round of qualifying, Ricky Craven, Johnny Benson and Jimmy Spencer all

(Above) When Todd joined the action, he suddenly found his brothers Brett (11) and Geoff (7), and the Brothers Bodine treated their hometown fans to some high-speed sibling rivalry. *(Left)* A bruised Kyle Petty, still sore from his accident last week at The Brickyard, wears a flak jacket to protect his ribs. Kyle was able to qualify his Coors Light Pontiac in 16th position and started the race, but gave way to relief driver Todd Bodine early in the event.

had problems that resulted in the teams readying spare cars for qualifying. Craven had further problems during qualifying, spinning out during his lap and failing to post a time in the first session.

When the qualifying period was over, the driver most people expected to win the pole was 10th — and the driver least expected to turn the fastest lap had claimed his second Busch Pole of the season.

Mark Martin, trying to win his fourth consecutive pole at The Glen, fought with his Valvoline Ford throughout the day and changes made to the car didn't produce the desired lap. Mark was on the outside of the fifth row.

On the other hand, Dale Earnhardt forgot his pain for just over 73 seconds and focused intently on the lap at hand. As a result, he set a new track record and grabbed his third career pole at Watkins Glen, the 22nd of his career. It was the surprise of the weekend. The broad smile under his trademark mustache lit up the press room following his lap.

It was another example of his determination to remain a factor in the point race, and it prompted admiring glances and awestruck remarks from many of his peers. It was a typical Earnhardt performance.

Jarrett made it an "all-Dale" front row with his lap, although it was more than two-tenths of a second off Earnhardt's pace. Ricky Rudd and Terry Labonte, two of the best road racers among the NASCAR Winston Cup ranks, claimed the second row, with Jeff Gordon and Rusty Wallace, another road course hot shoe, setting up shop in the third row. Ernie Irvan and Michael Waltrip made up the fourth row, while Joe Nemechek was alongside Martin.

Ken Schrader and Brett Bodine barely missed the top 10,

(including the 1987 IROC round and the 1986 Camel Continental GTO class with Jack Baldwin), Geoff Bodine had never won a NASCAR Winston Cup event in front of his home fans at The Glen. Raised just 30 miles down the road from the track, Geoff has long been one of the favorites here, and he harbored hope that one day he would claim victory in The Bud at The Glen.

Bodine was working on a 55-race winless streak, and Martin was seeking to "four-peat" after winning three consecutive Glen events. Most fans in the $1, $2 and $5 pools in the camping areas were encouraged when they pulled the number 6 from the passed cap, while those who drew number 7 frowned, figuring they had "donated" their money to the cause.

This, however, would be Geoff Bodine's homecoming party. He and crew chief Paul Andrews had planned it for a

(Left) Ken Schrader, who was hoping to end his own winless streak by taking Budweiser to the winner's circle in their own event, took the point on lap 68 and held it for 15 laps before yielding to eventual winner Geoff Bodine. (Below) Geoff Bodine fends off the challenges of point leaders Dale Earnhardt (3), Terry Labonte (5) and Jeff Gordon (24) in the closing laps of the race. His experience at The Glen, combined with sound pit strategy, created the right formula for success.

and Kenny Wallace was the final first-day qualifier. In the second round of qualifying, Bobby Hillin claimed the fastest lap of those who ran and grabbed 26th place, and Craven's troubles continued when he pulled onto pit road before taking the green flag for his lap. One look under the hood and the car was pushed back to the garage, forcing Craven to use a provisional to make the field. Morgan Shepherd and Dave Marcis were the other provisional starters. Elliott found the thrashing in the McDonald's Ford too much for his leg, and he handed his car over to Schroeder for the weekend. Dorsey qualified 19th and Leitzinger 17th, while Petty managed to wrestle himself into his Pontiac long enough to post the 16th-fastest lap.

Although he had won races at The Glen in the past

week, feeling they had lost their chance for a strong finish and perhaps a victory at The Brickyard by spending too much time on pit road. This would be a two-stop race. No more, no less. They would stick by the plan no matter what happened on the track and see where the cards fell at the end of the event.

For the longest time during the race, it didn't seem to matter what Bodine and Andrews had up their sleeves for the QVC Ford. Earnhardt, eschewing any assistance from relief driver Green, tucked himself into the Goodwrench Chevrolet and set sail on the field — at one time building his lead to more than 2.5 seconds.

Then halfway through the race, Bodine began rolling out his strategy, and it started to work for the QVC team. On

Richard Petty's STP Pontiac, with driver Bobby Hamilton aboard, sports a commemorative paint scheme used only once in Richard's illustrious career. Just days after signing with STP in January 1972, Petty, without time to add STP red to his already Petty-blue Plymouth, opened the season on the road course at Riverside in an all-blue car decorated with STP logos. Richard started second and went on to win his first race with the company and began an association that has lasted for 25 years.

lap 47, the third caution of the event flew from the flag stand, and all the lead-lap cars headed for pit road — except for Bodine. He remained on the track, taking over the point, trying to extend his window until he needed to make just one more stop. Despite the fact that the rest of the leaders had new tires on their cars, Geoff managed to keep them at bay, proving he could run against their new tires on his worn Goodyears. It was a lesson that immediately taught him that his car was good enough to win — if he continued his strategy and the breaks came his way.

On lap 62, his window arrived. Bodine pitted under green for tires and fuel, and when he returned, Earnhardt was back in the lead — but only until he pitted when the fourth caution came out on lap 64. At that point, many of the leaders headed for pit road, but Bodine remained on the track, lining up ninth for the restart and then chopping his way through the field to close on leader Ken Schrader. Geoff followed him for almost 10 laps, and then finally made his move in a place where longtime Glen watchers had never seen it done before.

Heading up into the narrow esses, Geoff drew alongside Schrader and the two cars bumped, sending Geoff sideways. He then recovered to take the lead. It was a gutsy move, one many Formula One drivers wouldn't dare take in their glory years at The Glen. It was the wrong angle, the wrong place, the wrong move, and there was no recovery room if it was needed. No one would have done it. But Geoff did. And he made it stick.

It put him into the lead, and when Schrader faded, Terry Labonte moved up to challenge but failed by just a few car-lengths. Bodine had achieved his dream in a strategic effort that had worked against the odds.

Martin came home third, failing to win his fourth straight, while Jeff Gordon soldiered around to finish fourth, ahead of Bobby Labonte and Earnhardt. Michael Waltrip, Nemechek, Shepherd and Wally Dallenbach claimed the final positions in the top 10, but Earnhardt's drive rated just as many headlines as Bodine. Dale had gone all the way in the race, and came home in sixth place as he desperately tried to protect his second place in the point standings. Jarrett, who finished in 24th place as the final car on the lead lap, took a big point hit after four straight top-three finishes.

Bodine's victory was hugely popular in front of the enormous crowd at The Glen, and as he celebrated with his team in victory lane, those who had tucked away the slip of paper with the number 7 on it headed to the pot to collect their winnings.

The Bud at The Glen

Fin. Pos.	Str. Pos.	Car #	Driver	Team
1	13	7	Geoff Bodine	QVC Ford
2	4	5	Terry Labonte	Kellogg's Corn Flakes Chevrolet
3	10	6	Mark Martin	Valvoline Ford
4	5	24	Jeff Gordon	DuPont Refinishes Chevrolet
5	14	18	Bobby Labonte	Interstate Batteries Chevrolet
6	1	3	Dale Earnhardt	GM Goodwrench Service Chevrolet
7	8	21	Michael Waltrip	Citgo Ford
8	9	87	Joe Nemechek	Burger King Chevrolet
9	38	75	Morgan Shepherd	Remington Arms Ford
10	31	15	Wally Dallenbach	Hayes Modems Ford
11	27	4	Sterling Marlin	Kodak Film Chevrolet
12	22	16	Ted Musgrave	Family Channel / PRIMESTAR Ford
13	19	94	Dorsey Schroeder	McDonald's Ford
14	12	11	Brett Bodine	Lowe's Ford
15	36	30	Johnny Benson	Pennzoil Pontiac
16	32	12	Derrike Cope	Badcock Ford
17	18	9	Lake Speed	Spam Ford
18	28	17	Darrell Waltrip	Parts America Chevrolet
19	33	23	Jimmy Spencer	Camel Cigarettes Ford
20	17	29	Butch Leitzinger	Cartoon Network Chevrolet
21	23	99	Jeff Burton	Exide Batteries Ford
22	29	98	Jeremy Mayfield	RCA Ford
23	16	42	Kyle Petty	Coors Light Pontiac
24	2	88	Dale Jarrett	Quality Care / Ford Credit Ford
25	11	25	Ken Schrader	Budweiser Chevrolet
26	15	37	John Andretti	Kmart / Little Caesars Ford
27	24	1	Rick Mast	Hooters Pontiac
28	39	71	Dave Marcis	Prodigy Chevrolet
29	26	77	Bobby Hillin	Jasper Engines / Federal-Mogul Ford
30	20	33	Robert Pressley	Skoal Bandit Chevrolet
31	25	81	Kenny Wallace	Square D / T.I.C. Ford
32	21	22	Ward Burton	MBNA America Pontiac
33	6	2	Rusty Wallace	Miller Ford
34	3	10	Ricky Rudd	Tide Ford
35	7	28	Ernie Irvan	Texaco Havoline Ford
36	37	41	Ricky Craven	Kodiak Chevrolet
37	35	8	Hut Stricklin	Circuit City Ford
38	30	43	Bobby Hamilton	STP Pontiac
39	34	90	Dick Trickle	Heilig-Meyers Ford

GM Goodwrench Dealer 400

Dale Jarrett and his team knew that their assault on the leaders in the championship point standings suffered a setback last week at The Glen. To get back in the hunt, they needed to perform well at Michigan – and they did. Here, the Quality Care crew gives Jarrett another superb pit stop, helping him secure his fourth win of the season and keeping his championship bid alive.
***(Right)** Jeff Burton proudly displays his first career Busch Pole Award after turning a fast lap of 185.395 mph on the two-mile Michigan oval. Jeff ran well during Sunday's race and obtained his eighth top-10 finish of the season.*

Dale Earnhardt's gutsy performance at The Glen, leading the first half of the event and going all the way to a sixth-place finish despite still suffering from his injuries received at Talladega, had kept him right in the thick of the battle for the NASCAR Winston Cup championship. When he arrived at Michigan International Speedway for the GM Goodwrench Dealer 400, he had his eyes set on his first victory since the spring.

Like Wallace at Pocono just a few weeks before, Earnhardt had extra incentive to win this race. His car sponsor was the event bankroller, and the last thing Earnhardt and Richard Childress' team was interested in was seeing a Ford in victory lane at the conclusion of a GM-sponsored race. Plus, a Goodwrench trophy would look great back home mixed in with the black-and-silver Goodwrench cars.

Earnhardt trailed Terry Labonte by 76 points after The Glen, losing just a few to Terry in the frantic last laps. Jeff Gordon had slipped to 119 behind but was now in third place. The 24th place that Dale Jarrett claimed at The Glen sent him spiraling backward to 147 behind after he had fought so hard to get back into contention with his string of

top-three finishes.

Still, there was a third of the season remaining to be contested, and anything could happen — just look at the results of the last four races!

During the week between The Glen and Michigan, Kyle Petty simply couldn't stand the pain any longer, and drove himself to a hospital near his Trinity, N.C., home. When the exams and X-rays were complete, Kyle found he had five broken ribs, a fractured shoulder blade and severely bruised muscles in his back and abdomen. It was clear he would not be racing at Michigan. When he arrived at the track, he found his Coors Light Pontiac in the garage stall and his crew standing around with nothing to do — and no driver for the car.

SABCO crew members began strolling through the NASCAR Busch Series garage area, asking drivers if they could spare some extra time to help the team. Most drivers were too involved in the NASCAR Busch Series point battle, and their car owners wouldn't let them take a chance in a NASCAR Winston Cup race. Others were unable to make the deal for one reason or another.

Kyle finally zipped up his driver's suit and struggled

that the team would run a second effort beginning in 1997. Team owner Larry McClure said he was talking with several potential sponsors and a short list of drivers, including Rick Mast.

The big news, however, belonged to the SABCO team. Owner Felix Sabates told the media he had signed Indy racing star Robby Gordon to replace Kyle in the Coors Light entry, beginning with the 1997 season. Gordon has been one of the drivers in the Ford pipeline for years, and the question of what kind of cars Felix would field for Gordon brought immediate speculation. Sabates answered the question in general terms, saying the team would campaign General Motors equipment in 1997.

One of the favorites to win the pole for the Michigan race was Bobby Labonte, who had swept both events at Roger

Pictures of concentration. (Top) Ernie Irvan focuses his attention as he waits for the start of the GM Goodwrench Dealer 400. The weekend marked the second anniversary of the accident that nearly took his life, and after a win and nine top fives in this, his comeback year, a win at Michigan would taste ever so sweet.
(Right) Wally Dallenbach's competitive fire is evident in his expression. Bud Moore's Fords with Wally at the controls had not performed up to expectations so far this season, and he was hoping to begin a turnaround this weekend.

through the window of the car, if for no other reason than to make sure the car was together when a driver finally was found. Kyle ran just a couple of laps, and then eased his way out of the car, white-lipped from the pain. Eventually, Jim Sauter became the driver for the weekend and Kyle became a spectator.

Bill Elliott was back behind the wheel of the McDonald's Ford, sure his healing leg could take the minimal stress of the short race on the wide two-mile oval. Dale Earnhardt also was determined to go the distance again, hoping for another strong finish to remain in the hunt for his eighth championship.

Ricky Craven and his wife Cathleen became parents for the second time on Monday after The Glen, welcoming their first son, Richard Everett, into the world. Also, the long-awaited date for the new California Speedway, under construction near Los Angeles, was announced for June 22 next season.

Other news that greeted the crews working in the garage area included an announcement by Square D that it had extended its sponsorship program with the FILMAR team and Kenny Wallace, tying the three entities together until the turn of the century. Morgan-McClure Racing gave credence to the rumors that had been circulating for weeks

Penske's immaculate facility the year before. Labonte did his best, but came up just a tick of the watch short. He stepped from the Interstate Batteries Chevrolet and walked over to the Exide Ford where he congratulated Jeff Burton on winning the first pole of his NASCAR Winston Cup career. They had battled on the NASCAR Busch Series tracks on their way to the NASCAR Winston Cup level, and now both had won poles in the most competitive form of the sport.

For Burton, the Michigan accomplishment was vindication for what he said was the biggest nightmare of his life — failing to make the field at Atlanta in the spring. He had arrived at the track in Georgia last March in second place in the point standings, but because his was a new team, he had no provisionals to use that early in the season. He and the Exide team had to load their Ford into the transporter and watch the Atlanta race on television.

The Thunderbird that claimed the Michigan pole was the same car that had failed at Atlanta, and Burton and his Jack Roush teammates were ecstatic with their accomplishment.

The second row went to Mark Martin and a surprising Dick Trickle, giving the boys on ESPN's SportsCenter something special to talk about that evening. Right behind the Martin/Trickle row were Bobby Hamilton, with the fastest Pontiac in the field, and Sterling Marlin in his Kodak Chevrolet. Of the four championship contenders, Jeff

Gordon had the best qualifying lap, taking the seventh-fastest lap and just beating Darrell Waltrip. Lake Speed and Michael Waltrip claimed the final top-10 positions, just ahead of Robert Yates Racing teammates Dale Jarrett and Ernie Irvan.

Earnhardt qualified 16th, but Terry Labonte didn't have the same good luck that his younger brother did during the first qualifying session. Terry was 22nd on the grid, while Wally Dallenbach claimed the final first-day position and would start 25th. Derrike Cope, hoping to secure another top-10 start, had his motor come apart during his qualifying run.

(Left) Dale Earnhardt drops his black Monte Carlo to the inside of Terry Labonte along Michigan's frontstretch as Bobby Labonte and Jeff Burton trail the action. After his superhuman effort last week at Watkins Glen, no one, not even point leader Labonte, doubted Earnhardt's resolve to climb back into the championship fight. *(Below)* On the opening lap, Dick Trickle (90) blasted out of his fourth-place starting spot and shot around front-row starters Jeff Burton (99) and Bobby Labonte (18) to take an early lead. Trickle led the first two laps and looked like a contender until his engine let go before mid-distance.

Dale Jarrett (88) drives past Rusty Wallace (2) and Lake Speed (9) while Dale Earnhardt (3) and Bobby Hamilton (43) look for an opening in the early stages of the race. Rusty ran well until the engine in his Miller Ford failed on lap 77. Lake led seven laps but his day ended when he was involved in an accident. Earnhardt looked competitive, but spun in the late going and finished 17th. Hamilton remained on the lead lap throughout the race, but was never in contention for the win.

After Jimmy Spencer claimed the second-day Busch fastest lap bonus, Jason Keller and Ron Hornaday Jr., who was mounted in Dale and Teresa Earnhardt's NASCAR Winston Cup car, failed to make the field after not posting fast enough qualifying laps. Jeremy Mayfield, the pole-winner at Talladega just three races ago, used a provisional to get into the field, as did Greg Sacks and Mike Wallace. Sacks was in the Cartoon Network Chevrolet, and Wallace drove the TriStar Ford.

Friday evening, following the pole-winning effort by Burton, crew chief Buddy Parrott and several of the Exide crew members were eating dinner in the same restaurant where Buddy's son Todd, Dale Jarrett's crew chief, and some of the Quality Care group were eating. Father warned son to be ready on Sunday "because our car is really good and we're going to give you a real butt-kicking." The good-natured jibe brought an "I don't think so" from Todd, and everyone was laughing as they left the restaurant.

Sunday, it was the younger Parrott who had the last laugh.

Despite Mark Martin's race-long dominance as he sought his first victory of the season, the race came down to a battle between the Valvoline Ford and the Quality Care Thunderbird. Victory in the "Back Yard 400" at Michigan is very important to the teams because it is the final time the cars compete on the manufacturers' home turf. The warmth of the win lasts long into the gray, dreary winter in Detroit.

As the laps wound down, it was clear that a Ford was going to win the GM Goodwrench 400, but the question remained whether it would be Martin's or one of the Robert Yates' Thunderbirds.

Martin led the final restart, with Jarrett and Irvan lined up behind him. For most of the race, Jarrett's car had been better on long runs rather than on short sprints. The final green flag came out with 11 laps to go, and Mark thought he might have victory in sight for the first time this year.

Jarrett had other ideas. He found a high groove in the first and second turns that allowed his Ford to free itself up just enough to get a run at Martin. By keeping his red-white-and-blue Thunderbird pinned to the bottom of the track in the third and fourth turns, Jarrett would be able to command the race if he could get past Martin.

Bill Elliott (94) and Ricky Rudd (10) look for a way past Mark Martin, but Mark was having none of it. His Valvoline Ford was dominant, leading 135 of 200 laps, including 88 after the halfway point. Mark's bid for his first victory of the season ended in disappointment, however, when Jarrett slipped past with only seven laps remaining in the race.

Todd Parrott and Dale Jarrett display their well-deserved Michigan trophies in victory lane. After working with the car throughout the race, adjusting it on every visit to pit road, they hit the combination at the perfect time. Jarrett took his first lead with seven laps remaining in the race and held on to take the checkered flag.

The chance came with just seven laps left in the race, and Dale drove to the outside of Martin heading down the frontstretch. He remained outside the Valvoline Ford in the first turn and then pulled ahead slightly while exiting the second turn. From there on, all he needed to do was mirror drive, making sure he had the track blocked, and his fourth victory of the season would go into the books.

He was able to make it work, and Martin had nothing to challenge with. Jarrett pulled away to win by a couple of car-lengths, while Martin held off a charging Terry Labonte and Irvan for second place. Jeff Gordon came home fifth, ahead of Bobby Labonte, and Johnny Benson posted yet another solid finish with a seventh place in the Pennzoil Pontiac, the highest-placed Grand Prix in the final results. Ricky Rudd was eighth, and Jeff Burton came home ninth, beating Jimmy Spencer for the spot.

Trickle, who had bolted to the lead on the first lap and then ran with the leaders for the first third of the race, fell victim to engine problems and finished 38th, but it had been a pleasure for everyone in the garage area to see Junie Donlavey's Ford running at the front.

Earnhardt, who never led the race, was classified 17th after he collided with Ken Schrader late in the race. The black Chevrolet spun and slid down the frontstretch into the infield grass, but Dale recovered and finished on the lead lap. He lost points, however, to the three others battling for the point lead.

Jarrett had needed a good finish after his Glen problems, but the victory did little to help him gain points. With Labonte third and Gordon fifth, Jarrett still found himself facing an uphill climb to reach a fighting position for the championship.

Crew members give Bill Elliott some help to return the McDonald's Ford to the race track. Elliott stayed on the lead lap, but never found the chassis combination to put him up among the leaders. He was listed 14th at the end of the day.

GM Goodwrench Dealer 400

Fin. Pos.	Str. Pos.	Car #	Driver	Team
1	11	88	Dale Jarrett	Quality Care / Ford Credit Ford
2	3	6	Mark Martin	Valvoline Ford
3	22	5	Terry Labonte	Kellogg's Corn Flakes Chevrolet
4	12	28	Ernie Irvan	Texaco Havoline Ford
5	7	24	Jeff Gordon	DuPont Refinishes Chevrolet
6	2	18	Bobby Labonte	Interstate Batteries Chevrolet
7	19	30	Johnny Benson	Pennzoil Pontiac
8	23	10	Ricky Rudd	Tide Ford
9	1	99	Jeff Burton	Exide Batteries Ford
10	26	23	Jimmy Spencer	Camel Cigarettes Ford
11	28	75	Morgan Shepherd	Remington Arms Ford
12	29	7	Geoff Bodine	QVC Ford
13	5	43	Bobby Hamilton	STP Pontiac
14	21	94	Bill Elliott	McDonald's Ford
15	18	25	Ken Schrader	Budweiser Chevrolet
16	32	1	Rick Mast	Hooters Pontiac
17	16	3	Dale Earnhardt	GM Goodwrench Service Chevrolet
18	38	41	Ricky Craven	Kodiak Chevrolet
19	14	77	Bobby Hillin	Jasper Engines / Federal-Mogul Ford
20	39	98	Jeremy Mayfield	RCA Ford
21	30	42	Jim Sauter	Coors Light Pontiac
22	8	17	Darrell Waltrip	Parts America Chevrolet
23	34	16	Ted Musgrave	Family Channel / PRIMESTAR Ford
24	27	12	Derrike Cope	Badcock Ford
25	10	21	Michael Waltrip	Citgo Ford
26	33	8	Hut Stricklin	Circuit City Ford
27	17	87	Joe Nemechek	Burger King Chevrolet
28	31	11	Brett Bodine	Lowe's Ford
29	41	19	Mike Wallace	Healthsource Ford
30	40	29	Greg Sacks	Cartoon Network Chevrolet
31	15	37	John Andretti	Kmart / Little Caesars Ford
32	9	9	Lake Speed	Spam Ford
33	6	4	Sterling Marlin	Kodak Film Chevrolet
34	25	15	Wally Dallenbach	Hayes Modems Ford
35	24	22	Ward Burton	MBNA America Pontiac
36	35	97	Chad Little	Sterling Cowboy Pontiac
37	13	81	Kenny Wallace	Square D / T.I.C. Ford
38	4	90	Dick Trickle	Heilig-Meyers Ford
39	20	2	Rusty Wallace	Miller Ford
40	37	71	Dave Marcis	Prodigy Chevrolet
41	36	33	Robert Pressley	Skoal Bandit Chevrolet

Goody's Headache Powder 500

Rusty Wallace blows by Derrike Cope (12) under the lights at Thunder Valley. Rusty lit up the track all night long, leading 353 of 500 laps including the last 161 to take his fifth win of the season. The victory was also his sixth career win at the track where he scored his first ever NASCAR Winston Cup victory in 1986. **(Right)** *As the final third of the season got underway at Bristol, Ricky Rudd was looking for, and beginning to find, the performance and consistency he expects from himself and his team. Rudd finished ninth at Bristol, his fifth top-10 in the last seven starts, and sat solidly in sixth place in the point standings.*

The stretch run for the title actually had been going on for some time, but the night race at Bristol has traditionally been the event that gets everyone psyched about the battle for the championship.

Teams had been racing every weekend since the Talladega event and would continue to be busy from now until Charlotte in a brutal grind comprised of 14 straight races before a free weekend. With four of those 14 events in the book, crew members were already beginning to look a bit worn around the edges. The championship contenders would be weeded from the pretenders in this stretch of races, and despite the long hours and weekly preparation, all of the drivers knew the test was upon them.

Survive, run well in this string of events — and the championship might come calling. Let up for a single minute, lose focus or concentration — and the chance for the crown would be gone.

Even though the crew members looked worn, Bristol Motor Speedway certainly did not. Purchased earlier in the year by Speedway Motorsports, Inc., the track was in the middle of a huge renovation that would eventually change the appearance of the half-mile and increase its seating capacity beyond what even the wildest dreamer had thought possible a year before. Gone was the hill on the backstretch. Over one million cubic yards of dirt and rock had been moved to fill in the steep drop behind the third and fourth turns. Now, the ground behind the turns was level to the top of the concrete wall, and new grandstands would be built on a site that previously had not been suitable to build on.

From the main entrance to the restrooms, concession stands, parking lots and walkways, the track was changing daily, and new General Manager Jeff Byrd asked fans to "pardon the dust" and give his crews the time they needed to complete the project. It would be worth it, he promised, and from what was already visible, Bristol would be totally different when the teams arrived for the 1997 spring event.

On the day practice opened, President Bill Clinton approved new regulations regarding tobacco products and triggered an angry wave of protest from millions of sports fans across the country. The news from Washington overshadowed Butch Mock's announcement that Rick Mast had signed on to drive his Remington Arms Fords, replacing Morgan Shepherd at the conclusion of this season. That announcement also took Mast out of the running for the

(Above) The grid starts off at the newly-named Bristol Motor Speedway as a television crew sends the excitement into living rooms across the nation. Saturday night racing at Bristol each August has become one of the most popular events on the NASCAR Winston Cup tour. (Left) Mike Wallace sits patiently in the GM Goodwrench pit in case he is called upon to drive in relief for the injured Dale Earnhardt. Despite the fact that Bristol is one of the most physically demanding tracks on drivers, Mike held little hope of climbing into the "3" car after witnessing Earnhardt's recent performances.

Terry Labonte appeared ready to take over command of the point race. His third place at Michigan, coupled with Hendrick Motorsports teammate Jeff Gordon's fifth place, had stretched Labonte's lead to 134, while Gordon moved into a tie for second place with Dale Earnhardt. Dale Jarrett's victory kept him in fourth place but, despite the win, he was still 137 points behind. Jarrett needed a few more wins, in conjunction with poor finishes (out of the top 10) by his rivals, to pull within striking distance of Labonte. Picking up five or ten points a race just wasn't going to get the job done.

For the last three events at Bristol, Mark Martin had found a way to put his Valvoline Ford on the pole for the event. He had been fast in practice for this year's second race at Bristol but was not at the top of the speed sheets. He knew that if he was to win a fourth consecutive pole, he needed to find something more in the car than he had shown during the practice sessions.

Crew chief Steve Hmiel and Mark conferred, and decid-

proposed second team from Morgan-McClure Racing, sending car owner Larry McClure scrambling to find a driver for the new team.

When Bobby Hillin moved from pit road to the track for the first practice session, a new crew chief was donning his headset for the "77" team. Troy Selberg, who left Mock's team earlier this year, had replaced Mike Hillman at Jasper Motorsports.

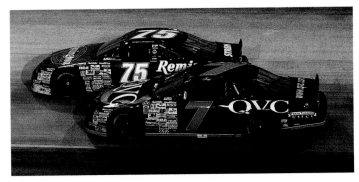

Geoff Bodine (7), revitalized after his win at Watkins Glen two weeks ago, pulls up on Morgan Shepherd, who works the outside groove in the early stages of the race. Bodine's enthusiasm was quashed when his QVC Ford developed an oil leak before mid-distance and sent him to the garage. He finished in last place. Shepherd survived the race but finished 19th, five laps off the pace.

ed not to try a drastic change on the Ford for the timed laps. Setups the team had used before had made the Thunderbird ultrafast, so the two turned to the notebooks and set the car up for qualifying the way it had been previously, and Mark rumbled out onto the track.

Just over 15.3 seconds later, he was back under the flag, and a huge roar greeted him as he climbed through the window of the Thunderbird. His lap was a mere .033 seconds faster than the time posted by Jeff Gordon, and when everyone had run, Mark had won his fourth straight Busch Pole at Bristol.

It wasn't an easy one, he admitted after the race. He had driven the Ford right on the edge of being out of control and was a "little shaky" as he emerged from the car. He said

he knew the lap was fast, but didn't know if it was good enough. "I was just relieved that we hadn't wrecked," he remarked.

In the second row, Terry Labonte and Ricky Craven, who had recently witnessed the birth of his second child, claimed the third and fourth qualifying spots, while Rusty Wallace and Michael Waltrip were right behind with their Thunderbirds. Kenny Wallace celebrated his 33rd birthday with the seventh-fastest lap, barely beating Ernie Irvan, and Dale Jarrett and Ken Schrader locked up the fifth row, ahead of Sterling Marlin and Geoff Bodine.

Dick Trickle snagged the final position in the first round, and John Andretti was the fastest of the second-round qualifiers, claiming the Busch prize money. Bobby Hamilton, Jeremy Mayfield, Derrike Cope and Chad Little, driving the Cartoon Network Chevrolet, used provisionals, and Bill Elliott chose to use a former champion's provisional to put

(Left) Terry Labonte makes a final adjustment to his rearview mirror – a critical piece of equipment at Bristol – before pulling off pit road from his third starting spot to begin the race. The current point leader scored his fourth consecutive top-five finish, but still lost ground to Gordon and Jarrett in the standings.
(Below) Brett Bodine (11) tries to follow Dale Earnhardt past Joe Nemechek (87) on the high banks. Earnhardt had problems throughout the race, including a brush with the wall and an overheating engine, but hung on to finish 24th.

Dale Jarrett (88) overtakes Jim Sauter, driving the Coors Silver Bullet for the second straight race while Kyle Petty recovers from the injuries he sustained at Indianapolis. Sauter had a rough night at Bristol and finally retired in 31st place after being involved in a accident. Jarrett drove to fourth place in the race and moved past Earnhardt to third in the point standings.

his McDonald's Ford in the field. Elliott decided discretion was the better part of valor, and chose not to subject his healing leg to the stress of 500 laps around Bristol. When Bobby Hillin failed to make the field, Elliott asked him to drive the red-white-and-gold Ford in the race. Hillin was pleased to accept and started shotgun on the field.

Martin led the field away from the flag under the lights Saturday night, but by the 10th lap, Gordon had fought his way past Mark and went on to lead the first fifth of the race. Behind him, Rusty Wallace had his Miller Ford on song, and after he finally moved to the front for the first time on lap 100, it became clear that Wallace had the right combi-

nation in his Ford to lead at will.

And lead he did. Nothing Gordon or any of the others in the field had for Wallace worked, and Rusty simply drove away from the field, dominating the race and administering a good thrashing to his competitors. He moved to the point for the last time on lap 340, and led the final 161 laps of the race. Wallace was brought back into contact with the field only through the appearance of two caution flags.

This night was his, and he registered his sixth career win at Bristol — the 46th of his NASCAR Winston Cup career. The win also marked his fifth victory of the season. After beating Gordon by six-tenths of a second, Wallace said his crew's selection of shocks and springs — unlike any combination they had run on the high-banked half-mile before — had been the perfect choice, allowing him to run wherever he needed to on the track.

Gordon finished second and Martin was a fighting third

(Right) Kenny Wallace (81) slips past a spinning John Andretti. Bobby Labonte (yet to enter the picture) was right behind but not as lucky as Wallace. Labonte couldn't avoid the Kmart car and the resulting accident put both drivers out for the night.
(Below) Pole-winner Mark Martin, who won this race in 1993, felt that this would be the night to score his first win in 1996. Starting on the outside of the front row, Jeff Gordon was also looking for a win – his seventh of the season. Both drivers led at some point during the race, but neither one could challenge Rusty Wallace for the win.

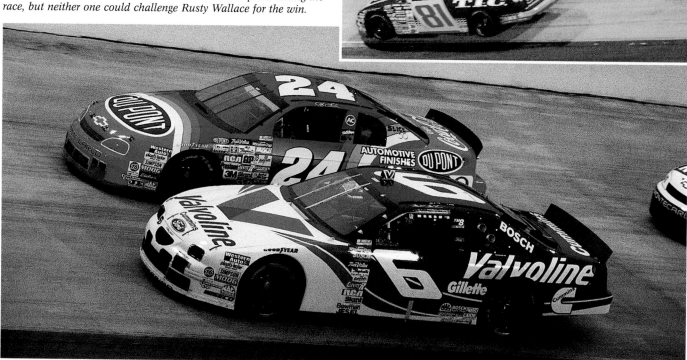

Ernie Irvan watches the action from his perch on a tire as the Texaco crew fixes his damaged Thunderbird after it was involved in an accident. Ernie returned to the race and was running at the end, but was listed 36th, 130 laps down.

in the final rundown as he continued to search for his first victory of the year. Mark's finish matched the same position he had posted in the spring event here and helped move him into fifth place in the point standings.

Dale Jarrett worked his way to fourth place, but he lost points to Gordon on the way. Terry Labonte was fifth, and Jarrett was beginning to shake his head. Here he was, finishing in the top four almost every race, and he simply couldn't close the gap on Gordon and Labonte because they finished in the top five week after week. It was getting frustrating for the Yates team.

Michael Waltrip and Jimmy Spencer both turned in extremely impressive runs with their Fords, while Ward Burton shook off the poor luck that had plagued him and his MBNA team all season, and came home eighth. Ricky Rudd and Bobby Hamilton claimed the final top-10 positions and were the only remaining cars on the lead lap at the conclusion of the 500 laps.

Where was Dale Earnhardt? He was struggling to a 24th-place finish. On lap 212, Dale and Lake Speed collided, and Earnhardt scraped the side of his car on the wall. Three laps later, leader Rusty Wallace went by, lapping the black Chevrolet. Dale tried to keep the car going on the track, but lost two more laps just after the halfway point of the race.

His crew finally got a chance to work on the car during the fifth caution flag of the night (on lap 268), but there were more problems with the Chevrolet. The fan had stopped working and the engine was overheating, and the team tried to cool off the engine with water from a hose. Almost immediately a valve stuck open, and water began spewing everywhere.

Dale ended up 24 laps behind, and it was evident from the expression on his face that he was none too happy with the entire situation. It marked the sixth time in the last seven races that he had been further back in the field than 12th place, and it cost him a bundle of points in the point chase — points he could not afford to lose with just nine races remaining in the season.

Dale fell to 198 points behind leader Terry Labonte, and although he admitted that he was not back to 100 percent, his frustration was showing. Entering Talladega, he had been just 12 points behind point leader Labonte and looked poised as the odds-on favorite to win his eighth championship. Now he was scratching and clawing, trying to stay within reach of the leader until he was fully healed and able to make a final, last-ditch effort to win the title.

Gordon's second place moved him to within 114 points of Labonte in the point battle, and Jarrett's fourth with a bruised Ford put him 13 points behind Jeff. Wallace may have claimed the headlines at Bristol, but for Gordon, Labonte and Jarrett, the war for the title now turned to Darlington.

Goody's Headache Powder 500

Fin. Pos.	Str. Pos.	Car #	Driver	Team
1	5	2	Rusty Wallace	Miller Ford
2	2	24	Jeff Gordon	DuPont Refinishes Chevrolet
3	1	6	Mark Martin	Valvoline Ford
4	9	88	Dale Jarrett	Quality Care / Ford Credit Ford
5	3	5	Terry Labonte	Kellogg's Corn Flakes Chevrolet
6	6	21	Michael Waltrip	Citgo Ford
7	15	23	Jimmy Spencer	Camel Cigarettes Ford
8	21	22	Ward Burton	MBNA America Pontiac
9	13	10	Ricky Rudd	Tide Ford
10	35	43	Bobby Hamilton	STP Pontiac
11	20	17	Darrell Waltrip	Parts America Chevrolet
12	28	16	Ted Musgrave	Family Channel / PRIMESTAR Ford
13	10	25	Ken Schrader	Budweiser Chevrolet
14	19	11	Brett Bodine	Lowe's Ford
15	7	81	Kenny Wallace	Square D / T.I.C. Ford
16	26	9	Lake Speed	Spam / Melling Ford
17	36	98	Jeremy Mayfield	RCA Ford
18	11	4	Sterling Marlin	Kodak Film Chevrolet
19	16	75	Morgan Shepherd	Remington Arms Ford
20	17	8	Hut Stricklin	Circuit City Ford
21	4	41	Ricky Craven	Kodiak Chevrolet
22	39	94	Bobby Hillin	McDonald's Ford
23	38	29	Chad Little	Cartoon Network Chevrolet
24	23	3	Dale Earnhardt	GM Goodwrench Service Chevrolet
25	32	15	Wally Dallenbach	Hayes Modems Ford
26	25	90	Dick Trickle	Heilig-Meyers Ford
27	24	71	Dave Marcis	Prodigy Chevrolet
28	29	30	Johnny Benson	Pennzoil Pontiac
29	37	12	Derrike Cope	Badcock Ford
30	27	95	Gary Bradberry	Shoney's Restaurants Ford
31	33	42	Jim Sauter	Coors Light Pontiac
32	22	18	Bobby Labonte	Interstate Batteries Chevrolet
33	31	33	Robert Pressley	Skoal Bandit Chevrolet
34	14	87	Joe Nemechek	Burger King Chevrolet
35	30	1	Rick Mast	Hooters Pontiac
36	8	28	Ernie Irvan	Texaco Havoline Ford
37	18	99	Jeff Burton	Exide Batteries Ford
38	34	37	John Andretti	Kmart / Little Caesars Ford
39	12	7	Geoff Bodine	QVC Ford

Mountain Dew Southern 500

Jeff Gordon douses himself with cold water after climbing from his car in Darlington's victory lane, while wife Brooke and crew chief Ray Evernham congratulate him on his win. Á la Richard Petty in 1966 and '67, once Jeff found the key to the storied superspeedway, he unlocked the door to three straight wins. (Right) Bobby Labonte (18) leads Jeff Gordon (24) and Hut Stricklin (8) as the trio prepares to put a lap on Dale Jarrett midway through the race. Note the flattened right side of Jarrett's car, damage sustained when he slapped the wall after slipping in oil on lap 46 while in the lead.

The journey had begun in February in Daytona when Dale Jarrett and crew chief Todd Parrott combined to win the Daytona 500, giving the new Robert Yates team, its sponsors and its crew a triumph in the "Super Bowl" of the sport.

In the Winston Select 500 at Talladega in May, the Ford Quality Care and Red Carpet Leasing team almost took the second step toward the Winston Select Million, the $1 million bonus posted by Winston to a driver able to win three of the four selected events in the program in a single year. Jarrett failed to win the race by a hairsbreadth, coming home a challenging second to Sterling Marlin.

At Charlotte, Jarrett and his team did take the second step toward the Million, winning the Coca-Cola 600 in the day-into-night race and putting themselves in the position to claim the bonus with a victory in the Mountain Dew Southern 500.

It all sounds so simple. Win three of four events and take home the pot of gold. But, in reality, it may be the hardest prize to win in any sport. With competition at its highest level in history, it is difficult to win even one race on the NASCAR Winston Cup tour. Furthermore, attempting to win at Daytona, Talladega, Charlotte or Darlington presents a different challenge than the other races because of the degree of difficulty each of the four tracks presents to the teams. To win two of those events in a season is a great accomplishment. To win three of the specified races in a single year is monumental. That's why the Winston Select Million rates so high with drivers and teams. Claiming the bonus clearly puts a driver head and shoulders above his peers.

Only one driver has won the award since it began in 1985 — Bill Elliott grabbed it the first time it was offered. Since then, several drivers have won two of the four select races and the $100,000 consolation prize, but no one has been able to claim the million-dollar check.

This year, it was Jarrett's opportunity to chase the Winston Select Million, and his Robert Yates Racing team had done its work, testing at venerable Darlington and fine-tuning the red-white-and-blue Thunderbird until it had turned the fastest laps of the pre-event testing. Jarrett and the team were ready for the challenge when they arrived at the tricky track.

While teams were preparing to qualify for the Darlington

NASCAR officials broke from tradition and announced the 1997 season schedule during the Darlington weekend. Normally, the schedule is not released until the December NASCAR Winston Cup awards banquet, but with the additions and changes to the schedule for the coming season, teams and fans needed to begin making hotel reservations. The new schedule included dates for Texas and California, as well as a second date for New Hampshire. Talladega had received its wish to be moved from the late July date. The DieHard 500 will now be held in mid-October, offering fans and teams a break from the sweltering, sauna-like conditions of Alabama in July.

(Above) Dale Jarrett's helmet bears a million dollar bill with his likeness, signifying his opportunity to win The Winston Select Million with a Southern 500 victory. Jarrett showed every intention of taking the coveted prize when he won the pole and drove to an early lead in the race. Lady Luck did not smile on him, however, and Winston's bonus money went up in smoke. (Right) The only winner of the million-dollar prize is Bill Elliott (right), who discusses the handling of his McDonald's Ford with crew chief Mike Beam. Elliott won the $1 million in 1985, the first year it was offered.

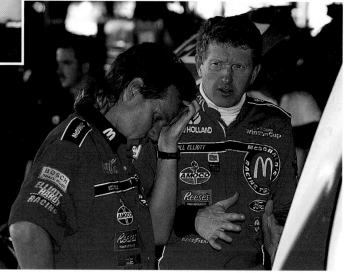

race, rumors swept through the garage area that one of the first "trades" in the history of the sport was about to occur — John Andretti and Jeremy Mayfield were switching rides. It was clear that the Kranefuss/Haas team wanted Mayfield for the 1997 season and that Jeremy was headed for the Kmart car. Cale Yarborough had considerable interest in Andretti, who was almost a perfect choice because he resides in Indianapolis, home to sponsor RCA. No one was saying much, but by the end of the weekend, word had been obtained that the trade would indeed take place, beginning with the next event at Richmond.

While the schedule was being made available, teams were checking the practice times and finding that Jarrett and his Ford were right at the top of the list. Dale's pre-event testing speeds had been carried into practice, and he became one of the favorites to win the pole for the event.

As he belted into the Ford, crew chief Parrott leaned inside the car and told Dale that he had been watching others on the track as they tried to post fast laps prior to Jarrett's run. Parrott said drivers were attacking the first turn too hard, causing their cars to wash up the track slightly and keeping them from jumping back into the throttle quickly. Jarrett nodded his understanding, reached over, flicked the ignition switch and headed out for his lap.

Jarrett heeded Parrott's advice and let his Ford roll into the corner, carrying more speed than it had during practice. When the car took its set in the first turn, Jarrett was already back in the throttle. He blasted out of the second turn, and then was careful with the third and fourth turns, squeezing the accelerator just enough to carry his speed but not enough to send him into the fourth-turn wall. He

John Andretti (left) and Jeremy Mayfield seem pleased about their impending "trade," but it's obvious new uniforms will have to be ordered! It had been rumored that the driver switch would take place after the season, but both teams decided to get a jump on 1997 by making the move in the coming week at Richmond.

flashed across the line, and the tactic had worked. He had won his second career NASCAR Winston Cup pole — just barely — over Jeff Gordon.

Gordon, winner of last year's Mountain Dew Southern 500 and the spring TranSouth 400 this year, thought he had the Busch Pole with his lap, but he was .017 seconds behind Jarrett. Still, Gordon had displayed that he had a mount ready to run at the front of the pack.

Geoff Bodine's fine effort resulted in the third-fastest lap, while Ken Schrader and Sterling Marlin put their Chevrolets fourth and fifth on the list. Mark Martin had another strong run to claim the outside of the third row, while Chad Little gave the Cartoon Network Chevrolet a strong starting spot with the seventh-fastest lap, just ahead of Terry Labonte's effort. Rick Mast was in the fastest Pontiac during the first round of qualifying and Hut Stricklin had a great lap to qualify 10th, ahead of an equally

(Right) Lake Speed, driving his Spam Thunderbird, takes a peek to see if there is enough room to get by Geoff Bodine's QVC Ford. The two drivers went in opposite directions over the course of the race as Bodine qualified third and jumped to an early lead but faded to a 21st-place finish. Speed, on the other hand, started back in 37th position but drove to 10th by the end of the event. *(Below)* The Valvoline crew hustles through a green-flag pit stop in a bid to score their first win of the season. Mark Martin, the 1992 Southern 500 winner, finished third – the team's sixth consecutive top-five finish.

impressive time posted by Derrike Cope. Dale Earnhardt's lap was just a tick behind Cope's.

Bobby Hillin claimed the final position during the first day, while Ward Burton's qualifying lap came to an abrupt end when he smacked the fourth-turn wall, causing a brief fire. Ricky Rudd, awaiting his qualifying run, was one of the first over the pit wall to help Ward out of his wrecked MBNA-sponsored Grand Prix. Joe Nemechek also banged the wall between the first and second turns, and was unable to complete his lap.

Burton returned the next day with another car and posted the fastest time of the second-round qualifiers, grabbing the Busch second-day bonus. Jeff Burton, winner of the Michigan pole, was forced to use a provisional to make the field, as were Ricky Craven, Kyle Petty and Robert Pressley. Nemechek failed to make the field as well, but because others ahead of him used all the available provisionals, the Burger King Chevrolet was loaded into the transporter for the trip back to the shop. Jay Sauter, driving Felix Sabates' second Pontiac, also failed to qualify, as did Randy

Jimmy Spencer considers his car's setup for Sunday's race. Apparently, his thoughts were well directed: Jimmy led three times for 69 laps and looked as though he would contend for victory until a cut tire caused him to spin and hit the wall while leading the race.

MacDonald in his Diamond Rio Ford.

From the drop of the green flag at Darlington, Jarrett looked set to chase down the bonus. He led the field under the flag stand and took command of the race, seemingly on cruise control until the 46th lap. Then he slipped in some oil dropped by another car, and the Thunderbird was instantly into the wall. His dream of joining Bill Elliott in the elite Winston Select Million winner's club was gone. His crew worked frantically to repair the damage and he was able to return to the track three laps down. He went on to make up one of those laps before the event ended.

At that point, it appeared that Jimmy Spencer was headed for victory lane. He kept his Smokin' Joe's Thunderbird comfortably at the point for the bulk of the next 120 laps, but his hopes for victory disappeared in a cloud of tire

During the second half of the event, Hut Stricklin (inset) was overpowering in the Stavola Brothers' Circuit City Ford. (Below) With the laps winding down in the race, Jeff Gordon stalks the leader, looking for an opportunity to slip by. Stricklin's Thunderbird, on the verge of overheating, could not hold off the defending champion and yielded the lead with 15 laps to go. Hut finished second in an outstanding performance.

Jeremy Mayfield (98) was determined to end his tenure with Cale Yarborough Motorsports on a high note, and it appeared he might do just that until he hit a spinning Earnhardt and suffered a premature end to his day. Bobby Hamilton was able to avoid the incident and continued on his way to a 19th-place finish. Earnhardt also continued, but suffered yet another setback in his championship hunt with a 12th-place finish.

smoke. Spencer spun and hit the second-turn wall, losing a lap he could never regain.

Then, the race became the Hut Stricklin show. Hut and the Stavola Brothers' Circuit City Thunderbird had struggled at times during the season, but on this wonderful fall afternoon at the pioneer superspeedway, the Alabama native took the crimson Thunderbird to the point and appeared ready to win his first career NASCAR Winston Cup event.

But Gordon was hardly out of the hunt. He and Stricklin traded the lead back and forth during green-flag pit stops, and after the final stop, Stricklin seemed to have the measure of the DuPont Chevrolet. He eased past Gordon and began to pull away slightly, building a two-second lead.

Just as Stricklin began practicing his trophy acceptance speech, the handling began to go away and the engine began to overheat in the Circuit City Ford. As it did, Gordon applied what he had been saving in the Chevrolet. Bit by bit, car-length by car-length, Gordon narrowed the gap, finally pulling onto Stricklin's rear bumper with 37 laps remaining in the race. Jeff stalked the Ford for 11 laps — looking here, searching there, trying to find the weakness he needed to exploit.

He finally found it on lap 352 and zipped past Stricklin. As Hut's problems mounted, Gordon pulled away and finally won by just over five seconds — an eternity in the highly competitive world of NASCAR Winston Cup racing.

Stricklin managed to finish second, ahead of Martin and Schrader, with Andretti fifth in his final appearance in the Kmart Ford. Bobby Labonte and Ernie Irvan were sixth and seventh, ahead of Marlin, Elliott and Lake Speed.

Where were the other championship contenders? Jarrett was classified 14th, and Dale Earnhardt hit the wall but fought his way to 12th place, two laps behind. Terry Labonte ran in the top five throughout the afternoon until the final 100 laps, when his Kellogg's Chevrolet developed an oil leak, sending a plume of smoke out behind the car and forcing Terry to pit road for repairs. He was unable to get back up to full speed once he returned to the track, and fell to 26th in the final rundown.

The victory made Gordon only the second driver in the history of the storied track to win three consecutive events at Darlington. Only Dale Earnhardt had accomplished the feat before, and it gave Gordon three wins in just eight career starts at the track.

More importantly to the defending NASCAR Winston Cup champion, the combination of finishes between the DuPont and Kellogg's Chevrolets had moved Gordon to within 24 points of Terry Labonte's championship lead.

Mountain Dew Southern 500

Fin. Pos.	Str. Pos.	Car #	Driver	Team
1	2	24	Jeff Gordon	DuPont Refinishes Chevrolet
2	10	8	Hut Stricklin	Circuit City Ford
3	6	6	Mark Martin	Valvoline Ford
4	4	25	Ken Schrader	Budweiser Chevrolet
5	15	37	John Andretti	Kmart / Little Caesars Ford
6	21	18	Bobby Labonte	Interstate Batteries Chevrolet
7	13	28	Ernie Irvan	Texaco Havoline Ford
8	5	4	Sterling Marlin	Kodak Film Chevrolet
9	26	94	Bill Elliott	McDonald's Ford
10	37	9	Lake Speed	Spam / Melling Ford
11	27	30	Johnny Benson	Pennzoil Pontiac
12	12	3	Dale Earnhardt	GM Goodwrench Service Chevrolet
13	14	81	Kenny Wallace	Square D / T.I.C. Ford
14	1	88	Dale Jarrett	Quality Care / Ford Credit Ford
15	16	27	Todd Bodine	David Blair Motorsports Ford
16	18	10	Ricky Rudd	Tide Ford
17	41	42	Kyle Petty	Coors Light Pontiac
18	25	77	Bobby Hillin	Jasper Engines / Federal-Mogul Ford
19	31	43	Bobby Hamilton	STP Pontiac
20	7	29	Chad Little	Cartoon Network Chevrolet
21	3	7	Geoff Bodine	QVC Ford
22	9	1	Rick Mast	Hooters Pontiac
23	17	23	Jimmy Spencer	Camel Cigarettes Ford
24	38	75	Morgan Shepherd	Remington Arms Ford
25	36	15	Wally Dallenbach	Hayes Modems Ford
26	8	5	Terry Labonte	Kellogg's Corn Flakes Chevrolet
27	42	33	Robert Pressley	Skoal Bandit Chevrolet
28	19	11	Brett Bodine	Lowe's Ford
29	20	16	Ted Musgrave	Family Channel / PRIMESTAR Ford
30	29	71	Dave Marcis	Prodigy Chevrolet
31	39	99	Jeff Burton	Exide Batteries Ford
32	34	17	Darrell Waltrip	Parts America Chevrolet
33	22	21	Michael Waltrip	Citgo Ford
34	11	12	Derrike Cope	Badcock Ford
35	32	95	Gary Bradberry	Shoney's Restaurants Ford
36	30	90	Dick Trickle	Heilig-Meyers Ford
37	24	98	Jeremy Mayfield	RCA Ford
38	28	2	Rusty Wallace	Miller Ford
39	33	60	Ed Berrier	Berrier Racing Ford
40	35	22	Ward Burton	MBNA America Pontiac
41	23	19	Loy Allen	Healthsource Ford
42	40	41	Ricky Craven	Kodiak Chevrolet

Miller 400

When Rusty Wallace arrived at Richmond, he unveiled this special paint scheme that he would carry for the rest of the season to commemorate Miller's 25 years in motorsports. Wallace, the favorite of many to win the race for his sponsor, was never a factor during the event. **(Right)** *Ernie Irvan raises his fist in triumph after climbing from his car in Richmond's winner's circle. Ernie, who had been a contender in the race during the last 100 laps, shot past Johnny Benson to take the lead with 18 laps to go, then held off Jeff Gordon's charge to cement his second win of the year.*

A fifth, a second and a victory in his last three outings had pulled defending NASCAR Winston Cup Champion Jeff Gordon to within 24 points of his teammate, Terry Labonte, in the battle for this year's championship. When Gordon's Rainbow Warriors unloaded the DuPont Chevrolet at Richmond, they were still basking in the glow of their driver becoming only the sixth in history (after Herb Thomas, Bobby Allison, Cale Yarborough, David Pearson and Dale Earnhardt) to win back-to-back Mountain Dew Southern 500s.

It's a good thing the DuPont team members had that victory to keep them warm because the entire Richmond area had been lashed by Hurricane Fran, with 53 mph winds, two inches of rain and a loss of power at the track on September 6 ending any hope of activity there. Power was out all over the Capital City area, and the speedway's problems were well down the power company's priority list, which needed to take care of other facilities — like hospitals — first. The track management simply shut the place down, using portable generators to run the phone system for a while.

The hurricane had also closed the airport, and many crews, along with tens of thousands of spectators, were unable to arrive for the events Friday. Thursday evening, the rain associated with the leading edge of the hurricane brought a premature end to the NASCAR Craftsman Truck Series race, and Richmond's bout with the winds and heavy rain began at approximately 4 a.m. Friday morning.

The huge storm system had turned the NASCAR Winston Cup portion of the weekend into a one-day affair, and Friday night's NASCAR Busch Series event was rescheduled for Sunday. That meant the entire grid for the Miller 400 would be determined within one qualifying period. A brief practice session would precede qualifying, with "Happy Hour" scheduled to follow and a short break for preparation of the cars for the race under the lights Saturday night.

It would be a long day for the teams and drivers, but Mark Martin made the most of the limited time, although after the 90-minute practice, he felt he had a middle-of-the-pack mount at best. Few were more surprised than Martin when the lap he turned became the Busch Pole-winning speed — his second pole in the last three races and his third in the last eight.

He said he was much more concerned about which pits

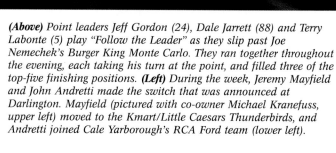

(Above) *Point leaders Jeff Gordon (24), Dale Jarrett (88) and Terry Labonte (5) play "Follow the Leader" as they slip past Joe Nemechek's Burger King Monte Carlo. They ran together throughout the evening, each taking his turn at the point, and filled three of the top-five finishing positions.* (Left) *During the week, Jeremy Mayfield and John Andretti made the switch that was announced at Darlington. Mayfield (pictured with co-owner Michael Kranefuss, upper left) moved to the Kmart/Little Caesars Thunderbirds, and Andretti joined Cale Yarborough's RCA Ford team (lower left).*

would be left to choose from when it was finally his turn to pick than his pole speed, but as it turned out, he was the second to select after reigning champion Gordon. Jeff was just a fraction of a second behind Martin and claimed the outside of the front row for the start.

Jeff Burton and Bobby Labonte grabbed the second row slots, but Labonte was disappointed, having bobbled at both ends of the track during his lap and feeling it had cost him a shot at the pole. Still, he was pleased to start from fourth place, ahead of Ward Burton and Joe Nemechek. The sixth-fastest lap, Nemechek's best qualifying effort of the season, came one week after he failed to make the field for the Mountain Dew Southern 500 at Darlington.

Bill Elliott and Dale Jarrett had their Fords on the fourth row, ahead of two more Thunderbirds driven by Ted Musgrave and Rusty Wallace. With Martin, Jeff

Dale Earnhardt sprints out of pit row as Mark Martin (6) and Ernie Irvan (28) finish up their stops. Martin surprised many, including himself, when he won the pole — his second in the last three races and his third in the last eight.

Burton and Musgrave all in the top nine, it was an outstanding performance by the teams of Jack Roush. Ken Schrader and Bobby Hamilton just missed the top 10, while Ricky Rudd, Morgan Shepherd, Hut Stricklin and Bobby Hillin used provisionals to make the field. Stacy Compton, Jay Sauter and Gary Bradberry all were unable to run fast enough in the qualifying session and were forced to watch the race from the sidelines.

The John Andretti/Jeremy Mayfield trade had been consummated, and the Richmond event marked the first race for the two drivers with their new teams. Andretti qualified 31st in the RCA Ford and Mayfield was two rows behind him, taking over the 35th starting spot in the Kranefuss/Haas Kmart Thunderbird.

While teams were working their way through the pre-race checklists, word spread through the garage that Caterpillar was stepping up its sponsorship efforts with the NASCAR Busch Series-leading team owned by Buz McCall. The team will move to the NASCAR Winston Cup level next season with driver David Green. The University of Nebraska is also due to join the NASCAR Winston Cup tour by becoming the new sponsor of Harry Melling's Cup

team, with Lake Speed behind the wheel. Spam, the team's sponsor for the past two years, will remain in the sport, but with a team yet to be announced.

The biggest whispers, however, centered on Ken Schrader and the Skoal team, soon to be owned by Andy Petree. Speculation had it that Schrader would leave the Hendrick Motorsports team (if a suitable replacement could be found to Budweiser's liking) and move over to take the seat to be vacated by Robert Pressley. Talk centered around Ricky Craven as Schrader's replacement, although no one could figure out how Craven could become a Hendrick dri-

In a battle of the beer labels, Kyle Petty blasts his Coors Light Pontiac on the inside groove as he overcomes Ken Schrader's Budweiser Chevrolet. Both teams had mediocre runs in the race, with Ken finishing 13th and Kyle coming home 18th.

ver, particularly after the announcement at New Hampshire just a few weeks ago that Ricky had become half-owner of the Larry Hedrick Kodiak team.

None of the talk mattered a few hours later when four drivers belted into their cars with championship hopes dancing in front of their eyes. While Gordon's three-race string of excellent finishes had pulled him right onto Terry Labonte's bumper, Dale Jarrett had continued to work his way back into contention, sparked by the victories at Michigan and Indianapolis. D.J. was now 91 points behind

From the drop of the green flag, it looked like Gordon had the car to beat. The defending champ blasted past Martin in the second lap and immediately began stretching out his lead. One by one, however, his challengers emerged, with two of them surprising the capacity crowd with their powerful runs. Virginian Jeff Burton stunned the crowd by running to the front with his Exide Ford — and staying there. And Johnny Benson continued to impress, moving his Pennzoil Pontiac all the way from 34th place to the point.

Most expected Gordon to be able to put away Burton

The Interstate Batteries crew works quickly to get Bobby Labonte back on the track at Richmond. Labonte, still running hot after his sixth-place finish in the Mountain Dew Southern 500 the week before, started from the outside of the second row but was unhappy with that position after he bobbled during qualifying. He went on to finish 11th.

Terry, and it appeared that he truly had become a contender for the title. On the other hand, Dale Earnhardt's hopes continued to sink into the morass. He now trailed Terry by 161 points and time was beginning to run out for the proud seven-time champion.

In addition, Chevrolet's seemingly invulnerable position at the top of the Manufacturer's Championship table had eroded over the last eight races, with Fords winning six times and tying the Bowtie Brigade with 11 wins each in the first 22 races of the year. Chevrolet, on the basis of Gordon's Mountain Dew Southern 500 victory, had pulled back into the lead after losing it at Bristol, but the difference was only a single point between the two combatants.

and Benson with the greatest of ease, but he couldn't, and the two challengers hung with the leaders throughout the evening, leading when they could and putting themselves into contention for the win. Ernie Irvan also came to the front and, by the three-quarter mark, the Texaco Ford was at the point and looking very strong, indeed.

Benson had other ideas and whistled his bright yellow Pontiac to the outside of Gordon and latched onto Irvan's bumper. During the final pit stop of the night, the Bahari crew responded with an outstanding effort, and sent Benson back onto the track in the lead.

Irvan, Terry Labonte and Gordon were lined up behind Benson on the restart, and it took just a few laps for Benson

Ernie Irvan and his Texaco Havoline Ford led the field for a total of 88 laps – including the final 19 – on his way to posting his second Richmond victory and the 14th of his career.

to realize that the chassis adjustment the team had gambled with during the final stop was the wrong one. With 18 laps to go, Irvan went past Benson. Two laps later, Gordon moved past Benson as well to resume his duel with Irvan for the victory. Johnny continued to fall backwards and eventually finished in 10th place, however, his finishing position in no way reflected the brilliant race he had driven.

Gordon gave chase, but, despite a final yellow flag in the last 15 laps, Jeff had nothing left to challenge Irvan with. Ernie held his line, diced with Gordon in the final laps, and emerged with a three-quarter car-length victory, his second win of the season. The finish had the huge throng in the grandstands on its feet, roaring its approval of the outstanding duel, and Irvan was delighted with the victory. So was Gordon, who knew that his competitors would find these kinds of finishes in the stretch run to the title impossible to beat. If he could keep finishing in the top two or three, he would be back at the head table at the NASCAR Winston Cup awards banquet in New York.

Jeff Burton was as brilliant at Richmond as Hut Stricklin had been at Darlington, and it was strange to hear the Virginian and his team complain about a third-place finish. Still, it showed the competitive spirit within the team and its driver and, although the team members were smiling, it was clear that nothing short of a victory would please them this season.

Dale Jarrett fought his way to fourth place, while Terry Labonte, blocked by slower traffic in the final laps, was not able to mount a charge that would move him any further to the front and finished fifth. He maintained his point lead — but it was now a mere four points over his teammate Gordon. For all intents and purposes, the two were deadlocked in their battle for the title.

Rusty Wallace, debuting his new paint scheme celebrating Miller's silver anniversary in motorsports, surprised everyone by never being a factor in the race and finishing sixth. Bobby Hamilton had yet another solid short-track performance in the STP Pontiac, and Derrike Cope brought the Badcock Ford home in eighth place, finally working his way past the poor racing luck that had plagued him and his team throughout the year. Martin took ninth place, ahead of Benson.

For yet another race, Dale Earnhardt fell victim to problems. The handling of his Goodwrench Chevrolet was terrible, he said succinctly after the race, noting that the car wouldn't steer where he wanted. He was lapped twice and finished 20th, the ninth consecutive race he had finished out of the top five. The last time that string had occurred was in 1983, and it was obvious that something good needed to happen very quickly for Richard Childress and his team. Dale had fallen to 218 points behind Terry Labonte, and the quicksand was getting deeper.

Miller 400

Fin. Pos.	Str. Pos.	Car #	Driver	Team
1	16	28	Ernie Irvan	Texaco Havoline Ford
2	2	24	Jeff Gordon	DuPont Refinishes Chevrolet
3	3	99	Jeff Burton	Exide Batteries Ford
4	8	88	Dale Jarrett	Quality Care / Ford Credit Ford
5	24	5	Terry Labonte	Kellogg's Corn Flakes Chevrolet
6	10	2	Rusty Wallace	Miller Ford
7	12	43	Bobby Hamilton	STP Pontiac
8	18	12	Derrike Cope	Badcock Ford
9	1	6	Mark Martin	Valvoline Ford
10	34	30	Johnny Benson	Pennzoil Pontiac
11	4	18	Bobby Labonte	Interstate Batteries Chevrolet
12	37	10	Ricky Rudd	Tide Ford
13	11	25	Ken Schrader	Budweiser Chevrolet
14	22	21	Michael Waltrip	Citgo Ford
15	9	16	Ted Musgrave	Family Channel / PRIMESTAR Ford
16	7	94	Bill Elliott	McDonald's Ford
17	30	7	Geoff Bodine	QVC Ford
18	19	42	Kyle Petty	Coors Light Pontiac
19	21	1	Rick Mast	Hooters Pontiac
20	23	3	Dale Earnhardt	GM Goodwrench Service Chevrolet
21	17	4	Sterling Marlin	Kodak Film Chevrolet
22	36	17	Darrell Waltrip	Parts America Chevrolet
23	38	75	Morgan Shepherd	Remington Arms Ford
24	39	8	Hut Stricklin	Circuit City Ford
25	26	11	Brett Bodine	Lowe's Ford
26	29	33	Robert Pressley	Skoal Bandit Chevrolet
27	15	90	Dick Trickle	Heilig-Meyers Ford
28	25	41	Ricky Craven	Kodiak Chevrolet
29	35	37	Jeremy Mayfield	Kmart / Little Caesars Ford
30	28	23	Jimmy Spencer	Camel Cigarettes Ford
31	13	9	Lake Speed	Spam / Melling Ford
32	40	77	Bobby Hillin	Jasper Engines Ford
33	33	15	Wally Dallenbach	Hayes Modems Ford
34	27	71	Dave Marcis	Prodigy Chevrolet
35	14	27	Todd Bodine	David Blair Motorsports Ford
36	31	98	John Andretti	RCA Ford
37	5	22	Ward Burton	MBNA America Pontiac
38	20	81	Kenny Wallace	Square D / T.I.C. Ford
39	6	87	Joe Nemechek	Burger King Chevrolet
40	32	29	Chad Little	Cartoon Network Chevrolet

MBNA 500

*Reigning NASCAR Winston Cup Champion Jeff Gordon moves into first place in the point race after a solid run at Dover brought him his third consecutive win at the track. Jeff started the race on the inside of row two, alongside teammate and chief championship challenger Terry Labonte. **(Right)** Front-row starters Bobby Labonte and Rick Mast lead the field for the start of the MBNA 500. The younger Labonte broke a track record with his qualifying run of 155.086 mph. Mast had his best run of the season so far and finished sixth.*

With Fords winning eight of the last 12 races (a string stopped only by Sterling Marlin's rain-shortened victory in the Pepsi 400 and Jeff Gordon's three victories), NASCAR officials announced that there would be some changes made on the Thunderbirds and Monte Carlos by the time they arrived at Dover Downs for the MBNA 500.

The Chevrolets were allowed to raise their rear spoilers and drop their noses a fraction of an inch, while the Fords were forced to shave their rear spoilers and raise the ride height of their noses. NASCAR hoped to put the two makes on equal footing for the remainder of the year.

Ernie Irvan's Richmond victory had put the Ford teams back on top by two points in the tight Manufacturer's Championship, and tied Ford and Chevrolet with 12 victories each. It looked like a dogfight for the remainder of the year for the prestigious title.

Jeff Gordon and Terry Labonte were just four points apart at the top of the standings when they arrived to do battle at Dover Downs. However, Gordon seemed to have just a little more incentive for victory than his Hendrick

Motorsports teammate. Although this race was the MBNA 500, it was at Dover, and DuPont executives had made the quick journey south from Wilmington to share in the excitement of the weekend with their driver. Jeff had won this race last year, and it had been a key moment in his successful quest for the championship. He hoped to repeat the race victory in front of his DuPont friends and take a major stride toward a second straight championship.

After his fourth place at Richmond, Dale Jarrett was within striking distance of Labonte and Gordon at 86 points behind leader Labonte. But with seven races left, he needed to begin making his move. He seemed well clear of Dale Earnhardt, whose poor finishes had continued at Richmond. The chase for the title had begun to take on the look of a three-driver battle, unlike the situation just three or four races ago.

If the battle for the top spot in the standings was hard-fought, the struggle for positions five through 10 was just as tight. The likes of Mark Martin, Ricky Rudd, Ernie Irvan, Ken Schrader, Rusty Wallace and Sterling Marlin were locked in furious battle, and the positions changed with

ference between Labonte and Mast was just a tenth of a second — not even measurable by the human eye. Mast blamed himself for not winning the pole. He had told the team to make one slight chassis adjustment for qualifying, and that had caused the Pontiac to push enough in the second and fourth turns to keep him from a lap that would have put the Grand Prix on the pole.

Gordon showed he was ready to rumble by claiming the inside of the second row — and Terry Labonte left no doubt that he would be a major player in the 500-mile test Sunday, lining up right alongside his teammate. Geoff Bodine and Rusty Wallace were in the fastest Fords under the new regulations, but Bodine was more than a mile per hour off the pole speed. Dick Trickle's outstanding seventh-fastest lap gave Junie Donlavey and the Heilig-Meyers folks plenty to smile about, while Mark Martin slotted his Valvoline Ford alongside Trickle into the fourth row.

Dale Jarrett had the ninth-fastest lap, and John Andretti showed he was much happier with his RCA Ford, putting the red-and-

(Above) Dale Earnhardt guides his ride to the track before the race. A series of poor finishes had mired Dale in fourth place in the point standings, apparently out of contention for his eighth NASCAR Winston Cup championship. He finished a disappointing 16th at Dover. (Right) After claiming his fourth career pole position, Bobby Labonte talks strategy with crew chief Jimmy Makar. Labonte worked his way to a fourth-place finish.

each race. Ernie and Ken were separated by just two points, while Rusty and Sterling were a mere six points apart. Only 127 points separated positions six through 10 as the teams prepared for the first qualifying session at the Monster Mile.

When the first session was completed, all the superstitions had been thrown to the wind by the Interstate Batteries team. Who cared about the old wives tale that green cars are unlucky at race tracks? So what if it was on Friday the 13th? What did it matter if Bobby Labonte had become the 13th different Busch Pole winner of the season?

Using the same chassis the team had raced at Pocono and Darlington, Bobby had whipped around the one-mile oval at a track speed record of 155.086 mph and he needed every bit of it to claim his fourth career pole position.

Right on his tail on the speed sheet was Rick Mast, who had Richard Jackson's Hooters Pontiac humming. The dif-

white Thunderbird on the outside of the fifth row, just ahead of Hut Stricklin and Ken Schrader.

Wally Dallenbach was the final first-day qualifier, while Sterling Marlin became the fastest second-session runner and claimed the Busch second-round bonus. Of the 16 drivers trying to find a spot in the field, 10 stood on their Friday times, while Jimmy Spencer, Bobby Hamilton and Darrell Waltrip took provisionals. Eric Smith, hoping to make the race with his Ford, crashed during the morning practice session and was unable to make a qualifying lap during the second session.

The abrasive concrete surface at Dover presents a huge challenge to Goodyear, whose goal is to make a tire that provides excellent grip on the surface of the track while also lasting from one full fuel stop to the next under the lead-footed charges of today's drivers. It's a very difficult compromise. After Saturday's NASCAR Busch Series race, NASCAR officials decided to order a mandatory yellow flag early in the MBNA 500 so teams and Goodyear officials would have a good reading on how long a set of tires would last. The mandatory yellow came on lap 70, and the only

(Above) Geoff Bodine (7) works on the inside of Rusty Wallace. Rusty challenged Jeff Gordon for the win until lapped cars prevented him from pulling ahead. *(Right)* In single file formation, Terry Labonte (5) leads brother Bobby, Jeff Gordon, Rick Mast, Rusty Wallace and Mark Martin, but had an off day at the Monster Mile as a pair of cut tires and subsequent green-flag pit stops pushed him back to 21st place, and dropped him from the point lead.

problem found was on a right-front tire on Robert Pressley's car. Later in the race, however, cut tires contributed to poor finishes by Terry Labonte and Dale Earnhardt, sending Terry out of the point lead and all but taking Earnhardt out of contention for his long-sought eighth championship.

With 14 yellow flags interrupting the action on the track, the race took more than 150 laps to sort out, and finally Ernie Irvan emerged as the likely favorite to win the race. Gordon was mired in the middle of the field early in the race, struggling with a mismatched set of tires that made every lap an adventure.

Then, on lap 200, Irvan tangled with Derrike Cope, and Ernie was into the wall and out of the race.

Pit work then came into play, and for the rest of the event, Gordon was able to take advantage of his first pit stall nearest the pit exit. Three times during the remainder of the race, his Rainbow Warriors completed their work and Gordon nosed his Monte Carlo across the line first to take the lead for restarts. The quick pit work and the strategy of choosing the pit stall at the end — the prerogative of the reigning champion — had made him a contender for victory again.

His team turned him out for the last time on lap 449, and with four more caution flags during the final 50 laps and 13 cars on the lead lap, Gordon simply remained at the front of the field, preferring track position over stops for fuel and tires.

The strategy worked perfectly, and even with Rusty Wallace dogging his rear bumper on each of the final restarts, Gordon was able to

Jeff Gordon (24) takes the green flag on a late-race restart in front of Rusty Wallace (2). Gordon's win pleased the DuPont executives who were visiting the track from nearby headquarters in Wilmington, Del.

maintain command of the race and neutralize Wallace's challenge. During the first three of those four final restarts, there were lapped cars for Rusty to deal with before he could run Gordon down, but the final one came with just four laps to go, and there were nothing but lead lap cars behind Jeff. He was wary of Wallace but equal to the challenge. At the end, he beat Wallace by nearly a half-second.

The victory was his third straight at Dover in front of the DuPont executives and employees. It also moved him into the point lead and brought a $70,000 bonus from the pot posted by Winston payable to the current leader in points if he also wins the race. The $10,000 prize per race had rolled over for seven events.

With Terry Labonte finishing 21st in the event after a pair of cut tires resulted in green-flag pit stops and lost laps, Gordon now had command of the point chase. He moved to 76 points ahead of Labonte, and Terry could only grit his

teeth and hope that Martinsville would be more kind to him in his quest for a second NASCAR Winston Cup championship.

Dale Jarrett finished third and capitalized on Labonte's misfortune. Jarrett and his Qualify Care Ford now trailed Gordon by 97 markers — but had moved to within 21 points of Labonte's runner-up position.

Gary Bradberry (95) races on the outside of Ward Burton, who hoped to have a good finish in the race backed by his car sponsor, MBNA America. Starting from 33rd place, Burton turned the bad luck that has followed him all season around and streaked to a seventh-place finish.

On this beautiful September afternoon in Delaware, a capacity crowd packed the grandstands that encircle nearly the entire one-mile concrete oval.

Behind Jarrett, Bobby Labonte finished fourth in the event, just ahead of Martin, who posted his ninth consecutive top-10 finish. Rick Mast and Ward Burton finished sixth and seventh, both having strong runs devoid of the bad luck that has followed them all season, while Kyle Petty and Michael Waltrip battled for eighth place. Kyle won the skirmish, and the two drivers bumped each other in frustration on the "cool-down" lap. Neither, however, was cool when they emerged from their cars on pit road, and after some angry words, the two close friends stalked off in separate directions. Bobby Hamilton posted his seventh top 10 of the season and moved to within four points of Ted Musgrave in their battle for 12th place in the point standings.

When Earnhardt's right-rear tire came apart on lap 277, the pieces of the tire ripped the crush panels and the sheet metal, sending Dale to pit road for repairs. He lost two laps and finished 16th in the event. It had been another difficult day for Earnhardt and his team — now 279 points behind Gordon — and they faced a huge uphill battle.

Jimmy Spencer in his Camel Ford zips along the outside of Rusty, who was fighting not only for the win but also for position in the fifth- through 10th-place spots in the ongoing point battle, which was shaping up to be a dogfight between Mark Martin, Ricky Rudd, Ernie Irvan, Ken Schrader, Sterling Marlin and himself.

Geoff Bodine and Bobby Hillin just missed top-10 runs, and were on the lead lap throughout the day. Hillin had been in the top 10 late in the race, but an air pressure adjustment in a tire during a pit stop had been the wrong way to go, and he fell back to 12th. Still, it was a strong performance from Hillin and crew chief Troy Selberg, who was working his third race with Hillin.

Gordon's victory moved Chevrolet back into the lead in the Manufacturer's Championship standings, with Ford now one point behind. The win was the 13th for the Monte Carlos this season.

MBNA 500

Fin. Pos.	Str. Pos.	Car #	Driver	Team
1	3	24	Jeff Gordon	DuPont Refinishes Chevrolet
2	6	2	Rusty Wallace	Miller Ford
3	9	88	Dale Jarrett	Quality Care / Ford Credit Ford
4	1	18	Bobby Labonte	Interstate Batteries Chevrolet
5	8	6	Mark Martin	Valvoline Ford
6	2	1	Rick Mast	Hooters Pontiac
7	33	22	Ward Burton	MBNA America Pontiac
8	24	42	Kyle Petty	Coors Light Pontiac
9	23	21	Michael Waltrip	Citgo Ford
10	40	43	Bobby Hamilton	STP Pontiac
11	5	7	Geoff Bodine	QVC Ford
12	34	77	Bobby Hillin	Jasper Engines Ford
13	21	9	Lake Speed	Spam / Melling Ford
14	10	98	John Andretti	RCA Ford
15	36	37	Jeremy Mayfield	Kmart / Little Caesars Ford
16	20	3	Dale Earnhardt	GM Goodwrench Service Chevrolet
17	26	4	Sterling Marlin	Kodak Film Chevrolet
18	13	75	Morgan Shepherd	Remington Arms Ford
19	16	31	Mike Skinner	RealTree Camouflage Chevrolet
20	18	81	Kenny Wallace	Square D Ford
21	4	5	Terry Labonte	Kellogg's Corn Flakes Chevrolet
22	12	25	Ken Schrader	Budweiser Chevrolet
23	7	90	Dick Trickle	Heilig-Meyers Ford
24	30	30	Johnny Benson	Pennzoil Pontiac
25	35	87	Joe Nemechek	Burger King Chevrolet
26	38	71	Dave Marcis	Prodigy Chevrolet
27	37	11	Brett Bodine	Lowe's Ford
28	27	94	Bill Elliott	McDonald's Ford
29	25	15	Wally Dallenbach	Hayes Modems Ford
30	39	23	Jimmy Spencer	Camel Cigarettes Ford
31	15	12	Derrike Cope	Badcock Ford
32	28	33	Robert Pressley	Skoal Bandit Chevrolet
33	17	16	Ted Musgrave	Family Channel / PRIMESTAR Ford
34	14	10	Ricky Rudd	Tide Ford
35	22	41	Ricky Craven	Kodiak Chevrolet
36	19	28	Ernie Irvan	Texaco Havoline Ford
37	32	95	Gary Bradberry	Shoney's Restaurants Ford
38	11	8	Hut Stricklin	Circuit City Ford
39	41	17	Darrell Waltrip	Parts America Chevrolet
40	29	99	Jeff Burton	Exide Batteries Ford
41	31	29	Chad Little	Cartoon Network Chevrolet

Hanes 500

Rusty Wallace (2) shows John Andretti (98), Terry Labonte (5) and Jeff Burton how to negotiate a tight corner at Martinsville Speedway. Rusty started from the outside of the front row and led the first 35 laps but eventually finished last after he lost the water pump in his Miller Ford. Andretti, on the other hand, had a good day. He started the race in sixth place and ran well until the last lap of the race when he lost two positions coming through the last turn. He finished fifth. (Right) A familiar sight – Jeff Gordon in victory lane. After coming home either first or second in the four races prior to Martinsville, Jeff adds yet another win to his vast collection acquired this season and will take an 81-point lead over his closest competitor, Terry Labonte, to the next race at North Wilkesboro.

For Jeff Gordon and his Rainbow Warriors, the stretch run toward defense of his NASCAR Winston Cup title had been nothing short of sensational. The string of races in the last third of the season that sorts the contenders from the pretenders is one of the year's toughest struggles, with race after race piled on weekend after weekend.

There is no break, and the stress of running at every type of track — from the fastest superspeedway to the road course to the brutal 500 laps around a one-mile oval — quickly helps decide who will wear the champion's crown at the conclusion of the season. The attitude and chemistry within the team are tested and called into play. Crucial strategy is an important part of victories or top finishes. Team management — from car preparation to last-minute adjustments during the race — plays a huge role in the success of a group during the stretch run.

For Gordon, team manager Ray Evernham and the remainder of the Warriors, this stretch would be one to look back at and savor when the season was completed. If the championship came, that would make reminiscing even better. But simply from the standpoint of preparation and finishing positions, this string of races had been a beauty so far.

Since Gordon's Brickyard problems, the team had finished fourth at Watkins Glen, fifth at Michigan, second at Bristol, posted a victory at the Mountain Dew Southern 500 at Darlington, finished second at Richmond and then won at Dover. For six races, the team had not been out of the top five. The last four times the DuPont Chevrolet had gone to the line, it had come home either first or second.

No wonder the Warriors were pumped when they arrived at Martinsville. Their short-track program had improved tremendously during the season, and since North Wilkesboro last fall, the team had not finished out of the top five at a short track. Gordon now had some breathing room over teammate Terry Labonte, with a spread of 76 points between the two Hendrick Motorsports Chevrolets. Ford-driving Dale Jarrett was working on his own fine stretch run, finishing first, fourth, fourth and third in four of his last five races. Only the Mountain Dew Southern 500, when he had unsuccessfully chased the Winston Select Million, was a black mark on his record. Yet, he was just 97 points behind Gordon and hoped to close the gap even more.

Dale Earnhardt's hopes for an eighth title were all but history. With just six races left in the season, he was well off

Bobby Hamilton (43) chases Rusty Wallace in the opening laps of the race. The two front-row starters would go head-to-head early until Bobby took the lead on lap 36. The STP Pontiac team dominated much of the race until pit road problems took them out of contention for the victory.

the pace at 279 behind Gordon, and although he was recovering slowly from the injuries he suffered in the DieHard 500 at Talladega, he simply was not up to full strength. And full strength was what he needed right now, with Gordon, Labonte and Jarrett showing no signs of faltering.

While teams were working their way through the practice sessions leading to qualifying, Jimmy Spencer, Kyle Petty and Michael Waltrip found their wallets a little lighter after NASCAR officials assessed fines totaling $17,000 on the three drivers for their antics during the heat of battle at Dover. Spencer was hit for $10,000 for his actions regarding Wally Dallenbach, while Kyle was levied a $5,000 fine and Waltrip $2,000 for their post-race activities both on the track and off.

For the longest time during the first round of qualifying, it appeared that Rusty Wallace was headed for his first pole position in nearly two years. He had locked up his left-front brake heading into the third turn during his run but still managed to post the quickest lap of the session — until Bobby Hamilton made his run.

Hamilton had already claimed the pole for the NASCAR Craftsman Truck Series event to be held Saturday at Clay Earles' magnificent half-mile, and he had been very fast in the Petty Enterprises Pontiac during the morning practice sessions for the Hanes 500. He had claimed the pole at Michigan earlier in the season, but the team's best Martinsville car had been wrecked at Pocono only weeks before. Hamilton's new mount was a good one — but whether it would be good enough to beat Wallace's lap was the question.

Bobby rolled out in the STP Pontiac, put a great lap together, and came back to pit road grinning. The lap was good enough to beat Wallace's mark and was a mere .002 seconds off the track record owned by Ted Musgrave, set in 1994.

It was the second pole of the season and of Hamilton's career, and it marked the first time a Petty Enterprises car had won more than one pole in a season since 1977. It was also the first time a Petty-entered car had claimed the pole at Martinsville since 1974.

the field for the start of the Hanes 500. Mark Martin and Dale Jarrett slotted themselves in the second row, while Morgan Shepherd and John Andretti, with a fine performance in Cale Yarborough's RCA Ford, claimed the third row.

Bobby Kennedy celebrated being named crew chief for SABCO's Coors Light effort by giving Kyle Petty a Pontiac strong enough to claim the seventh starting position. Dick Trickle continued his solid qualifying performances in Junie Donlavey's Heilig-Meyers Fords by grabbing the outside of the fourth row.

(Inset) After the race, a member of the Square D/T.I.C. crew slices open a tire to see if the intense braking that is characteristic at Martinsville melted the bead. After qualifying 24th, Square D driver Kenny Wallace had a solid run to tenth place. (Above) Geoff Bodine (7) heads the pack through the corner as Wally Dallenbach and Dale Earnhardt (3) do a little rubbing. Rick Mast (1) and Robert Pressley follow closely on the track's inside groove. Dale's hopes of chasing down the point leaders diminished with his 15th-place finish.

Hamilton became the first driver in history to win the pole for a NASCAR Craftsman Truck Series race and a NASCAR Winston Cup race during the same weekend, and it gave the Petty team plenty of reason to celebrate when the crew members headed for dinner Friday night!

Wallace was also on the front row, in his best qualifying position since Phoenix two years ago. Although he had wanted to win the pole, he was pleased to be at the front of

Bill Elliott and Gordon made up the fifth row, just ahead of the Labontes, with Terry beating younger brother Bobby by .005 of a mile per hour for the inside of the sixth row.

At Martinsville, only the fastest 18 cars are pitted on the frontstretch, and Earnhardt's qualifying lap, good for 19th place, meant that the Goodwrench Chevrolet was relegated to the backstretch pits. He had good company. Watkins Glen winner Geoff Bodine, Musgrave, Johnny Benson,

A game of tug-of-war for the lead ensued between the "43" and "24" cars during the Hanes 500. (Above) Here, Bobby Hamilton leads Jeff Gordon down the front straight on the half-mile track, but the Pontiac owned by Petty Enterprises could not keep up the challenge for the win. (Right) An air wrench problem kept Hamilton from making a quick pit stop and then a mismatched set of tires left him unable to work his way through the pack back to the front.

Michael Waltrip, Darrell Waltrip, Ricky Rudd, Sterling Marlin, Ricky Craven and Spencer were all back there with him.

Rudd, Marlin, Craven and Spencer were forced to use provisionals to make the field, while Derrike Cope, Brett Bodine, Billy Standridge, Gary Bradberry and Chad Little were all forced to watch from the sidelines when the green flag fell on the field Sunday afternoon.

Fans pulling for the "43" car were slightly disappointed when Rusty bolted to the point on the first lap, and continued to lead for the first 35 laps. But Hamilton simply was watching to see what Rusty's Miller Ford had. On the 36th lap, the Pontiac took over the lead and the standing-room-only crowd responded with a roar that echoed off the duck ponds outside the fourth turn. Those hoping to see the first Petty Enterprises victory since 1984 had plenty of reason to cheer.

Hamilton was simply sensational, and once the STP

Pontiac was in front with clean air on its nose, Bobby was in command. Gordon was carving his way to the front and would present a substantial challenge, particularly with his use of the champion's pit choice. Other than a single lap led by Terry Labonte during a cycle of green-flag pit stops, the battle was left to Hamilton and Gordon.

Both drivers were superb, and their mounts ready for victory. The undoing of Hamilton's brilliant run came during a pit stop, when an air wrench problem kept the red-and-blue Pontiac in the back of the pack. Then a mismatched set of tires kept him from working his way back to the point.

That left Gordon in position for his third victory in his last four outings, and not even a late caution brought on by

Martinsville could have spelled disaster for the Kellogg's Corn Flakes team. Terry Labonte (5) lost a lap after loosening a piece of shifting linkage in the early going and had to fight through the field for the rest of the race. He not only made up the lap, but also streaked to a second-place finish.

Dallenbach's spin with five laps remaining could derail the Gordon express. The caution did, however, let the field bunch up for a restart. With a single lap to go, the Kellogg's Monte Carlo was right behind the DuPont Chevrolet. Jeff expected a severe challenge from teammate Labonte, but it didn't materialize in the final circuit.

The win went to Gordon by less than a half-second. On the final lap, some frantic bumping and shuffling while exiting the fourth turn dropped Andretti from third place to fifth. Hamilton, who had applied the bump that moved John out of the way, fought his way to third. Rick Mast, with one of his best runs of the year in the Hooters Pontiac, also found a way past Andretti in the closing yards of the race to capture fourth. John was forced to settle for fifth, but his performance behind the wheel of the RCA Ford had been outstanding throughout the race. He ran with the leaders and looked set for at least third place until the final corner of the last lap.

Strong running Morgan Shepherd and Geoff Bodine were sixth and seventh, respectively, while Kyle Petty ran to eighth place, his second straight top 10 in his lame-duck situation with the Coors Light Pontiac. Mark Martin and Kenny Wallace, in the first cars that were a lap in arrears, completed the top 10.

Terry's second place was a tribute to his team and his driving ability. Early in the race, a piece of his shifting linkage had come undone, and by the time he got the car up to speed, he had lost a lap. With just over a quarter of the race in the books, Terry hunkered over the wheel and fought his way back through the field, eventually regaining his lost lap and then driving all the way to the runner-up position. That's the stuff of which champions are made.

Other challengers fell by the wayside during the afternoon in southern Virginia. Rusty lost the water pump in his Ford, Ricky Rudd had transmission problems that brought an end to his 34-race string of finishes, and Dick Trickle, who had a brilliant run with Junie Donlavey's Ford, eventually fell from the battle for victory with clutch problems.

Earnhardt's hopes of closing the point gap on the leaders backfired. The handling of the Goodwrench Chevrolet was suspect right from the beginning of the race, and before the 100-lap mark, Dale had been lapped. He fell another lap behind and finished the race in 15th position, seeing his dream of an eighth championship all but disappear with just five races left in the season.

"The Other Dale" also struggled at Martinsville, falling two laps off the pace during the race. Jarrett finished one position behind Earnhardt and, after fighting to get within reach of challenging for the championship, lost ground to the Hendrick Chevrolet drivers.

Hanes 500

Fin. Pos.	Str. Pos.	Car #	Driver	Team
1	10	24	Jeff Gordon	DuPont Refinishes Chevrolet
2	11	5	Terry Labonte	Kellogg's Corn Flakes Chevrolet
3	1	43	Bobby Hamilton	STP Pontiac
4	29	1	Rick Mast	Hooters Pontiac
5	6	98	John Andretti	RCA Ford
6	5	75	Morgan Shepherd	Remington Arms Ford
7	20	7	Geoff Bodine	QVC Ford
8	7	42	Kyle Petty	Coors Light Pontiac
9	3	6	Mark Martin	Valvoline Ford
10	24	81	Kenny Wallace	Square D Ford
11	17	99	Jeff Burton	Exide Batteries Ford
12	18	28	Ernie Irvan	Texaco Havoline Ford
13	8	90	Dick Trickle	Heilig-Meyers Ford
14	26	21	Michael Waltrip	Citgo Ford
15	19	3	Dale Earnhardt	GM Goodwrench Service Chevrolet
16	4	88	Dale Jarrett	Quality Care / Ford Credit Ford
17	22	30	Johnny Benson	Pennzoil Pontiac
18	9	94	Bill Elliott	McDonald's Ford
19	35	23	Jimmy Spencer	Camel Cigarettes Ford
20	21	16	Ted Musgrave	Family Channel / PRIMESTAR Ford
21	12	18	Bobby Labonte	Interstate Batteries Chevrolet
22	14	15	Wally Dallenbach	Hayes Modems Ford
23	30	17	Darrell Waltrip	Parts America Chevrolet
24	31	77	Bobby Hillin	Jasper Engines Ford
25	25	8	Hut Stricklin	Circuit City Ford
26	36	41	Ricky Craven	Kodiak Chevrolet
27	27	87	Joe Nemechek	Burger King Chevrolet
28	28	9	Lake Speed	Spam / Melling Ford
29	32	71	Dave Marcis	Prodigy Chevrolet
30	16	25	Ken Schrader	Budweiser Chevrolet
31	34	4	Sterling Marlin	Kodak Film Chevrolet
32	15	33	Robert Pressley	Skoal Bandit Chevrolet
33	23	46	Stacy Compton	First Union Chevrolet
34	13	37	Jeremy Mayfield	Kmart / Little Caesars Ford
35	33	10	Ricky Rudd	Tide Ford
36	2	2	Rusty Wallace	Miller Ford

Tyson Holly Farms 400

North Wilkesboro Speedway, which has hosted races since 1948, lost both of its track dates earlier in the year and will close its doors to the NASCAR Winston Cup series at the end of the season. The drivers that made the field for the final NASCAR Winston Cup race at North Wilkesboro Speedway pose for a parting shot. Every driver would go on to take the checkered flag – only the third time in NASCAR history that all cars were running at the end of the race. (Right) Jeff Gordon is surrounded by Robert Pressley (33), Jeff Burton (99), and Lake Speed (9) as he makes his way through one of the sweeping North Wilkesboro corners. Jeff started from the outside of the first row and won the race by more than 1.7 seconds over Dale Earnhardt, keeping him in the lead in the point race and earning him his 10th victory of the season.

When the gates opened in 1947, the track was little more than a dirt oval carved in a farmer's field. Old clapboard fences made of rough-sawn one-by-eights standing on end and nailed to cross members lined the outside of the turns.

The track had its beginnings before William H.G. "Big Bill" France founded NASCAR and before the formation of the "strictly stock" class of cars that would evolve into NASCAR Winston Cup racing.

North Wilkesboro started out hosting weekend gatherings of some of the fastest moonshine cars in the area, driven by some of the most daring young men ever to climb behind the wheel of a car.

The rumbling, sliding, lumpy-looking cars of back then hold little resemblance to the glistening, hand-built thoroughbreds fielded weekly in the sport today. But at North Wilkesboro, the racing has always been the same: Hard. Fast. Elbows flying. Sheet metal scraping. It has always been devil-take-the-hindmost racing and has ranged from one- and two-lap shoot outs in the closing moments to tongue-wagging endurance tests of 400 nonstop, green-flag laps.

Bobby Allison and Richard Petty fought to one of the most storied finishes in the history of the sport there in 1972 when they thumped each other during the closing laps in a pounding, earthshaking battle that made fans wonder if either car could possibly make it to the finish.

"It was among the most difficult of all race tracks," Fred Lorenzen recalls. "It was a combination of short track and superspeedway. It was simply the best. You found out just how good a racer you were when you went there. There was no quarter asked — and none given. You simply had to be at the very top of your game if you were to win at North Wilkes, and I can't tell you how disappointed I am that the track now is gone from the schedule."

That's right, gone. Home to races since 1948, the site of dual NASCAR events since 1951, and one of the most unusual tracks on the circuit with its uphill and downhill straights and its five-eighths-mile length, North Wilkesboro Speedway saw the curtain go up for its final NASCAR Winston Cup event with the running of the Tyson Holly Farms 400 on September 29, 1996.

After track owner Enoch Staley died in May 1995, many race fans wondered what would happen to the track. The answer came quickly when Bruton Smith purchased one-

half of the track from the Combs family, and Bob Bahre, chairman of New Hampshire International Speedway, bought the other half from the Staley family. Both men wanted one of North Wilkes' two NASCAR Winston Cup dates. Bahre hoped to add a second weekend to his lovely one-mile oval in New Hampshire, and Smith wanted to secure a date for his 1.5-mile facility under construction near Ft. Worth, Texas.

The negotiations were completed by the time the NASCAR Winston Cup teams rolled into the garage area at North Wilkesboro. Smith had obtained an April date for his track in Texas, and the second date Bahre had hoped for had been granted to New Hampshire for September. All that was left was the running of the Tyson Holly Farms 400.

Defending NASCAR Winston Cup Champion Jeff Gordon, fresh from his victory at Martinsville, brought his 81-point lead over Hendrick Motorsports

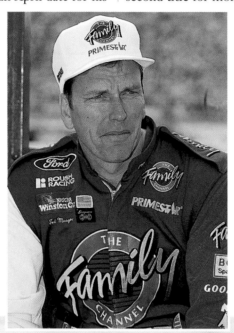

(Right) Ted Musgrave toppled Jeff Gordon from the top of the scoring pylon during qualifying to win his second straight fall pole at the legendary track and the fifth of his career. Musgrave's luck ran out on race day, however, as he never led a lap and finished 19th. (Below) It was a packed house for the final race at North Wilkes. Fans will miss the famed track, which retired NASCAR Winston Cup Champion Benny Parson likened to a "favorite grandfather."

teammate Terry Labonte to North Wilkesboro. With three victories and two second-place finishes in his last five races, Gordon looked poised to put a second straight NASCAR Winston Cup on his mantle.

But Labonte couldn't be counted out yet. He had fought his way back from a lap behind at Martinsville to finish in the runner-up position, which kept his hopes for a second career championship alive. Twelve years had passed since he won his first crown in 1984, and Terry was not about to let this chance slip away. The cool Texan knew, after chasing a second title for more than a decade, that a driver may not have many chances to win the championship. He was determined to capitalize on any opportunity when the battle was this close and with the end of the season looming on the horizon.

Dale Jarrett had seen his chances for a championship take a roundhouse right to the temple at Martinsville with his 16th-place finish, and he fell to 162 points behind Gordon. With just five races remaining on the schedule, his hopes seemed fleeting, at best. At least he had hope. That wasn't the case with Dale Earnhardt, whose chances for an eighth title had, in reality, ended in the accident at Talladega in late July. Earnhardt was now 341 points behind Jeff, and merely hoped to return to victory lane before the

time sheets. Then, it was Ted Musgrave's turn. When his laps were over, the Family Channel/Primestar Ford was the fastest car in the garage area and he had won his second straight October pole at North Wilkesboro and the

(Left) Bobby Hamilton leads Jeff Gordon, Mark Martin and Ernie Irvan. Hamilton qualified third for the race but was knocked out of contention for the win on lap 71 when he and Irvan collided with Kyle Petty. (Below) The Exide Batteries team had to be pleased with driver Jeff Burton's run in the Tyson Holly Farms 400. He challenged Jeff Gordon for the lead with less than 50 laps to go and finished an impressive fourth. (Bottom) New dad Rick Mast and his Hooters Pontiac also had a good day, coming from the 28th starting spot to finish sixth.

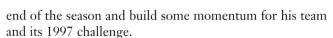

end of the season and build some momentum for his team and its 1997 challenge.

After notching his second pole position of the season the previous weekend at Martinsville, Bobby Hamilton seemed to have the measure of the field during the first qualifying session — the STP Pontiac was on rails. Although Hamilton said after his lap that he felt he had missed the shock absorber setup in the rear of the car, he was the fastest of the first 28 drivers to make their qualifying laps. Then as he was pulling down off the track, he saw sprinkles of rain hit his windshield, and qualifying was delayed for two and a half hours.

Gordon was the first driver out after the rain stopped, and he immediately sent Hamilton to second place on the

Dale Earnhardt (3) fights Jeff Gordon (24) from the outside for the lead as Dale Jarrett (88) and Bill Elliott (94) follow close behind. Earnhardt mounted a late-race challenge to Gordon but couldn't muster enough juice to pass him. Jeff won his third straight race, making him the first driver to do so since Rusty Wallace in 1994.

fifth of his career. Roush Racing teammate Mark Martin was fourth fastest, while Ernie Irvan and Johnny Benson claimed the third row.

Derrike Cope was behind them in row four after another strong qualifying performance with Bobby Allison's Badcock Furniture Ford, beating an equally impressive lap from Bobby Hillin. Rusty Wallace and Michael Waltrip posted laps good enough to make up the fifth row, just ahead of Earnhardt and Bill Elliott.

In the second round of qualifying, Hut Stricklin turned the fastest lap of the six cars attempting to make the field, and provisionals went to Geoff Bodine, Lake Speed, Robert Pressley and Jeff Green, who was driving the Cartoon Network Chevrolet. Darrell Waltrip used a former champion's provisional to start shotgun on the field, and Ward Burton, Dick Trickle and Gary Bradberry were forced to watch Sunday's event from the sidelines.

From the drop of the green flag at North Wilkesboro, it appeared that the race would be a battle royal between Gordon, Hamilton and Ernie Irvan. Gordon bolted past Musgrave on the first lap, then Hamilton showed his heels to Gordon on the second lap. It wasn't long before Irvan stormed to the front, taking the point on lap 13. However, the challenges for victory from Irvan and Hamilton ended on lap 71 when Kyle Petty slipped while exiting the fourth turn and tangled with Ernie and Bobby. The Texaco Ford headed for the garage area, and hopes for one final Petty

Enterprises victory at North Wilkesboro ended, as well.

That left the event to Gordon, and the youngster set sail, eventually leading more than half of the 400 laps. He still had a few skirmishes left in the final portion of the race, first having to beat back an effort from Jeff Burton with less than 50 laps to go, and then having to watch in his rearview mirror as Earnhardt charged to the front, passing Burton and mounting his own challenge.

Dale managed to chop into Gordon's lead in the final laps but could not close the gap enough to make a serious run at the reigning champion. At the end, the margin between the DuPont and Goodwrench Chevrolets was just over 1.7 seconds, and Gordon had won his 10th race of the season — a remarkable feat.

The effort by Gordon and his Rainbow Warriors had been rock solid, and the win gave Jeff his third straight victory. He became the first driver to win three consecutive races since Rusty Wallace did it in 1994, and the triumph put Gordon into both the history and trivia books as the final winner at the storied North Wilkesboro track.

For Earnhardt, second place was almost as good as a victory. It was the first top-five finish for the seven-time champion since the Pepsi 400 at Daytona back in July, some 12 races ago. Despite the runner-up finish, however, Dale fell another 10 points behind in the point standings.

Dale Jarrett posted an outstanding run to come from his 30th starting position to finish third, but, like Earnhardt, he

Robert Pressley (33) and Dave Marcis (71) demonstrate the perils of side-by-side competition through North Wilkes' flat turns as Jeff Green, driving the Cartoon Network Chevrolet, John Andretti (98) and Jeremy Mayfield (37) take notes. Kyle Petty trails the action as he waits for an opening to occur.

also lost points in the battle for the title. Leaving North Wilkesboro, Jarrett trailed Gordon by 182 points, and there were only four races left on the schedule to make up the difference. Apparently, his (and Ford's) hopes for a championship were over.

With a strong run in the Exide Ford, Burton battled his way to fourth place ahead of Terry Labonte, Rick Mast, Ricky Rudd, Hamilton, Martin and Rusty Wallace. Sterling Marlin was the final car on the lead lap, coming home 11th.

Labonte's fifth place reflected a stalwart performance from the Kellogg's team. Fighting a car that refused to handle throughout the race, Terry managed to wrestle the Monte Carlo back to fifth after dropping away from the battle at the front of the pack in the middle of the event.

He lost 30 points to Gordon with his fifth place, and now trailed by 111 as the teams loaded their transporters for the final time in the North Wilkesboro garage area and began heading out through the back gate.

"We're still in the point race, and we've got four races to go, all at tracks where we run pretty well," Labonte said after the event. "We had a top-five finish and still lost points to the leader. That's just the way it goes."

Labonte and Gordon may have been Hendrick teammates, but the heat of the title run was beginning to show. Now was the time for the every-man-for-himself mentality to prevail between the two factions in the remaining races. That was made clear by Labonte's crew chief, Gary DeHart.

"All they've (the "24" team) got to do is slip up just one time — and we can catch back up," DeHart said. "We're not quitting, by any means. The guys on this team are pumped up, and we still have a chance. All we need is one opening."

Jeff Burton and Dale Earnhardt looked to be menaces to Gordon's run in the late stages of the race but neither posed a significant threat. Dale's second-place finish was especially sweet since he hadn't finished in the top five since the Pepsi 400 at Daytona in July.

Tyson Holly Farms 400

Fin. Pos.	Str. Pos.	Car #	Driver	Team
1	2	24	Jeff Gordon	DuPont Refinishes Chevrolet
2	11	3	Dale Earnhardt	GM Goodwrench Service Chevrolet
3	30	88	Dale Jarrett	Quality Care / Ford Credit Ford
4	14	99	Jeff Burton	Exide Batteries Ford
5	16	5	Terry Labonte	Kellogg's Corn Flakes Chevrolet
6	28	1	Rick Mast	Hooters Pontiac
7	21	10	Ricky Rudd	Tide Ford
8	3	43	Bobby Hamilton	STP Pontiac
9	4	6	Mark Martin	Valvoline Ford
10	9	2	Rusty Wallace	Miller Ford
11	13	4	Sterling Marlin	Kodak Film Chevrolet
12	10	21	Michael Waltrip	Citgo Ford
13	18	18	Bobby Labonte	Interstate Batteries Chevrolet
14	19	75	Morgan Shepherd	Remington Arms Ford
15	27	81	Kenny Wallace	Square D Ford
16	26	8	Hut Stricklin	Circuit City Ford
17	6	30	Johnny Benson	Pennzoil Pontiac
18	24	25	Ken Schrader	Budweiser Chevrolet
19	1	16	Ted Musgrave	Family Channel / PRIMESTAR Ford
20	32	23	Jimmy Spencer	Camel Cigarettes Ford
21	12	94	Bill Elliott	McDonald's Ford
22	20	41	Ricky Craven	Kodiak Chevrolet
23	31	11	Brett Bodine	Lowe's Ford
24	23	98	John Andretti	RCA Ford
25	34	9	Lake Speed	Spam / Melling Ford
26	29	87	Joe Nemechek	Burger King Chevrolet
27	37	17	Darrell Waltrip	Parts America Chevrolet
28	15	37	Jeremy Mayfield	Kmart / Little Caesars Ford
29	22	71	Dave Marcis	Prodigy Chevrolet
30	33	7	Geoff Bodine	QVC Ford
31	25	42	Kyle Petty	Coors Light Pontiac
32	36	29	Jeff Green	Cartoon Network Chevrolet
33	35	33	Robert Pressley	Skoal Bandit Chevrolet
34	17	15	Wally Dallenbach	Hayes Modems Ford
35	8	77	Bobby Hillin	Jasper Engines / Federal-Mogul Ford
36	5	28	Ernie Irvan	Texaco Havoline Ford
37	7	12	Derrike Cope	Badcock Ford

UAW-GM Quality 500

Throughout the weekend, it was unclear who would take the reins in the Racing for Kids Chevrolet, fielded by Dale and Teresa Earnhardt. In the end, it was off-road racing standout and IndyCar driver Robby Gordon, who will move to the NASCAR Winston Cup series full-time next season to drive the Coors Light Monte Carlo for Felix Sabates. **(Right)** *Robby gives a thumbs up before qualifying for the UAW-GM Quality 500. Gordon slotted himself into the 13th starting position Wednesday night, but crashed his car in practice the next day and, after a turn of events, ended up driving Joe Nemechek's Chevrolet (with "14" on the side) for the race on Sunday.*

The October race weekend at Charlotte traditionally attracts the largest media coverage of all the races in the second half of the season, and teams and sponsors take advantage of that situation by announcing their plans for the coming season.

This year, it was no different, and the announcements were stacked on top of each other during the five-day Charlotte speedfest. Mike Wallace and sponsor Spam showed the new colors of the Pro-Tech team, and Ken Schrader and Andy Petree revealed that, as anticipated, they would be pairing in the future in Skoal Chevrolets fielded by the former Leo Jackson team that now belonged to Petree. Diamond Ridge told the world that Robert Pressley had been signed to drive the Cartoon Network Chevrolets for 1997. Fred Flintstone and Barney Rubble had served their time and would be replaced by Scooby Doo and Shaggy for the new season.

Derrike Cope and Skittles joined forces, and Derrike tossed out samples of the candy to the crowd as the new Pontiac was unveiled. Ricky Craven was formally introduced (via press release) as the new Hendrick Motorsports driver, taking Schrader's place in the Budweiser Chevrolets.

Steve Grissom already had been named to replace Craven in the Kodiak Chevrolets owned by Larry Hedrick.

A variety of other announcements were made regarding NASCAR Busch Series teams, but the headline event of the weekend was the scenario involving Joe Nemechek, Felix Sabates, Robby Gordon and Dale and Teresa Earnhardt's NASCAR Winston Cup entry.

At Charlotte, the Earnhardts would field their Racing for Kids Chevrolet for Gordon, providing seat time for Sabates' 1997 driver before next season. At the same time, Sabates and Nemechek found a way to work NEMCO Motorsports, Nemechek's family-owned team, into the Sabates stable as part of the overall package needed to secure sponsorship that would be announced in Atlanta at year's end.

Robby Gordon impressed many garage-watchers with his 13th place in the first round of qualifying, but he crashed the car in practice the next day after slipping in oil leaked by another car. At the same time, Nemechek was unable to qualify for the race. When Gordon found himself with no backup car, the Nemechek Chevrolet was hastily enlisted, and the number changed from "87" to "14" for Robby. Gordon practiced in the car, didn't like the way it drove,

(Above) Bobby Labonte (right) and Jeff Gordon (left) lead the field for the start of the race. Although Bobby captured the pole, he lost his engine and finished a disappointing 40th. (Left) NASCAR champion crew chief and new team owner Andy Petree (right) gets a new driver for his Skoal Chevrolet for 1997. Ken Schrader, seen here announcing the deal, will make the move to the "33" car from his Budweiser Monte Carlo. (Below) During raceweek at Charlotte, three-time NASCAR Winston Cup champion Cale Yarborough cemented his place in history on the Walk of Fame at the Charlotte Motor Speedway.

and decided not to compete in the Charlotte race. Nemechek then appeared to be the substitute driver for the now "14" Monte Carlo.

The plot thickened. Gordon headed for an off-road race in Nevada on Saturday. Nemechek prepared to drive No. 14 while Sabates updated the media daily on the car's driver status. Then, after a chiding telephone call from Earnhardt, Gordon returned to Charlotte. Nemechek ran the car in the final practice session, but Robby ended up driving the car in the race. The episode seemed to be the soap opera of the weekend.

Pole qualifying for the Charlotte events is held under the lights, giving those fans who work during the day the opportunity to see the action in the evening firsthand. The night session also means that the drivers who draw the higher numbers in the qualifying order can expect

Two Pontiacs with up-and-coming star drivers go head-to-head as Bobby Hamilton takes the high route and Johnny Benson goes low in one of Charlotte's banked turns. Hamilton qualified his STP Pontiac fourth for the race but finished 19th, two laps off the pace. The Pennzoil team didn't have much luck either as Benson came home 14th, three spots better than his 17-th place start.

better running conditions — improved adhesion to the asphalt for the Goodyear Eagles and more horsepower from the engines — due to the cooler night air.

The odds-on favorite for the pole was point-leader and defending NASCAR Winston Cup Champion Jeff Gordon, who was tied with Bill Elliott among active drivers for the most Charlotte poles with four. Surprisingly, Jeff had struggled during the afternoon practice session, and crew chief Ray Evernham ordered a series of changes for the DuPont Chevrolet in preparation for qualifying. The changes worked, and Gordon clawed his way to the fastest lap — until Bobby Labonte flashed what he had up on the scoreboard.

After having a talk with his teammates about finishing the season on a high note, Bobby had scorched the Monster Mile at Dover to post his first Busch Pole of the season.

Under the Charlotte lights, running 26th in the 48-car field during the first qualifying session, he had another fast lap up his green-and-black sleeve. When he whipped under the flagstand, he was almost 1.5 mph faster than Jeff and clinched the team's second pole in the last four races.

The difference had come in the suspension package under the Interstate Batteries Chevrolet. Bobby and crew

A DuPont crew member hurriedly throws open the hood of Jeff Gordon's Chevrolet to pinpoint what has gone wrong with the Monte Carlo. Gordon started from the outside of row one but, on lap 177, left the race with a cracked cylinder head. He finished 31st and watched his point lead disappear.

chief Jimmy Makar knew they had found the secret to making the Monte Carlo jump off the exits of the corners, the key to superior speed down the straights.

Behind the front row, Jeremy Mayfield slapped the Kmart/Little Caesars Ford on the inside of the second row, and for the third consecutive race, Bobby Hamilton was in the top four in qualifying, underlining the growing competitiveness of Petty Enterprises. The red-and-blue STP team was inching closer and closer to victory with each race, and Hamilton was grinning from ear to ear when he slid through the Grand Prix's window after his run.

Todd Bodine, driving David Blair's Thunderbird, had another sparkling run to grab the inside of the third row,

straight week, Darrell Waltrip chose to use a former champion's provisional and started last for the UAW-GM Quality 500.

In addition to Nemechek, Gary Bradberry, Dave Marcis, Robby Faggart and Delma Cowart failed to turn fast enough laps to gain a place in the event.

When the green flag fell on the field at Charlotte, it rapidly became clear that this race was going to belong to the Monte Carlos. Gordon, both Labontes and Craven were clearly the class of the field, leading all but two of the first 210 laps. Kenny Wallace and Jimmy Spencer each had their Fords in front of the field for a single lap — but those came under the second caution of the race. When the race

Ricky Craven, Terry Labonte and Mark Martin prepare for a restart during one of the race's five caution periods. Craven and Labonte spent much of the race swapping the point, while Mark, driving the strongest Ford in the field, gave chase.

while Jeff Green, filling the seat of the Cartoon Network Chevrolet for the weekend, completed the surprising third row. Two more youngsters, Jeff Burton and Ricky Craven, rocketed to the fourth row, while Robert Yates Racing teammates Ernie Irvan and Dale Jarrett plunked their Thunderbirds into the fifth row, just ahead of the Fords of Michael Waltrip and Mark Martin.

Rick Mast was absent from his Hooters Pontiac during the first qualifying session, choosing instead to return to his home in Virginia where his wife, Sharon, later delivered twin daughters, Kaitie and Sarah.

The second round of qualifying was held in the daytime, making the track hotter and slower, and John Andretti became the only driver to make the field with his timed lap during the session. A total of 11 drivers tried, and those needing provisionals to make the field were Ricky Rudd, Kyle Petty, Kenny Wallace and Pressley. For the second

went green again, the Chevrolets were back in command. And when the race was over, the Monte Carlos had fronted the field for all but 69 of the 334 laps.

Jeff Gordon, carrying a 111-point lead over Terry Labonte into the event, appeared headed for a fourth consecutive victory, although it was clear he would have challenges from the other three leading Chevrolets. However, Gordon's engine started to overheat and he abruptly slowed on the track on lap 177 and headed for pit road. The hood of the DuPont Chevrolet went up, and a cracked cylinder head was diagnosed. Jeff was left to limp around the track for the remainder of the race, hoping the engine would hold together long enough to give him a decent finishing position. He had fallen to 31st place, 15 laps behind, by the end of the race.

Two laps after Gordon's troubles began, Bobby Labonte also headed for pit road, but his problems were more exten-

Race winner Terry Labonte receives congratulations as he celebrates his win in the UAW-GM Quality 500. The victory is his first NASCAR Winston Cup points win at Charlotte Motor Speedway. Labonte went into the race 111 points behind point leader Jeff Gordon but proved he deserves his nickname "Ice Man" by erasing that lead down to a single point.

sive than Gordon's. The Interstate Batteries Chevrolet, after appearing strong enough to go to victory lane for the first time this season, suffered engine failure, and Bobby could only stand beside the car, frustration written all over his face.

That left the battle to the Kellogg's and Kodiak Chevrolets, and Ford's sole hope for victory, Mark Martin, who took the lead on lap 211. Following the fifth and final caution flag of the race, Martin managed to maintain his lead until Craven flashed past to take the point on lap 266.

Some 13 laps later, however, the Kodiak Chevrolet was on pit road, the first of the leaders to make a final green-flag stop. The final set of Goodyears was mismatched and turned Craven's green-and-white Chevrolet into a handful.

One by one, the contenders for victory made their final stops, and when Jeff Burton became the last of the hopefuls to visit pit road with 27 laps left in the race, the lead fell to Terry Labonte and his newly-painted Kellogg's Honey Crunch Corn Flakes Monte Carlo.

No one could challenge him in the final laps, and he rolled to a victory by more than three seconds over Martin, posting his 12th consecutive top-10 finish. Dale Jarrett fought his way to third place at the end of the race despite running over a piece of debris on the track, and then damaging the front end of his Ford in a bump-and-run collision with Jeff Green. Behind Dale, Sterling Marlin posted a solid fourth place, while Craven held on to beat Earnhardt for fifth place.

Ward Burton, Rusty Wallace and Michael Waltrip came home seventh, eighth and ninth, respectively, ahead of Bill Elliott's McDonald's Ford, which beat Jeff Burton and Lake Speed for the final position in the top 10. Speed's Spam Ford was the last car on the lead lap.

While Labonte celebrated his first Charlotte points victory in 37 tries — he won the non-points 1988 running of The Winston Select all-star race for Junior Johnson — the other side of the Hendrick Motorsports camp was in a gloomy mood.

Gordon's engine problems had cost him most of his hard-fought and well-earned point margin. His 31st-place finish, combined with Labonte's victory and bonus points for leading the most laps in the race, had cut Gordon's margin to a single point with three races remaining.

To add to Jeff's problems, Jarrett had driven through the obstacles in his path, and the Ford Quality Care driver had moved back into the point hunt. He entered the race 182 points behind but now trailed by just 92. Gordon had lost 110 points in a single race and if that happened again, Jarrett could capitalize and be right in the thick of the battle for the championship that he and his team wanted so desperately.

UAW-GM Quality 500

Fin. Pos.	Str. Pos.	Car #	Driver	Team
1	16	5	Terry Labonte	Kellogg's Corn Flakes Chevrolet
2	12	6	Mark Martin	Valvoline Ford
3	10	88	Dale Jarrett	Quality Care / Ford Credit Ford
4	33	4	Sterling Marlin	Kodak Film Chevrolet
5	8	41	Ricky Craven	Kodiak Chevrolet
6	34	3	Dale Earnhardt	GM Goodwrench Service Chevrolet
7	14	22	Ward Burton	MBNA America Pontiac
8	23	2	Rusty Wallace	Miller Ford
9	11	21	Michael Waltrip	Citgo Ford
10	21	94	Bill Elliott	McDonald's Ford
11	7	99	Jeff Burton	Exide Batteries Ford
12	20	9	Lake Speed	Spam / Melling Ford
13	39	10	Ricky Rudd	Tide Ford
14	17	30	Johnny Benson	Pennzoil Pontiac
15	18	1	Rick Mast	Hooters Pontiac
16	28	23	Jimmy Spencer	Camel Cigarettes Ford
17	19	16	Ted Musgrave	Family Channel / PRIMESTAR Ford
18	36	12	Derrike Cope	Badcock Ford
19	4	43	Bobby Hamilton	STP Pontiac
20	26	7	Geoff Bodine	QVC Ford
21	5	27	Todd Bodine	David Blair Motorsports Ford
22	30	97	Chad Little	Sterling Cowboy Pontiac
23	15	75	Morgan Shepherd	Remington Arms Ford
24	35	40	Greg Sacks	First Union Chevrolet
25	24	8	Hut Stricklin	Circuit City Ford
26	6	29	Jeff Green	Cartoon Network Chevrolet
27	32	78	Billy Standridge	Diamond Rio Ford
28	22	11	Brett Bodine	Lowe's Ford
29	27	25	Ken Schrader	Budweiser Chevrolet
30	41	81	Kenny Wallace	Square D Ford
31	2	24	Jeff Gordon	DuPont Refinishes Chevrolet
32	42	33	Robert Pressley	Skoal Bandit Chevrolet
33	37	15	Wally Dallenbach	Hayes Modems Ford
34	38	19	Loy Allen	Healthsource Ford
35	29	90	Dick Trickle	Heilig-Meyers Ford
36	25	77	Bobby Hillin	Jasper Engines Ford
37	9	28	Ernie Irvan	Texaco Havoline Ford
38	13	14	Robby Gordon	Racing For Kids Chevrolet
39	31	98	John Andretti	RCA Ford
40	1	18	Bobby Labonte	Interstate Batteries Chevrolet
41	40	42	Kyle Petty	Coors Light Pontiac
42	43	17	Darrell Waltrip	Parts America Chevrolet
43	3	37	Jeremy Mayfield	Kmart / Little Caesars Ford

ACDelco 400

With a near-perfect stop, Terry Labonte's Kellogg's crew, led by crew chief Gary DeHart, won the annual Unocal 76/Rockingham Pit Crew competition Saturday. The team performed a penalty-free stop for four tires and fuel in 22.056 seconds, beating second place Jeff Gordon's DuPont team by a half-second. Rick Mast and the Hooters crew were third in the competition, three-tenths of a second behind the Rainbow Warriors. **(Right)** *Ricky Rudd revels in his victory in the ACDelco 400. The win, Rudd's first of the season, stretches his streak of winning at least one race per season to 14 years.*

With three races remaining on the schedule, the closest battle in the history of the NASCAR Winston Cup Series headed for Rockingham and the newly renovated North Carolina Motor Speedway. When crew members arrived at the Sandhills track, they could hardly believe their eyes.

Since the March race here at the 1.017-mile oval, Chris Browning and his troops had continued the transformation of the track into a modern facility ready to carry forward the long tradition of The Rock. A new press box, control tower and hospitality suite complex had replaced the spider-webbed concrete block structure that had been the heart of the facility for decades.

The gleaming edifice heralded a new beginning for The Rock. The superb new garage area in the infield would help the track maintain its position on the NASCAR Winston Cup tour well into the future. Rockingham's management team had taken the steps needed to keep the track from falling by the wayside as the North Wilkesboro track had. Browning promised new seats and more suites, and said that these changes would bring the increase in purses needed to keep Rockingham part of the tour.

The changes at Rockingham weren't the only headlines during the weekend. Wally Dallenbach was named as the driver of Felix Sabates' third team for the 1997 season and was slated to drive a minimum of 15 races with backing from First Union bank. Bobby Labonte and his Joe Gibbs-owned team were due to switch to Pontiacs for the coming season. NAPA had signed on as the presenting sponsor of the new race at California Speedway in June next year, and Hooters had formally announced it was withdrawing as a sponsor in NASCAR Winston Cup racing after being a primary sponsor with one team or another since 1992.

Todd Bodine changed driver's suits for the Rockingham race, zipping into a green-and-white outfit with Skoal emblazoned across the chest. With Robert Pressley given an early release to join the Cartoon Network/Diamond Ridge team for the final three races of the season, Todd agreed to drive the Skoal Bandit for Andy Petree for the remainder of the year.

Some of the biggest news stories, however, were generated by crew chiefs rather than drivers. Richard Childress said that David Smith, who had worked as the at-track crew chief for Dale Earnhardt's effort this year, would be moved

Dale Jarrett (88), with a lap-down Jeff Gordon (24) on his left, prepares the field for an early-race restart along Rockingham's frontstretch. The newly renovated North Carolina Motor Speedway has a shiny new press box, control tower and hospitality suite complex for fans to enjoy, and the management promises more improvements for the coming season.

into the team manager's role for Mike Skinner's new NASCAR Winston Cup team in 1997 and that a new crew chief for Earnhardt would be named later. At the same time, Jimmy Fennig went to work in a Valvoline uniform for the first time since he left the Bobby Allison/Derrike Cope team to join Roush Racing as Mark Martin's crew chief. Fennig's move freed Steve Hmiel to become the general manager of the Roush endeavor and oversee all three teams.

The huge shocker came Saturday morning when Morgan-McClure Racing owner Larry McClure met crew chief Tony Glover at the garage gate and told him not to report for work. Glover, the crew chief for the Kodak Chevrolet since 1983, had accepted an offer to go to work for Sabates and Robby Gordon's team beginning in 1997 but had planned to remain with the Kodak crew through the end of the current season. After a team meeting Friday evening, McClure had decided to allow Glover to begin his new employment immediately. Engine builder Sheldon "Runt" Pittman, who had worked as a crew chief in the old Hoss Ellington days, would serve as Sterling Marlin's crew chief until a decision was made regarding who would lead the Kodak team in 1997.

The white-hot battle for the championship, with Hendrick Motorsports teammates Jeff Gordon and Terry Labonte separated by just one point, erased the 1979 battle between Darrell Waltrip and Richard Petty as the closest struggle in history with three races remaining on the schedule. Richard had trailed Darrell by 17 points at that point in the season, and came back to win the championship in the final event at Ontario, Calif., by 11 points.

Following the North Wilkesboro race, Labonte's

The Valvoline crew was headed by crew chief Jimmy Fennig for the first time during the ACDelco 400. Fennig (right), who left Bobby Allison's team and driver Derrike Cope to join the Roush Racing organization, looks on with driver Mark Martin as his new team completes pre-race preparations.

crew chief, Gary DeHart, said that if Gordon and his DuPont Chevrolet faltered just once, the Kellogg's crew could catch up and make a championship battle out of the remainder of the season. He received his wish the following week at Charlotte when Gordon cracked a cylinder head and finished 31st. Now, the teams were on equal terms and the title would go to whichever team ran the best in the three remaining races.

Gordon's problem also breathed new life into the Robert Yates Racing effort and third-place Dale Jarrett. A third at Charlotte had pulled the red-white-and-blue Ford back into contention, and Jarrett was only 92 points behind Jeff. His problem, Dale conceded, was that both Gordon and Labonte would need to have problems in the remaining races, and that situation wasn't

(Right) Exide Batteries Ford driver Jeff Burton (99) wowed the fans at Rockingham with his performance during the race. Starting 22nd on the grid for the day, Burton hung with the lead pack – even making a run at Ricky Rudd for the point in the last 74 laps – and finished a respectable fifth.
(Below) Ernie Irvan (28) fights off a challenge from John Andretti (98) as Ricky Rudd (10) and Derrike Cope (12) follow close behind. Seeking to avenge a 37th-place finish at Charlotte two weeks before, Irvan ran strong all day and worked his way from his 20th qualifying slot to finish fourth.

likely. One driver might have problems, but probably not both. Still, he had a fighting chance — and that was all his Todd Parrott-led team had asked for in the closing stretch of the season.

Jarrett and the Yates team had tested at Rockingham in the week between Charlotte and the ACDelco 400, and the intensive session obviously paid off during the first round of qualifying. Jarrett ran late in the session, knocked Jeff Gordon's quick lap off the top of the scoring pylon, and then withstood a challenge from Ricky Rudd to win his second Busch Pole of the season. Rudd, staring the end of his

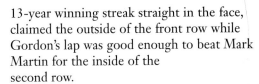

13-year winning streak straight in the face, claimed the outside of the front row while Gordon's lap was good enough to beat Mark Martin for the inside of the second row.

Bobby Labonte continued his strong qualifying performances as he claimed the fifth-fastest lap, barely ahead of John Andretti and Robby Gordon, who was driving Sabates' First Union Chevrolet this week. Kenny Wallace put his Square D Ford on the outside of the fourth row alongside Robby, while Ted Musgrave and Todd Bodine grabbed the fifth-row slots in front of Kyle Petty and Hut Stricklin. Terry Labonte had an uncharacteristic struggle during qualifying and was buried midway in the field in 19th place.

Bobby Hamilton's string of top qualifying performances ended when he failed to make the

The Tide crew works furiously on Ricky Rudd's Thunderbird. Rudd was consistently frustrated by his pit stops throughout the day, which led him to stay on the track during the final caution period of the race. Ricky's decision gave him the lead, which he held for the race's remaining 74 laps.

field during the first round of qualifying. On the second day, however, he turned the fastest lap of the session, and, although his lap was good enough to be tied for the 14th fastest time in the field, he started 26th.

Johnny Benson and the Pennzoil team were struggling. Crew member Eddie Crotchfelt had passed away since the last race, and the team had attended his funeral service. Then Benson lost the primary car to a qualifying accident during the first round. The spare Pontiac was rolled off the truck,

(Above) *Ricky Rudd in his Tide Ride fends off a challenge from Terry Labonte driving his Kellogg's Corn Flakes Chevrolet (with its special Honey Crunch paint scheme).* **(Right)** *Jeff Gordon (24) is able to use the outside groove on Rockingham's high-banked turns to overtake Ted Musgrave (16) and Robert Pressley (29). Pressley, with Scooby Doo gracing his hood, had made an early move to his ride for next season, but did not fare well as he tangled with Lake Speed in the last third of the race and finished 37th.*

and Johnny managed to get it into the field. Before the weekend was over, that car would also be wrecked.

Morgan Shepherd, Joe Nemechek, Ward Burton and Bobby Hillin all used provisionals to get into the ACDelco 400 field, while Ed Berrier, Norm Benning and Terry Byers were forced to load up and watch the race after not making the grid.

Few drivers had been more frustrated throughout the long season than Rudd. He came into the year with high hopes after finishing fifth and then ninth in the final point standings in the first two years of his team's existence. This was to be, Rudd had hoped, the breakthrough year, but it hadn't worked out that way. For a variety of reasons, his cars hadn't been as good as he had planned and, although

he was solidly in the top seven in points, he simply had not been able to run at the front, where he felt his Tide Fords should be.

Imagine, then, how his frustration mounted as, pit stop after pit stop, he fell backward through the field during the race. There was little question that his Thunderbird was among the

best cars in the field this fall Sunday at Rockingham, and after the disappointing performances on pit road, Rudd would grimly grip the wheel and begin working his way through the field again. By the end of the run or when a caution would interrupt, Ricky, who had just worked his way back to the front to challenge for the lead, would head for pit road where he would lose everything he had taken 50 or 60 laps to gain.

Dale Jarrett (88) glides past Yates Racing teammate Ernie Irvan (28). Jarrett had a good day at the track as he took his second Busch Pole of the season at Rockingham, led the most laps and battled to a second-place finish, bringing him to within 76 markers of point leader, and third-place finisher, Terry Labonte.

While Rudd was fighting off the gremlins, the battle at the front of the pack for the ACDelco victory appeared ready to be decided among Ford drivers Ernie Irvan, Dale Jarrett and Jeff Burton, who was having an outstanding day in the Exide Ford. Jarrett and Irvan were exceptionally strong, and even with Rudd working his way back up through the field, most expected to see a repeat of the final laps of the Brickyard 400, where Dale had finally beat Ernie in the closing moments of the race.

With Derrike Cope out of the race due to an early accident with Bobby Hamilton, several members of Bobby Allison's crew joined Rudd's Tide forces on pit road. However, when Ricky pitted under the sixth caution of the afternoon on lap 301 after Robert Pressley and Lake Speed tangled, the stop was not much better than the previous ones. Making matters worse, Ricky was held by NASCAR officials because of a loose lug nut, and when he returned to the track, he was 12th in line once again.

The seventh yellow flag waved on lap 315 for an accident involving Wally Dallenbach, Hillin and Jeremy Mayfield, and when pit lane opened on lap 321 after the cleanup, all the leaders headed for pit road for tires and fuel — except Rudd. Ricky chose to run the distance on the tires he had on the Ford, rather than risk another pit road problem.

That choice turned out to be the turning point of the race. Rudd led the remaining 74 laps on his used tires, fought off the challenges from all comers — including runs by Jeff Burton and Terry Labonte — and emerged as the winner by more than three seconds ahead of Jarrett. Dale had tried his best to overtake the Tide Ford in the final laps but couldn't muster the juice that was needed.

The daring call from the cockpit had paid off, and Rudd had won his first race of the season, continuing his streak of winning at least one race each season to 14 years, second only to Earnhardt's 15-year mark.

Jarrett led the most laps in the race and finished second, and Terry Labonte came home third, ahead of Irvan and Jeff Burton. Bobby Labonte finished sixth, beating Martin, Rusty Wallace and Earnhardt and while Jimmy Spencer claimed 10th place, his Camel Ford the final car on the lead lap.

The battle for the championship had taken another turn. Point leader Gordon struggled with a poor-handling Chevrolet early in the race, losing a lap in the process and never being in a position to regain it. His 12th-place finish, combined with Labonte's third place dropped the reigning champion to second in the standings, 32 points behind Labonte. Jarrett pulled to 76 points behind the leader and, with a little luck, could still claim the title. The race was tight — and only two events remained on the schedule.

ACDelco 500

Fin. Pos.	Str. Pos.	Car #	Driver	Team
1	2	10	Ricky Rudd	Tide Ford
2	1	88	Dale Jarrett	Quality Care / Ford Credit Ford
3	19	5	Terry Labonte	Kellogg's Corn Flakes Chevrolet
4	20	28	Ernie Irvan	Texaco Havoline Ford
5	22	99	Jeff Burton	Exide Batteries Ford
6	5	18	Bobby Labonte	Interstate Batteries Chevrolet
7	4	6	Mark Martin	Valvoline Ford
8	25	2	Rusty Wallace	Miller Ford
9	15	3	Dale Earnhardt	GM Goodwrench Service Chevrolet
10	14	23	Jimmy Spencer	Camel Cigarettes Ford
11	12	8	Hut Stricklin	Circuit City Ford
12	3	24	Jeff Gordon	DuPont Refinishes Chevrolet
13	28	4	Sterling Marlin	Kodak Film Chevrolet
14	34	21	Michael Waltrip	Citgo Ford
15	13	7	Geoff Bodine	QVC Ford
16	17	11	Brett Bodine	Lowe's Ford
17	41	22	Ward Burton	MBNA America Pontiac
18	9	16	Ted Musgrave	Family Channel / PRIMESTAR Ford
19	8	81	Kenny Wallace	Square D Ford
20	10	33	Todd Bodine	Skoal Bandit Chevrolet
21	24	17	Darrell Waltrip	Parts America Chevrolet
22	29	41	Ricky Craven	Kodiak Chevrolet
23	31	25	Ken Schrader	Budweiser Chevrolet
24	40	87	Joe Nemechek	Burger King Chevrolet
25	11	42	Kyle Petty	Coors Light Pontiac
26	6	98	John Andretti	RCA Ford
27	32	95	Gary Bradberry	Shoney's Restaurants Ford
28	26	43	Bobby Hamilton	STP Pontiac
29	39	75	Morgan Shepherd	Remington Arms Ford
30	37	71	Dave Marcis	Prodigy Chevrolet
31	21	90	Dick Trickle	Heilig-Meyers Ford
32	16	94	Bill Elliott	McDonald's Ford
33	42	77	Bobby Hillin	Jasper Engines / Federal-Mogul Ford
34	33	37	Jeremy Mayfield	Kmart / Little Caesars Ford
35	23	9	Lake Speed	Spam / Melling Ford
36	36	15	Wally Dallenbach	Hayes Modems Ford
37	30	29	Robert Pressley	Cartoon Network Chevrolet
38	18	1	Rick Mast	Hooters Pontiac
39	27	12	Derrike Cope	Badcock Ford
40	38	30	Johnny Benson	Pennzoil Pontiac
41	35	78	Billy Standridge	Diamond Rio / Hanes Ford
42	7	40	Robby Gordon	First Union Chevrolet

Dura Lube 500

The field flashes past the majestic Arizona mountains that provide a picturesque backdrop for Phoenix International Raceway. (Right) Bobby and Debbie Hamilton celebrate Bobby's first career NASCAR Winston Cup victory. The win marked the first time that Richard Petty – now a car owner – had been to victory lane since the 1984 Firecracker 400 at Daytona, when he won his 200th career NASCAR Winston Cup race.

Buddy Jobe's Phoenix International Raceway has become one of the most welcome fixtures on the circuit since the NASCAR Winston Cup tour's inaugural visit to the Valley of the Sun in 1988.

Those who haven't visited the oddly shaped one-mile oval and enjoyed the wonderful hospitality of the entire Phoenix area should put it on their calendars as a "must" for the future. The track's management continues to make improvements for competitors and fans, and, with the Grand Canyon, the artisans of Sedona, fabulous golf, and outstanding hotels and restaurants nearby (not to mention the quick, low-priced air shuttle jump to Las Vegas), the area is perfect for an extended vacation. Most important, however, is the attitude of the Phoenix residents, who greet the Cuppers and fans with a week-long celebration.

Almost every year since that first race, when Alan Kulwicki won his first NASCAR Winston Cup event and celebrated with a backwards victory lap, the Phoenix contest has played a role in the outcome of the NASCAR Winston Cup championship. This year would be no different.

On the strength of his Rockingham finish, Terry Labonte carried his 32-point bulge over Hendrick Motorsports

teammate Jeff Gordon into the Sonoran Desert. Terry expected to have a slight edge at Phoenix — he has run extremely well here in the past, including a victory just two years ago. The team had brought the "Iron man" car used at North Wilkesboro because the Kellogg's crew felt it would respond well to the flat track. The car was painted in the gray colors that Terry had taken to victory lane earlier this year at North Wilkes, and most garage-watchers expected Labonte to come "off the truck" in great shape for qualifying and the race.

After the first practice session, however, none of that mattered. The throttle hung wide open as Terry headed into the third turn, and he had no options. The Monte Carlo drilled the concrete wall, and, somehow, Terry's left hand got tangled up in the steering wheel on impact. The resulting injury, a broken metacarpal (the bone between the wrist and the first knuckle) leading to his forefinger, was extremely painful, and furthermore, the Chevrolet was ready for the junk pile. Labonte, a left-hander, became the focus of the media for the next three days. Many thought Terry's championship hopes were gone.

A group of sports medicine specialists and other doctors

1996
NASCAR Winston Cup Series
Dura-Lube 500
Presented by Auto Value
CHAMPION
Phoenix International Raceway
October 27, 1996

worked around the clock to find ways for Terry to continue competing during the weekend. By Sunday, he was able to run at nearly 100 percent with the help of a special steering wheel used by Dale Jarrett several years ago after he had suffered a broken left wrist. The steering wheel was

(Right) The Kellogg's Corn Flakes Chevrolet displays the damage it suffered after Terry Labonte smashed into the third turn wall during the first practice session for the Dura Lube 500. (Below) Labonte broke a bone in his left hand and had to go to his backup car, equipped with a special steering wheel, for the race. The injury didn't seem to deter Terry – even though he qualified 30th, he finished third.

found in Bobby Labonte's Interstate Batteries shop in Charlotte and put on a plane to Phoenix, where it was installed in the backup Kellogg's Monte Carlo.

As teams worked their way through the first practice session in preparation for qualifying, there were some different team combinations in the garage area. Troy Selberg had resigned from the Jasper team early in the week and Bobby Hillin found himself working for the first time with engine builder Bob Dell as his interim crew chief. Robby Gordon was on hand to drive Felix Sabates' First Union Chevrolet, and Tony Glover, after joining the team earlier in the week, was calling the shots as Robby's new crew chief.

While Glover and Dell were getting acquainted with their drivers, Kyle Petty moseyed over to the media center to announce that his new team for the coming season would field Pontiacs and be sponsored primarily by Mattel toys' Hot Wheels line. That announcement

Who is that masked man? Why, it's Geoff Bodine, waiting out the pre-qualifying sandstorm. Like Terry, Geoff qualified low (28th) but went on a tear and ran at the point in the closing laps of the race before he was overtaken by Bobby Hamilton.

ended considerable speculation regarding Petty's future and resolved the situation that had hung over Kyle since July's Pepsi 400, when he and Sabates said they would part company at the end of the season.

As Friday qualifying approached, a freak sandstorm blew through the area — one of only a handful like it experienced in the Phoenix area in the last three decades. With winds blowing at 25 mph and gusting to 40 mph, there was no way NASCAR officials were about to let the cars onto the track. Visibility was so poor, it was hard to see the backstretch from the frontstretch and, for the first time in history, first-round qualifying was postponed due to a sandstorm!

Another bizarre incident in the desert occurred Saturday morning. The cold weather that followed the storm left frost on everything. When the teams arrived at the track, drivers and crew members faced a one-shot chance to make the race. Only one qualifying session could be sandwiched into the schedule that also included a NASCAR Craftsman Truck Series event.

Mike Skinner, the defending truck series champion who will move to NASCAR Winston Cup next season in a Lowe's-sponsored second team under the Richard Childress banner, bumped Ricky Rudd off the top of the scoring pylon midway through the qualifying session. As driver after driver made their runs, it looked more and more like Skinner might pull off the pole position for the Dura Lube 500. Then, with just two drivers left to qualify behind him, Bobby Labonte rolled out in his green-and-black Chevrolet and won his third Busch Pole in his last six tries.

Beside Rudd, Ken Schrader slotted his Budweiser Chevrolet into the outside of the second row, while Dale Jarrett, hoping to narrow the 76-point distance between himself and point leader Terry Labonte, claimed the inside of the third row. Mark Martin, in search of his first victory of the season, sat on the outside of Dale.

Kenny Wallace had another strong qualifying performance to claim the seventh starting position, barely beating Rick Mast, who again had the Hooters Pontiac starting from the top 10. Rusty Wallace and Jeremy Mayfield shared the fifth row, just ahead of Bill Elliott and Ernie Irvan.

Where were Jeff and Terry? Gordon struggled during qualifying and could only manage the 19th starting position, while Terry, with his battered left hand and backup Chevrolet, found himself 30th for the start of the race. Winston West competitors Lance Hooper and Jeff Krogh completed the field as Ricky Craven, Hut Stricklin, Ward Burton and Hillin took provisionals. Westers Mark Krogh, Scott Gaylord, Larry Gunselman, Rich Woodland Jr., Joe Bean and Bill McAnally all failed to make the Phoenix field.

(Left) Pole-winner Bobby Labonte leads Ernie Irvan and Mark Martin through the flat turns at Phoenix International Raceway. The younger Labonte took his third pole in the last six races and looked ripe for his first victory of the season as he led the first 32 laps of the race. Ultimately, Bobby couldn't hold on and finished ninth.
(Below) Felix Sabates' First Union Chevrolet with Robby Gordon behind the wheel leads a pack of challengers. Gordon, with new crew chief Tony Glover calling the shots, took an early exit from the race after he was involved in an accident. He was classified 42nd in the final rundown.

Although Mark Krogh's car failed to qualify, it actually started the race when brother Jeff wrecked his car in the final practice session. Jeff had sold his backup car the previous week, so Mark volunteered his Chevrolet for the event.

With postcard-blue skies welcoming the teams and the largest crowd at a sporting event in Arizona history on hand to watch the drop of the green flag, the first two-thirds of the Dura Lube 500 looked like the race would shape up to be a dogfight between Bobby Labonte, Martin, Jarrett, Geoff Bodine and maybe Bobby Hamilton. Terry Labonte had clawed his way through the field to challenge as well, but it wasn't until the fifth caution flag of the race that the real story began to develop.

During the Friday and Saturday practice sessions, Hamilton and the STP team had concentrated their work on making the Pontiac respond when exiting the corners. They believed that if the car could run at the bottom of the track throughout the race and pull off the corners, it would be highly competitive.

That's exactly what happened as the Dura Lube 500 played directly into the hands of the Petty Enterprises team.

(Right) Kyle Petty leads Dale Earnhardt (3), Kenny Wallace (81) and Hut Stricklin (8) around Dave Marcis (71) and Bill Elliott (94). Kyle announced earlier in the weekend that in 1997 he would campaign his own car sponsored by Mattel's Hot Wheels. (Below) The STP Pontiac returns to a once-familiar position on the track – in front. Bobby Hamilton took over the point in the last 30 laps of the race and that winning feeling returned to Petty Enterprises at last.

While most of the lead pack made its final pit stop under the yellow flag on lap 260, Geoff Bodine remained on the track, hoping his older tires would hold up at the front of the group. While the drivers fought for position behind him, they would quickly wear off the edge of their new sticker tires. Bodine was gambling that track position would reward him with his second victory of the season. For the first few laps following the restart of the race, he appeared to have made the right move.

Everyone attending the winners' celebration at Phoenix was warmed by a familiar sight and a familiar smile. Finally, The King had returned to victory lane.

Terry and Mark, followed by Hamilton and Bobby Labonte, were lined up behind the black QVC Ford. Hamilton started a charge that moved him past Martin, then Terry, and he finally challenged Bodine for the point in just 12 laps. Hamilton took more than a lap to work his way past Geoff's Thunderbird, but when he finally did, he began easing away. Behind him, Terry also managed to find a way past Bodine, who was beginning to slip and slide on his used tires, and the Kellogg's Chevrolet started hunting down the STP Pontiac.

Labonte cut the gap to less than a second with nine laps left in the race, then looked in his mirror and saw Martin all over his rear bumper. The battle for second place gave Hamilton just a touch of breathing room, and he watched behind him as Terry and Mark staged a brilliant battle for the runner-up position. Mark finally prevailed on the next to last lap, and Labonte was forced to settle for third place after a spectacular performance.

Ted Musgrave had a sparkling run to fourth place, and Jeff Gordon, after fighting his DuPont Chevrolet for the entire distance, gritted out a fifth place, rallying from mid-field at the halfway mark of the race. Bodine beat Ernie Irvan for sixth place, and Jarrett came home eighth, ahead of Bobby Labonte. Darrell Waltrip, who had one of his better races of the second half of the season, closed out the top 10.

Few in the garage area could have been happier with the results of the race, even if they had won it themselves. The fact that Petty Enterprises was headed for victory lane for the first time in 13 years — 355 races — was reason enough to celebrate the trip to the Valley of the Sun.

This was Hamilton's first career victory, and it came in his 167th NASCAR Winston Cup start. There is a special pleasure felt by everyone throughout the garage area when a driver gets his first career victory. To have it come in the STP Pontiac — after the team had fought, struggled, worked and gone home week after week, year after year, many times without hope for a win — made the event even more special.

The win gave Richard Petty his first trip to victory lane since 1984, when he won at Rockingham and Daytona for Curb Motorsports. This time, he held the trophy as a car owner and posed alongside the STP Pontiac with his driver.

The winner's circle activities overshadowed the state of the point race. Terry's gutsy performance and third-place finish brought him 15 more points in the tight battle with his teammate. Gordon had failed to lead a lap and now headed for Atlanta trailing by 47 markers. Jarrett, desperately trying to close ground in the point battle, now found himself 99 points behind Labonte with just a single race left. He would need a miracle in Atlanta if he was to claim the championship.

Dura Lube 500

Fin. Pos.	Str. Pos.	Car #	Driver	Team
1	17	43	Bobby Hamilton	STP Pontiac
2	6	6	Mark Martin	Valvoline Ford
3	30	5	Terry Labonte	Kellogg's Corn Flakes Chevrolet
4	25	16	Ted Musgrave	Family Channel / PRIMESTAR Ford
5	19	24	Jeff Gordon	DuPont Refinishes Chevrolet
6	28	7	Geoff Bodine	QVC Ford
7	12	28	Ernie Irvan	Texaco Havoline Ford
8	5	88	Dale Jarrett	Quality Care / Ford Credit Ford
9	1	18	Bobby Labonte	Interstate Batteries Chevrolet
10	18	17	Darrell Waltrip	Parts America Chevrolet
11	13	33	Todd Bodine	Skoal Bandit Chevrolet
12	24	3	Dale Earnhardt	GM Goodwrench Service Chevrolet
13	2	31	Mike Skinner	RealTree Camouflage Chevrolet
14	3	10	Ricky Rudd	Tide Ford
15	20	15	Wally Dallenbach	Hayes Modems Ford
16	31	21	Michael Waltrip	Citgo Ford
17	26	75	Morgan Shepherd	Remington Arms Ford
18	37	23	Jimmy Spencer	Camel Cigarettes Ford
19	14	98	John Andretti	RCA Ford
20	29	90	Dick Trickle	Heilig-Meyers Ford
21	11	94	Bill Elliott	McDonald's Ford
22	41	22	Ward Burton	MBNA America Pontiac
23	34	52	Jack Sprague	Pedigree Pontiac
24	38	71	Dave Marcis	Prodigy Chevrolet
25	16	87	Joe Nemechek	Burger King Chevrolet
26	35	11	Brett Bodine	Lowe's Ford
27	15	4	Sterling Marlin	Kodak Film Chevrolet
28	33	9	Lake Speed	Spam / Melling Ford
29	22	42	Kyle Petty	Coors Light Pontiac
30	40	8	Hut Stricklin	Circuit City Ford
31	21	99	Jeff Burton	Exide Batteries Ford
32	23	30	Johnny Benson	Pennzoil Pontiac
33	43	07	Lance Hooper	Cinema / Unocal Pontiac
34	39	41	Ricky Craven	Kodiak Chevrolet
35	4	25	Ken Schrader	Budweiser Chevrolet
36	36	29	Robert Pressley	Cartoon Network Chevrolet
37	7	81	Kenny Wallace	Square D Ford
38	8	1	Rick Mast	Hooters Pontiac
39	42	77	Bobby Hillin	Jasper Engines / Federal-Mogul Ford
40	9	2	Rusty Wallace	Miller Ford
41	44	01	Jeffrey Krogh	Clearwater Forest Industries Chevrolet
42	32	40	Robby Gordon	First Union Chevrolet
43	27	12	Derrike Cope	Badcock Ford
44	10	37	Jeremy Mayfield	Kmart / Little Caesars Ford

NAPA 500

The final start of the season saw Bobby Labonte on the pole, his fourth time in that position since the second Dover race only two months ago. Not far behind Bobby in the second, third and fifth positions were the contenders for the NASCAR Winston Cup championship – Jeff Gordon, Terry Labonte and Dale Jarrett – proving that right from the start of the weekend the competitive fire was burning fiercely. **(Right)** *Winning the championship is "grrreat!" In a rare display of emotion, newly crowned NASCAR Winston Cup Champion Terry Labonte begins the celebration by opening a bottle of champagne – with a broken hand no less – while crew members, well-wishers and Kellogg's mascot Tony the Tiger cheer him on.*

Terry Labonte and his Kellogg's Corn Flakes teammates had made more than the best of a difficult situation two weekends ago at Phoenix. Despite Terry's injury to his left hand in a practice accident, which was causing him considerable pain, and despite having to work a backup Chevrolet into competitive shape, the team found a way to bring home a third-place finish.

The painkilling injections had done their job during the race at Phoenix, but the pain had returned by the time Terry climbed aboard the airplane headed for North Carolina and a series of appointments with specialists to determine the status of the broken bone.

However, he could find consolation in the fact that he would arrive at Atlanta Motor Speedway for the final race of the season with an increase in his point lead after a weekend in the desert sun that could have been disastrous. Now, if he could finish eighth or better in the NAPA 500 in Atlanta, he would claim his second career NASCAR Winston Cup championship.

Twelve long years had passed since Terry claimed his first NASCAR Winston Cup in the final race of the 1984 season at Riverside, Calif. Since then there had been drives with sev-

eral teams that showed the promise of race wins and championships, but a second title had proven to be very elusive.

Even the victories had disappeared. For a four-year stretch, the Texan had gone winless, something no one in the garage area could understand. There never had been a question of his talent or his maturity behind the wheel. Still, the whispers went through the garage area, and many wondered if he would ever win again.

Then, Rick Hendrick came calling after Ricky Rudd decided to leave Hendrick Motorsports and form his own team. Kellogg's followed Terry to the Hendrick compound, and Corn Flakes replaced Tide on the Chevrolets. Hendrick's gamble now looked ready to pay off. Labonte led the championship standings, with defending champion and teammate Jeff Gordon only 47 points behind.

Gordon, with 10 victories in a spectacular season that rivaled his championship year in 1995, was clearly the driver Labonte had to deal with at Atlanta. The smallest slip by Labonte — a cut tire, a miscue on pit road, a bump from another driver, a small mechanical malfunction — could put the point leader in the middle of the pack at the finish of the race. Then Gordon would only need a strong finish

Hot running Ernie Irvan was planning to end his comeback season with a victory until he cut a tire and drilled the wall with 70 laps remaining in the race. When Irvan's Texaco Havoline Ford was retired to the garage on the back of a flatbed truck, all eyes turned to the strongest in the lead pack – Dale Earnhardt, Jeff Gordon, Bobby Labonte and brother Terry.

near the front to claim the championship as his own. And to ensure that, Gordon's Rainbow Warriors had held one of their test dates for Atlanta. In the week between Phoenix and the NAPA 500, the team had brought a selection of its best cars to the track for Jeff to test, hoping to find the edge that would allow him to catch his teammate and post back-to-back championships.

The only other driver with an outside shot at the title was Dale Jarrett. Although he was 99 points behind Terry, it was still possible for Dale to claim the title. Dale would have to run well and both Terry and Jeff would have to have problems and fall from the race early. He had the longest of shots, Dale acknowledged early in race week, but he and the Quality Care team had nothing to lose — and everything to gain. Like Gordon, the red-white-and-blue Ford team tested at Atlanta prior to the race.

The Atlanta weekend, like many racing weekends before it, was filled with announcements regarding 1997. The opener for the weekend's press conferences was the unveiling of a second NASCAR Craftsman Truck Series team from Geoff Bodine's shop, with NASCAR Slim Jim All-Pro Series hot shoe Tammy Jo Kirk stepping up on the competition ladder to wheel the electric pink Lovable Ford F-150 for the entire season.

Brett Bodine's sponsorship package for the next three years had come together, and, although the exact details were not available at the time of the announcement, there

was little question that Brett would be much more competitive beginning with the Daytona race in February. Felix Sabates announced that SABCO would field Chevrolets for Wally Dallenbach, Robby Gordon and Joe Nemechek for the coming season. Wally will carry First Union's green-white-and-silver colors in its limited season of competition, and Gordon will drive the Coors Light Monte Carlo. Nemechek's BellSouth-sponsored Chevrolet was also unveiled in the company's hometown of Atlanta, and BellSouth Mobility will continue to sponsor his limited schedule of NASCAR Busch Series appearances.

The real work of the weekend — preparing for the first round of qualifying — was well underway in the garage area, and, when the timed session was completed, the stage had been set for Sunday's struggle for the title.

Gordon, Labonte and Jarrett were all clearly on form, with Gordon claiming the outside of the front row, barely ahead of Terry, who qualified with the third-fastest lap despite pain from his left hand. Jarrett was fifth, just a tick of the watch slower than Mark Martin, and Ernie Irvan underlined the competitiveness of his Texaco Ford with the sixth-fastest time.

The fourth row held a pair of surprises. Todd Bodine, in his final appearance in the Skoal Chevrolet, claimed the seventh position, and Greg Sacks plopped the First Union Pontiac on the outside of Todd. Bobby Hamilton, fresh from his Phoenix victory, turned the ninth-fastest lap, just

.006 seconds faster than Chad Little's fine lap, which was enough to grab the final top-10 position from Hut Stricklin.

The pole winner? None other than Bobby Labonte, who claimed his fourth Busch Pole since the second Dover race with a rocket ship run of 185.887 mph! Over the final third of the season, the team had been rounding into form, and many in the garage area felt the Interstate Batteries team was ready to win — not just set fast laps during qualifying.

The rest of the top 25 drivers who made the field in the first round included even more surprises. Jack Sprague claimed the 12th-fastest lap with his Pedigree Pontiac, Gary Bradberry had a strong qualifying run with the Shoney's Restaurants Ford, and Billy Standridge made the field the first day in his Diamond Rio Ford. Elton Sawyer, pressed into service in Harry Ranier's Ford when Tony Stewart was unable to drive the car, put the LaFayette Ford-sponsored Thunderbird on the list in 24th place. Randy Baker's time was good enough for 27th place on the grid.

When the second round of qualifying was completed,

Ken Schrader, Jeff Burton, Jimmy Spencer and Morgan Shepherd were forced to use provisionals to make the field. That left Dick Trickle, Jeremy Mayfield, Ron Barfield, Kenny Wallace, Kyle Petty and Derrike Cope all on the sidelines for the final event of the season Sunday afternoon. Petty missed his chance to run his final race with the Coors Light Pontiac, and Cope had expected to drive the Badcock Furniture Ford for Bobby Allison Motorsports one last time.

If there was any question regarding Jeff Gordon's determination to win a second straight NASCAR Winston Cup championship, the answer came early in the NAPA 500.

On lap 11, he headed for pit road

with a strange vibration coming from the rear of the car that he first thought was a suspension or rear-end problem. After slowing on the track, Jeff worked his way to his pit stall, and his crew hastily changed tires. When the left-rear wheel was examined, it was evident that the lug nuts had not been tightened properly and the wheel had been wobbling on the studs. Jeff returned to action, but was two laps behind the field. Many in the huge crowd thought the DuPont Chevrolet driver's chances for both a race victory and his second title were gone.

Gordon, however, had another opinion. An early caution and some exceedingly sportsmanlike moves by Darrell Waltrip and Robert Pressley allowed Jeff to move to the front of the line of lapped cars for the restart. Gordon set sail, moving onto the tail end of a lap down when the green flag flew. Some 30 laps later, another yellow flag appeared, and Gordon made up one of his two lost laps.

He again moved to the front of the lapped pack and, on the restart, again bolted ahead of the leaders. When Baker spun and brought out the third yellow flag of the day on lap 54, Gordon had made up his second lap and was back on track with the lead group.

(Left) When the final caution of the race flew, it appeared that Bobby Hamilton might get his second consecutive – and second career – win. As the rest of field pitted for a splash of gas, Hamilton, Ricky Rudd and Michael Waltrip, in no need of fuel, stayed on the track. Hamilton took the lead and stayed there for 12 laps but was overtaken on lap 287 by a determined Bobby Labonte, going all out to end a winless season. (Below) Jeff Gordon slides his DuPont Monte Carlo into its pit for a late-race stop. The talents of his Rainbow Warriors were tested at Atlanta as Jeff lost two laps early in the race after some lug nuts worked loose and caused a severe vibration in the left-rear wheel. Some strategic driving and timely caution flags helped him catch back up to the leaders and challenge for the victory.

The Kellogg's Corn Flakes Chevrolet was rock-solid and ran within the top five for practically the entire race. As the laps wound down, it was clear that unless something untoward happened to the Corn Flakes Monte Carlo, it wouldn't matter where Gordon finished.

When Schrader shredded a right-front, leaving debris on the track, the battle lines were drawn. Bobby Hamilton, Ricky Rudd and Michael Waltrip had enough fuel to make the remaining distance, while the remainder of the leaders all headed for pit road for a splash of Unocal. When the green waved for the final time on lap 278, it appeared that Hamilton might be in position to win his second straight race, but Bobby Labonte had fought his way from fifth place to the point by lap 287, and the race was his to lose.

After winning three races in 1995 and going the entire current season winless, Bobby wasn't about to let this one get away from his green-and-black Interstate Batteries Monte Carlo. He pulled away from the pack and cruised to the victory while Jarrett mounted a charge that moved him from sixth to second, where he finished some four car-lengths behind.

Gordon drove to a heady third place, just ahead of a hard-charging Earnhardt, while Terry Labonte drove to fifth place, earning more than enough points to clinch his second NASCAR Winston Cup championship.

Hamilton and Martin finished sixth and seventh, respec-

The race had quickly changed. Instead of being two laps down and having no chance for the title, Gordon was now definitely a factor for the win. His car obviously was one of the fastest on the track — he had made up his two lost laps in less than 50 circuits. Although he was at the rear of the lead-lap pack, he began working his way through traffic, picking off one car at a time and moving to 15th place by lap 99.

With the field making green-flag pit stops, Gordon remained on the track and led the race for the first time on lap 108. For the final two-thirds of the race, he ran in the top five and even led at times.

But Jeff had his hands full with a hot-running Bobby Labonte and Ernie Irvan, until Ernie cut a right-front tire and drilled the second-turn wall with 70 laps remaining in the race. The Texaco Havoline Ford was brought back to the garage area on a flatbed, and the focus of the race turned to Dale Earnhardt, Gordon and the Labonte brothers.

tively, ahead of Ricky Rudd and Jeff Burton, who had an outstanding run from a provisional starting position to ninth place. Rusty Wallace, with some experimental settings on his Miller Thunderbird, beat Michael Waltrip for the final position in the top 10.

Terry's fifth place put him 37 points ahead of Gordon in the final point standings, and the considerable pain in his injured left hand was quickly forgotten. With every fan in the stands cheering the two winners on, Terry pulled alongside brother Bobby and they made a victory lap together. Then Bobby motored away to be the first of the Labontes to visit Atlanta's victory lane.

Jarrett finished third in the standings, 89 points behind the champion, and Earnhardt held onto his fourth position, ahead of Martin, Rudd and Wallace. Sterling Marlin, Hamilton and Irvan completed the top 10, and all earned invitations to the stage at the upcoming NASCAR Winston Cup banquet at the Waldorf-Astoria Hotel in New York City in December. Johnny Benson, despite struggling with the Pennzoil Pontiac throughout the afternoon, won the Rookie-of-the-Year title.

It was a spectacular afternoon for the Labontes. Bobby won nearly $275,000, including the Unocal 76 Challenge bonus award of $136,800 for winning from the pole, and captured the first victory of the season for the Joe Gibbs-owned team. At the same time, Terry clinched his second NASCAR Winston Cup championship and the minimum $1.5 million champion's share of the NASCAR Winston Cup Point Fund. When Terry won the 1984 title, his champion's share had been $150,000!

The past year of racing had provided many memorable occasions — Dale Jarrett had a storybook year, winning the Daytona 500, Brickyard 400 and Coca-Cola 600 with a new team and a rookie crew chief; Michael Waltrip had come from last place to win The Winston Select all-star race and its $200,000 prize; an accident in July had taken Dale Earnhardt out of contention for his eighth championship; Richard Petty won his first race since retiring as a driver; and the point race had been one of the tightest in history — a single point separated the leaders with only three races to go — and had ended with a veteran driver winning his second championship after a 12-year drought. An interesting season, indeed.

The turbulent 1996 season had come to a dramatic close in Atlanta, but as the teams made their way to their transporters for the trip home (and some well-deserved time away from the track), fans couldn't help but look forward to the 1997 season and wonder what lay ahead.

As the sun sets on another NASCAR Winston Cup season, Atlanta's scoring pylon shows the story of 1996 – the race between Dale Jarrett (88), Jeff Gordon (24), Dale Earnhardt (3) and Terry Labonte (5) for the championship that came down to a season-ending battle in the NAPA 500.

NAPA 500

Fin. Pos.	Str. Pos.	Car #	Driver	Team
1	1	18	Bobby Labonte	Interstate Batteries Chevrolet
2	5	88	Dale Jarrett	Quality Care / Ford Credit Ford
3	2	24	Jeff Gordon	DuPont Refinishes Chevrolet
4	17	3	Dale Earnhardt	GM Goodwrench Service Chevrolet
5	3	5	Terry Labonte	Kellogg's Corn Flakes Chevrolet
6	9	43	Bobby Hamilton	STP Pontiac
7	4	6	Mark Martin	Valvoline Ford
8	28	10	Ricky Rudd	Tide Ford
9	40	99	Jeff Burton	Exide Batteries Ford
10	30	2	Rusty Wallace	Miller Ford
11	33	21	Michael Waltrip	Citgo Ford
12	23	22	Ward Burton	MBNA America Pontiac
13	15	1	Rick Mast	Hooters Pontiac
14	41	23	Jimmy Spencer	Camel Cigarettes Ford
15	34	4	Sterling Marlin	Kodak Film Chevrolet
16	25	77	Bobby Hillin	Jasper Engines / Federal-Mogul Ford
17	11	8	Hut Stricklin	Circuit City Ford
18	8	40	Greg Sacks	First Union Pontiac
19	20	9	Lake Speed	Spam / Melling Ford
20	13	94	Bill Elliott	McDonald's Ford
21	19	11	Brett Bodine	Lowe's Ford
22	10	97	Chad Little	Sterling Cowboy Pontiac
23	24	20	Elton Sawyer	LaFayette Ford
24	31	98	John Andretti	RCA Ford
25	36	71	Dave Marcis	Prodigy Chevrolet
26	38	7	Geoff Bodine	QVC Ford
27	16	30	Johnny Benson	Pennzoil Pontiac
28	42	75	Morgan Shepherd	Remington Arms Ford
29	22	78	Billy Standridge	Diamond Rio Ford
30	39	25	Ken Schrader	Budweiser Chevrolet
31	35	16	Ted Musgrave	Family Channel / PRIMESTAR Ford
32	7	33	Todd Bodine	Skoal Bandit Chevrolet
33	18	29	Robert Pressley	Cartoon Network Chevrolet
34	21	87	Joe Nemechek	Burger King Chevrolet
35	26	41	Ricky Craven	Kodiak Chevrolet
36	6	28	Ernie Irvan	Texaco Havoline Ford
37	37	17	Darrell Waltrip	Parts America Chevrolet
38	14	95	Gary Bradberry	Shoney's Restaurants Ford
39	29	19	Loy Allen	Healthsource Ford
40	32	15	Wally Dallenbach	Hayes Modems Ford
41	27	02	Randy Baker	Miles Motorsports Chevrolet
42	12	52	Jack Sprague	Pedigree Pontiac

Reflections

Bobby Hamilton knocked on victory lane's door several times during the season, making it apparent that the competitive fire was burning hotter at Petty Enterprises. When the team unloaded at Phoenix for the 30th event of the season, a confident Hamilton kicked in the door and delivered the famed "43" to the winner's circle for the first time in more than 12 years, capturing his first career NASCAR Winston Cup win in the process.

(Left) Richard Petty stayed plenty busy in 1996 while overseeing the operations of both his NASCAR Winston Cup team and his NASCAR Craftsman Truck Series effort, in addition to running for political office in North Carolina. It was all worthwhile, however, and paid off handsomely at Phoenix as Hamilton's win highlighted the silver-anniversary season of the association between sponsor STP and The King.

Rusty Wallace and Robin Pemberton (here and below), in his second full season as crew chief for Rusty's Miller Fords, did not lack intensity during the 1996 NASCAR Winston Cup campaign. The pair logged five victories during the season — second only to Jeff Gordon's series-leading 10 wins. An uncharacteristic lack of consistency, however, largely due to mechanical failures and uncanny bad luck on the race track, kept Wallace from cracking the top five in the final point standings. Unlike 1995, when the team had turnover of personnel in several key areas, Rusty and his Miller Mates will remain largely intact for 1997.

(Right) John Andretti gets a "lift" on pit road from Darrell Waltrip's team manager Jeff Hammond. Andretti began the season driving the Kranefuss/Haas Kmart Fords, but switched to Cale Yarborough's RCA Thunderbirds during the summer in a driver swap that included Jeremy Mayfield. Earlier in the year Darrell Waltrip, yearning to return to his winning ways of the 1980s, brought longtime friend and crew chief Jeff Hammond back to Darrell Waltrip Motorsports.

(Left) Mark Martin spent much of the year wondering just what it would take to get his Valvoline Ford back to victory lane. Mark consistently had one of the strongest Fords at all types of tracks, and posted four poles, 14 top-five and 23 top-10 finishes to take fifth in the final point standings. The victory eluded him, however, as Mark posted his first winless season since 1988.

(Below) Lake Speed served as both driver and team manager for the Spam/Melling team and, as such, had occasion to make a few "minor" adjustments to his cars. Speed and Melling are scheduled to team up once again in 1997 with new sponsorship from the University of Nebraska.

(Right) Dale Earnhardt surveys the competition during qualifying at Talladega in April, one week after taking command of the point chase at Martinsville. Dale started the season on track to claim an unprecedented eighth NASCAR Winston Cup championship, and remained at the top of the standings for seven straight races until dropping to second behind Terry Labonte after the Jiffy Lube 300 at New Hampshire. Two weeks later he suffered injuries at Talladega and, despite his toughness, did not regain his competitive form consistently for the rest of the season, finishing a distant fourth in the championship points.

(Above) Todd Parrott showed uncommon knowledge, much of it gained during his tenure as Rusty Wallace's chassis specialist, talent and leadership ability with a brilliant year as rookie crew chief for Dale Jarrett and the Quality Care team. Todd's season got off to a fast start with wins in the Busch Clash and season-opening Daytona 500 in February, followed by three more victories, including the Coca-Cola 600 and the Brickyard 400. The team remained in the hunt for the championship right down to the final race of the season at Atlanta, and finished a very commendable third in the final standings, only 89 points behind Terry Labonte.

(Right) Bill Elliott (94), Ricky Rudd (10) and Jeff Burton (99) stack it three wide on Talladega's steep banks. Elliott moved his team from Dawsonville to Mike Beam's facility near Charlotte at the start of the season, and became the sole owner of the effort after buying former partner Charles Hardy's share at mid-season. He was able to collect just six top-10 finishes, however, and wound up 30th in the standings at season's end. Rudd kept his streak of winning at least one race a year alive at 14 with a victory late in the season at Rockingham and took sixth in the final points. Burton had a fine season in his first year with Roush Racing under crew chief Buddy Parrott, winning his first career pole at Michigan in August and collecting six top-five and 12 top-10 finishes.

(Below) Kyle Petty went winless in 1996 and decided it was time to sever his relationship with Felix Sabates and the SABCO team. At Phoenix near the end of the season, Kyle announced the formation of his new team – PE II – that will field Pontiacs in 1997 with primary sponsorship from Mattel's Hot Wheels. Richard Petty will be part owner of the team and will be involved in its operation.

(Above) Michael Waltrip truly enjoyed his visit to Charlotte's victory lane after his historic win in The Winston Select at Charlotte in May. Michael, after qualifying for the all-star event with a fifth-place finish in the preliminary race, The Winston Select Open, stormed from the last starting spot to the front of the pack to take the victory and a check for $211,000. The win put him in the history book with Darrell Waltrip, the 1985 winner, as the only brothers ever to win the prestigious event.

When Harry Hyde left us in May, a great void was created among his friends and peers within the NASCAR Winston Cup family. Harry was much more than simply a crew chief. He was a great "people" person, and helped many young drivers on their way in the sport. For years, he was one of the most innovative head wrenches, and longtime fans of the sport will always remember his feats with Bobby Isaac and Buddy Baker, to name just two, in the K&K Dodges of days gone by. Many will remember him for working with Tim Richmond, Geoff Bodine and Bobby Hillin, while others will recall the role of Harry Hogge, played by Robert Duval in "Days of Thunder," a character based on Hyde's career. His closest friends, however, will treasure their time with the warm-hearted Hyde and his wonderful story-telling ability. We all will miss him.

Harry Hyde

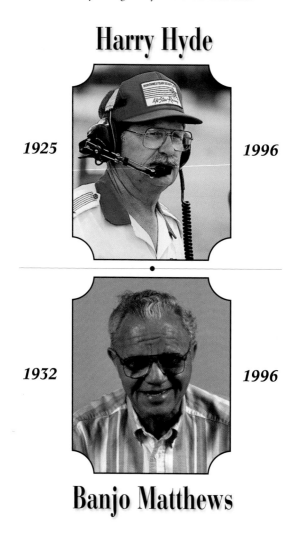

1925   1996

1932   1996

Banjo Matthews

Edwin "Banjo" Matthews was inducted into the National Motorsports Press Association's Hall of Fame in ceremonies at Darlington during the September Mountain Dew Southern 500 weekend. A month later, he left us after a lifetime dedicated to the sport. His nickname came from the thick lenses of his glasses, and, for his entire career, he was known in the garage area simply as "Banjo." He was one of the pioneer drivers in the sport and later became a team owner fielding factory-backed Fords. His legacy, however, may not lie in either the accomplishments he gained as a driver or a car owner, but rather as a car builder. The hallmark of his cars through the years was excellence, and drivers and car owners knew that when a chassis came from Banjo, it never left the shop until every detail had been checked, double-checked and triple-checked. Safety was of premier importance to Banjo. He and his team of builders simply would not deliver anything unless it was perfect in every way. That tradition continues in Banjo's absence. His life was racing, and the sport is better for the contributions he made throughout his career.

Autographs